From Yalta to Panmunjom

From Yalta
to
Panmunjom

Truman's Diplomacy
and the Four Powers, 1945-1953

HUA Qingzhao

East Asia Program
Cornell University
Ithaca, New York 14853

The *Cornell East Asia Series* publishes manuscripts on a wide variety of scholarly topics pertaining to East Asia. Manuscripts are published on the basis of camera-ready copy provided by the volume author or editor.

Inquiries should be addressed to Editorial Board, Cornell East Asia Series, East Asia Program, Cornell University, 140 Uris Hall, Ithaca, New York 14853.

TOWARD PEACE IN THE WORLD

Contents

Foreword

From Yalta to Panmunjom is a remarkable history of the early postwar world from the spring of 1945 to the beginning of 1953, as seen through a pair of Chinese eyes. It is also a painstaking account of the Truman diplomacy, thoroughly researched as well as illuminating. No other history, to my knowledge, contains such a wealth of new information backed by solid documentation.

Professor Hua has managed to present not only the Chinese point of view, but also, after lengthy research in the United States and Europe, the Western view. His year's work at the Harry S. Truman Library is an example of this academic diligence.

But what sets *From Yalta to Panmunjom* above other books goes beyond scholarly research. Professor Hua has been able to maintain an objectivity rarely encountered in works dealing with controversial subjects. The scope of this book, with its candid revelations of Chinese actions and motivations, based on material often unavailable to foreign historians, makes *From Yalta to Panmunjom* obligatory reading for any serious student of diplomatic history and for those who are interested in our era both in the author's home country and the rest of the world.

John Toland
Danbury
September 11, 1991

Acknowledgments

Any credit this book may merit should be shared with the individuals, institutions and depositories whose kind assistance has been instrumental in its completion.

I thank Bradley F. Smith, who taught me how to do research in the West; John and Toshiko Toland, the godparents of this book; and Stanley Vittoz, who polished the draft manuscript; Gabriel Kolko, who allowed me to use documents he collected during his own research projects and the Institute of World History at the Chinese Academy of Social Sciences, and the Tianjin Academy of Social Sciences, my two successive home institutions, without whose endorsements I would not have been able to research and write this book.

The US Government Fulbright Program and the British Council provided grant support. The Woodrow Wilson Center for International Scholars provided a guest scholarship. Stanford University and its History Department hosted me as a Fulbright Scholar. The Harry S. Truman Library and the HST Library Institute provided financial support and archival assistance—and made me feel at home.

For warmth, encouragement, assistance, hospitality and guidance given to me through the years, I thank: Dennis Bilger, Guenter Bischof, Chen Hansheng, Chen Zhongkuan, Gordon A. Craig, Charles F. Delzell, Mary W. Ernst, Robert Ferrell, Michael H. Haltzel, Haroldine Helm, Michael J. Lacey, Philip Lagerquist, Alan Lawrance, Meng Qinglong, Richard Miller, Erwin Mueller, Agnes F. Peterson, Jeff Safford, Liz Safly, Steve Schmeiser, Brent Schondelmeyer, Lord Sherfield, Sally Wood, Yang Shengmao, Zhang Zhilian, Zhao Fusan, Benedict K. Zobrist, Michael S. H. Chang, and Xu Xiaoguang.

Responsibility for any defects in the book is, of course, mine.

Hua Qingzhao
Tianjin, China
15 January 1993

Introduction

This is a book about the foreign policy of the United States during the Truman years. It is also about interactions of the foreign policy of the US with those of other countries—the Soviet Union, Britain and, especially, China. Though the author has tried to be as objective as possible, he nevertheless wants to emphasize that this is a picture of the early post-war world as seen through Chinese eyes.

During the Truman years, the world completed its transition from war to peace—but the world split into two spheres of influence, controlled by the US and the USSR. Despite a United Nations Organization intended to maintain peace, two former allies became rival superpowers, and their confrontation in the "Cold War" endured for more than four decades. Truman, although he inherited a part of Roosevelt's foreign policy, gave US foreign policy his own imprint. His diplomacy laid the foundation for US foreign policy during the Cold War era, and his legacy in this field persists to the present day.

In China, Truman remains a controversial figure. He supported Chiang Kai-shek during the civil war; indeed, the Chinese viewed him as Chiang's "backstage boss." Many Chinese still believe that Truman had imperialistic intentions and should be held responsible for mustering the UN efforts to invade Korea and threaten China. He is the only post-war president to have ordered American servicemen to fight against Chinese troops. Moreover, China was an arena for US-USSR rivalry during the Truman period, and the Chinese people were among the first victims of the Cold War. Naturally, they view this period of history quite differently from the Americans and the Soviets. It is especially important that they understand the origins and true dimensions of US foreign policy during this period.

To this day, few books on the Truman years have been written by Chinese scholars. Nor is there a book in English based on documentary research that gives Western readers a Chinese perspective on the

1

momentous events of those years. These facts motivated the effort that, over a period of more than six years, produced the pages to follow. This effort took the author to the US and the UK, as well as to research libraries in his native China. Among the US sources used for this study, the majority are available in the archives of the Truman Library in Independence, Missouri. Most of the British sources are available in the Public Record Office, Kew. Unfortunately, the diplomatic and military archives of the People's Republic of China are not open for general research; the author, ruling out unauthorized access to material, has relied upon official documents, unpublished papers, published articles in journals and newspapers, and books (memoirs, monographs, and official histories), many of which may be new to Western readers.

This book is organized more or less chronologically, in eleven chapters. In each chapter, the reader will find emphases and interpretations that differ from familiar Western scholarship and also from conventional wisdom in China.

The relationship between the US and PRC has never been smooth. In times past, the US blamed the PRC's ideology and conduct for souring Sino-American relations. Despite the First Amendment, the US government seems to feel that it has a right to decide what non-Americans around the globe should say and believe. Once Americans believe that other nations should adopt American values, understanding of other nations becomes impossible, and ignorance and insensitivity must lead to disastrous policy decisions on the part of the US. A review of US foreign policy from an unfamiliar perspective may help Americans understand the values, mentalities, and methodologies of others.

Many Chinese believe that Truman inherited a good China policy from Roosevelt and that Truman corrupted the legacy of his predecessor. Chapter 1 shows that this is incorrect. It also shows that China's praise for Stilwell was not entirely justified and it introduces to the Western reader the jarring notion that Yalta was little more than a meeting of robbers dividing their booty.

Eastern Europe—Poland in particular—was not, as Western scholars have long believed, the most important source of the Cold War. Chapter 2 shows that US-Soviet rivalry in Europe is a product of the Cold War, rather than its source, and the Cold War really originates in a deficient design for the post-war period. The UN, a key part of this design, could never overrule the actions of the two superpowers, whose conflicting interests and spheres of influence were bound to collide. The deficient design that precipitated the Cold War was itself a product of selfish pursuits on the part of the US and the USSR.

Chapter 3 examines the efforts of the US and the USSR to lure Chiang Kai-shek into following their design in China and traces their attempts to pressure the Chinese Communists. It also investigates how the US and the USSR became rivals in China.

Chapter 4 takes up the beginnings of "atomic diplomacy," arguing that the Potsdam conference of 1945 was not a crucial watershed.

The year 1946 was a year of preparation, leading up to declaration of the Cold War. The important events of this year are examined in Chapter 5, with special attention to Churchill's famous "Iron Curtain" speech and the differences that subsequently developed between Churchill and Truman; to Stalin's "war speech;" and to the so-called Clifford Paper, in which Clifford in fact played little part.

Contrary to prevailing views, there was no war crisis at all in the late 1940s. To support this view, Chapter 6 examines the Truman Doctrine, the Marshall Plan, Czechoslovakia, and the Berlin blockade.

Chapter 7 returns to China. The failure of Marshall's mediation in the Chinese civil conflict is traced to the Truman administration's categorical support for the Chiang regime. Unlike popular Chinese Communist Party (CCP) portrayals, however, the Communists at the time believed that Marshall did want to avert a Chinese civil war and that he was not entirely supportive of Chiang's excessive demands. Chapter 7 also relates a very significant, and totally neglected, incident involving the sexual assault on a Chinese woman by two US Marines and examines the ramifications of the incident.

Chapter 8 is a comparison of US diplomacy and Soviet diplomacy in China during the early post-war period. While the Americans threw in with Chiang's KMT, the Soviets kept one foot in each of the two boats—KMT and CCP. Whereas the Americans lost China when the KMT failed, the Soviets had positioned themselves to bargain with whichever party was in power. For a variety of reasons examined in this chapter, the US had no hope of establishing a working relationship with the CCP in 1949.

Truman started to change his policy toward China after the People's Republic was established in October 1949. He decided that the US should try to drive a wedge between the Chinese Communists and their Soviet comrades. Departing from its earlier stance, the Republican Party agreed in the spring of 1950 to bipartisanship in Far Eastern policy. The emergence of a bipartisan policy is traced in Chapter 9.

Contrary to both Chinese scholarship and Western revisionist historiography, Chapter 10 argues that Truman, as the President of the United States, responded justifiably when he sent troops to fight in the Korean War, but that there was no justification for sending warships to the Taiwan Straits, interfering in the Chinese civil war. Chapter 10 also examines the Chinese decision to cross the Yalu, Sino-Soviet relations during the war years, the activities of US intelligence agencies in China, and issues surrounding the treatment and repatriation of Prisoners of War.

Chapter 11 assesses the costs and benefits of the Korean War, for each of the major belligerents and for Japan and Taiwan. The big winner: the USSR.

A concluding chapter then summarizes, on the basis of the historical record examined in this book, the key factors influencing Truman's diplomacy. Despite each American president's placing his own imprint on foreign policy, tradition has played a significant part in US diplomacy overall. The most critical and perhaps controversial argument, however, is that ideology should not be considered a major determinant in relations between nations. The most important factors, here and almost always, are those involving existing or potential national interests.

1
FDR's China Legacy

News of President Franklin D. Roosevelt's death reached China on the morning of 13 April 1945. Chiang Kai-shek, Chairman of the Nationalist government, was at breakfast in his Chongqing mountain residence on the south bank of the Yangtze. Upon hearing the news, Chiang became visibly stunned, lost his appetite, and left the table. Roosevelt had backed him since before the US entered World War II, and Chiang had no idea of what to expect from the new President, Harry S. Truman.

When Roosevelt took office in 1933, Japan had occupied Manchuria for over a year. Though the Roosevelt government did not approve of Japanese expansion in China, the US joined the other western powers in policies of appeasement and compromise. Facing no western opposition, Japan encroached upon Chinese territory south of the Great Wall, precipitating China's declaration, on 7 July 1937, of a War of Resistance against Japanese Aggression. After war broke out, the US did not immediately come to China's aid; the Soviets were the first to help. In 1937 and 1938, the Soviet Union provided air support over East and Central China, extended loans to the Chinese government, and exchanged planes and other war materials for Chinese commodities.

The face of Chinese-Soviet relations changed in 1940, when the Soviet Union signed a non-aggression treaty with Germany. The Soviet air force went home, and the Soviet government refused to supply China with additional planes.[1] As reported by Lawrence Steinhardt, the US ambassador in Moscow, Vice Foreign Minister Vyshinsky told the Chinese that "while Soviet methods might have to undergo a change, the Soviet goal remains the same"—that is, that the Soviet Union remained China's ally and benefactor.[2] Still, Roosevelt and Secretary of State Cordell Hull were surprised at the cessation of Soviet aid to China and alarmed by Japan's control of the skies over major Chinese cities, among them Chongqing and Guilin.[3]

5

THE FLYING TIGERS

The first American to fight the Japanese in China arrived long before Pearl Harbor. Claire L. Chennault, a retired US Army Air Force captain, arrived in May 1937 to work for the Chinese Air Force. When the Sino-Japanese war broke out two months later, he stayed on as an advisor, instructing cadets and helping to direct combat missions.

Chiang Kai-shek sent Chennault back to the US in the winter of 1940, to recruit pilots and secure planes for China's air force. By this time, Roosevelt already felt compelled to aid China. US Ambassador to China Nelson Johnson, had been pressing for more aid to China to "prevent forcing them to choose between Japan and Communism."[4] In June, a senior State Department officer wrote a memo to Hull, outlining five possible avenues by which to aid China—extending currency stabilization loans, purchasing Chinese strategic materials, increasing appropriations to the Export-Import Bank, extending a rehabilitation and reconstruction loan, and freezing Chinese deposits in the US.[5] Chiang Kai-shek, of course, had been corresponding with Roosevelt all along, urging substantial US aid; in November 1940 he proposed US-China-UK cooperation, but the US government dismissed this idea.[6]

The US did decide to supply China with 100 P-40 Tomahawk fighters, to be flown by American volunteers. The planes had been allocated to Britain, but Britain agreed to let China have them in exchange for an allocation of 300 P-40s to be delivered several months later.[7] With 100 P-40s committed, Chennault recruited the necessary pilots and ground crews in the US, and secured support equipment. Although Chiang Kai-shek wanted to call the P-40 detachment a Special Air Unit of the Chinese Air Force, it was named the American Volunteer Group (AVG); Chennault was named its supervisor—in effect, its commander. The US Navy convoyed the P-40s to Burma, and the first AVGs entered combat in fall 1941. They fought very effectively, successfully blocking Japanese air raids directed at some Chinese cities and assisting British ground forces in Burma. Their prowess—and the vicious shark heads painted on the noses of their planes—led a Chinese news reporter to dub them the "Flying Tigers."

Meanwhile, Roosevelt's dealings with China were being complicated by frictions between Chiang's ruling Nationalist Party and the Chinese Communist Party (CCP). In 1937, after years of fighting, the two parties had formed a united front against Japan. Nominally, the Communist armed forces were under government military order, but in fact they reported only to the CCP. Moreover, large areas of interior China were under Communist control. Roosevelt sent Captain Evans Fordyce Carlson, a Marine who had been stationed in China as an intelligence officer, to serve as observer in the Communist-held areas. Carlson marched 2,000 miles with a unit of the Communist 8th Route Army, sending frequent reports to FDR. His frequent expressions of sympathy with the Communists and his admiration for their patriotism ultimately led to his resignation in 1939. (Carlson would later gain fame as leader of the Carlson Raiders, a Marine battalion that spearheaded the Guadalcanal landing; the Raiders functioned as a highly efficient and self-disciplined unit, with a philosophy of teamwork and sense of patriotism—in other words, in much the same manner as a Chinese Communist guerilla detachment.[8])

By the time the US entered the war in December 1941, China had been split into three zones: the Japanese Occupation Zone in the Northeast (Manchuria), most of North China, and parts of Central and South China; the Nationalist Zone, facing the Japanese along a front in Central and South China; and the Communists' Liberated Zone, in the Shaanxi-Gansu-Ningxia Border Region of interior China and in scattered patches to the enemy's rear.

US WARTIME AIMS AND ACTIVITIES IN CHINA

In 1944, Roosevelt approved a document defining the wartime aims of the US government in China: China should contain the bulk of the Japanese army and serve as a base for limited operations against Japan. Official US policy was "to keep China in the war and to make her an effective military ally by training her soldiers, sending supplies to her troops, giving air support to her armies and encouraging unity among diverse political groups."[8]

American wartime activities in China were threefold: providing supplies and economic aid; undertaking military and intelligence operations; and intervening in Chinese domestic politics, primarily Nationalist-Communist disputes. After Pearl Harbor, Roosevelt designated Lt.Gen. Joseph W. Stilwell as Commander of US forces in the China-Burma-India Theater and as Chief of Staff to the Supreme Commander of the Allied China Theater, Generalissimo Chiang Kai-shek. With these appointments, Stilwell was to orchestrate American military movements in East Asia.

The US government agreed with Chiang that equipment and materials would be of paramount importance, and promised to ship enough for thirty Chinese divisions. But because Japanese forces controlled the western Pacific and blocked overland communications through Burma, China was nearly sealed off from the US; war cargo could be transported into China only by flying it over the Hump of the Himalayas. With hopes of opening an overland route, the Americans started to equip and train Chinese troops in Ledo, India, and Chiang amassed a concentration of Chinese forces (the

"Y Forces") in Yunnan province, close to the China-Burma border. The American military was pushing for a joint US-UK-China effort to recapture Northern Burma. Chiang demanded a British amphibious offensive to aid the operations of Chinese troops in Burma and then, when the British insisted that such an offensive was not necessary, refused to deploy Chinese troops in Burma. This was a major topic of US-China consultations before, during, and after the Cairo Conference of November 1943. Although Chiang, under heavy US pressure, agreed to let three Chinese divisions already under Stilwell in India join the Burma venture, he never consented to send in his "Y Forces." The Hump airlift remained the only route between China and the Western Allies almost until V-J day.

During the Cairo Conference, Roosevelt and Chiang reached a secret agreement that, under Lend-Lease, the US would provide China with supplies and equipment for ninety divisions.[9] When this material was moved over the Hump, not all of it was used for the war effort against Japan. Chen Cheng, one of Chiang's top generals, said that "Every bullet received by the Chinese forces from American Lend-Lease has been and will be allocated only to those forces assigned to fight against Japan; however, if Central Government troops are attacked by any unfriendly forces, they must defend themselves with whatever weapons they have."[10] American military support, apart from helping China resist Japan, thus served also to widen the split between Chinese factions and to impel China toward civil war.

US air forces conducted the bulk of the American military operations in China, with three groups of bombers flying missions in Chinese skies. First, B-25s commanded by Col. James Doolittle took off from the carrier *Hornet* on 18 April 1942, bombed Japan, and then landed in China. Second, when the AVG ceased operations in July 1942, it was replaced by the China Air Task Force (CATF) under the US Army's 10th Air Force, stationed in India. In the spring of 1944, the CATF merged with the newly established US Army 14th Air Force; Chennault, promoted to Brigadier General, became commander of the 14th.[11] The 14th flew B-24s and B25s over China. Third, B-29 Superfortresses of the 20th Bomber Command under Brigadier General K.B. Wolfe operated from India and a base near Chengdu, in Sichuan province.

When Japanese troops launched a large-scale offensive in June 1944, they obliterated nearly all the bases of the 14th Air Force. The Japanese campaign advanced through Hunan and Guangxi provinces, entered Guizhou, and threatened Chongqing, the provisional national capital, and Kunming, site of 14th Air Force Headquarters and China terminal for the Hump airlift. The Joint Chiefs of Staff reported to FDR on 4 July 1944 that, "if the Japanese continue their advance to the west, Chennault's 14th

Air Force will be rendered ineffective, our Very Long Range Bomber airfields in the Chengtu [Chengdu] area will be lost, and the collapse of China must inevitably result." The JCS also stated that "the serious pass to which China has come is due in some measure to mismanagement and neglect of the Army. Until her every resource, including the divisions at present confronting the Communists, is devoted to the war against the Japanese, there is little hope that she can continue to cooperate with any effectiveness until the end of the war." The JCS recommended a very simple solution: appoint Stilwell to command all Allied ground forces in China. Roosevelt agreed, and sent a message to Chiang.[12]

The military brass in Washington were correct in assessing the causes behind the deteriorating situation, but they were mistaken in their solution. Generalissimo Chiang Kai-shek looked upon his army as the lodestar of his life, his "Precious Jade," and would never hand command over to anyone.[13] Moreover, even had Chiang agreed, no American officer would have been able to deal with the intricacies of commanding Chinese forces. Naturally, Chiang refused to yield his position, and as a countermeasure he asked Roosevelt to send a political representative to help iron out differences between the American and Chinese military establishments in China. FDR sent Patrick Hurley to bridge "political gaps."[14]

Though Roosevelt sent Evans Fordyce Carlson to the Communist-held areas in 1937 and 1938, he never had an official representative there. As foreign service officer John Paton Davies pointed out in a memo of 24 June 1943, the Communists constituted the most cohesive, disciplined and aggressive anti-Japanese group in the country. Increased contact with the CCP seemed an effective method of advancing the Allied war effort. So, in February 1944, the US Army proposed sending an observation mission to the Communist areas in North China to get information about Japanese military operations. Roosevelt endorsed the plan and sent a message to Chiang Kai-shek on 9 February asking for his support and cooperation.[15] Chiang replied two weeks later that he would welcome observers—but only in areas under his own control, a restriction that virtually denied US personnel passage into the Communist areas.

FDR, however, was just as much a master of diplomacy. On 1 March, he thanked Chiang for his communication, saying he would soon send the group without mentioning where it would go. Three weeks later, Roosevelt repeated his original request, and Chiang again refused to allow the observers' entrance. Only upon Vice President Henry Wallace's visit to China in June 1944 did Chiang finally agree in principle that an observers' group could be sent into Communist areas. By then, the Japanese were launching a strong offensive toward areas under Chiang's own control.[16]

The US Army Observer Group, known as the Dixie Mission, arrived at the Communists' headquarters in Yanan on 22 July 1944. The group was headed by Col. David D. Barrett, an old China hand, and—aside from military and intelligence personnel—included some foreign service officers, such as John S. Service. The inclusion of these officers constituted a kind of de facto recognition of the CCP, although the US could publicly deny that the group had any official political mission.

On 7 September 1944, Hurley arrived in Chongqing, along with Donald Nelson, who headed a mission on the economy. Hurley traveled to China by way of London and Moscow. He later told Truman that Roosevelt entrusted him with bringing Churchill and Stalin to an agreement on the US "China Policy," which consisted of three points: taking all necessary actions to bring about unification of the anti-Japanese forces in China; endorsing a free, united, and democratic Chinese government; and continuing to insist that Chiang make his own decisions and accept responsibility for his policies, thereby allowing China to work out her own destiny. According to Hurley, both Churchill and Stalin concurred in this Policy.[17] Also according to Hurley, Henry Wallace, after his visit to China in June, had informed Roosevelt that Chiang's government would soon collapse. Senators Brewster and Chandler, after their own visit to China in 1944, brought back a similar report. In view of US policy and the perceived situation in China, Roosevelt sent Hurley to prevent collapse of the Chinese government, keep Chinese armies in the war, smooth relations between the Chinese and American military establishments, and unify anti-Japanese forces in China.[18]

Immediately after Hurley arrived in Chongqing, Chiang informed the envoy that he was prepared to give Stilwell actual command of all Chinese forces in the field. The Americans may not have realized that Chiang's words were no more than a smoke screen. When fierce fighting between Allied and Japanese troops broke out in northern Burma, Stilwell protested to Chiang about his keeping the "Y" Forces in Yunnan. Roosevelt intervened to support Stilwell. But Hurley unwittingly undermined his efforts, by revealing to Chiang, FDR's apprehension about straining the harmony between China and the US. Chiang remained firm. On 25 September 1944, he requested that Stilwell be removed from the China theater, agreeing again to place all Chinese field armies under the command of an American other than Stilwell. Roosevelt yielded, and Stilwell was recalled.

Opinions concerning the recall of Stilwell are diverse, but center around three major lines of thought. First, Chiang Kai-shek himself claimed that Stilwell's attitude was intolerable; Hurley agreed. Second, Stilwell said he was recalled because Chiang was unwilling to continue fighting—a claim that many have supported. Third, Chiang later said that the real issues in the Stilwell affair were "the Communist demands: distribution of allied military aid to China and removal of the government's blockade around the Communist border area."[19] In the People's Republic, the prevailing view is that Stilwell was removed because of his sympathy for the Communists and his criticism of Chiang's reluctance to fight the Japanese.

While Stilwell's attitude toward Chiang was probably not the major factor in his recall, it was enough to cause Roosevelt some concern. Roosevelt told Army Chief-of-Staff George C. Marshall that, as Stilwell maintained, Chiang was very irritable, hard to deal with, and prone to constantly upping his demands; nevertheless, it was improper to address Chiang in a stern manner. "All of us must remember the Generalissimo came up the hard way....Besides, the Generalissimo finds it necessary to maintain a position of supremacy. You and I would do the same thing under the circumstances."[20]   Marshall tried to defend Stilwell, his former associate in the US Army 15th Regiment at Tianjin in the 1920s. He said that Stilwell had met with the "let the other fellow do it" attitude of the Chinese, and that "to correct this must be the primary objective of any representative dispatched to this theater to represent American interests." He also praised Stilwell's knowledge of China and the language, as well as the toughness that had brought him through the Burma campaign.[21]

The US government appointed new diplomatic and military representatives to China in late 1944.   Ambassador Gauss resigned in November, and Hurley succeeded him. Lt. General Albert C. Wedemeyer replaced Stilwell as Commander of the US Army in China.

HURLEY AS AMBASSADOR

American aid and military operations in China were certainly entangled with US involvement in Nationalist-Communist relations; sorting out the exact nature of this entanglement requires examination of the Soviet factor in FDR's China Policy.

After the failure of his mission to smooth relations between Chiang and Stilwell, Patrick Hurley turned his attention to facilitating negotiations between the Nationalists and Communists.   When he passed through Moscow in September 1944, Soviet Foreign Minister Molotov told him that some Chinese "called themselves Communists but were related to Communism in no way at all," and that the "Soviet Government should not be associated with these 'communist elements'."   When speaking with Donald Nelson, Molotov referred to the CCP as "so-called Communists."[22] Since the Chinese Communists could not defeat Chiang without Soviet aid, Hurley believed that it might be possible to reach a political agreement between the two sides. Prior to Hurley's assignment to Chongqing, the two sides were already negotiating the unification of their military forces. After his arrival, Hurley took measures to become a mediator between them. At the urging of John Paton Davies, on 7 November 1944 Hurley went to Yanan to confer with CCP leader Mao Zedong[23] The result of Hurley's visit to Yanan was a proposed five-point agreement between the Nationalist Government and the Communist Party, signed by Mao with Hurley as witness on November 10.

When Hurley took the draft agreement to Chongqing, the Nationalists deemed it unacceptable and counter-proposed a three-point agreement.[24] The major discrepancy between the two draft agreements concerned organization of the future government of China. The Communists demanded reorganization of the present national government into a coalition government embracing all the anti-Japanese parties and non-partisan political bodies, and establishment of a national military council by representatives of all the anti-Japanese armies. The Nationalists insisted upon incorporating the Communist forces into the national army and relegating the command of the Communists' troops to the Nationalist government, through a national military council. The Nationalist government would then select some Communists for membership on this council. The differences between the two draft agreements were never resolved. Again, Hurley's efforts to act as arbiter in China had proven fruitless. What is more, he had fallen considerably in the estimation of the Communists: a bounced check is worse than no check at all.

To push Chiang into serious negotiations, FDR instructed Hurley on 15 December 1944 to tell Chiang that both the Americans and the Russians thought a working arrangement between his government and the "North China forces" (the Communist troops) would greatly expedite ejection of the Japanese from China. The President told Hurley that "you can emphasize the word 'Russians' to him." Roosevelt meant that the Russians would soon come into the war, and that they would back the Chinese Communists if Chiang had not come to terms with Mao by then.[25] The fact that Roosevelt pressed Chiang to negotiate with the Communists by no means indicates that he was taking a neutral stand between the two sides.

That FDR did not remain neutral is also evidenced by his exchange with Harry Hopkins, concerning military equipment earmarked for the Nationalists. When Hopkins inquired as to the postwar fate of undelivered equipment, Roosevelt said: "They can buy it." Hopkins testified that one of the President's intentions was to strengthen Chiang's hand in dealing with "recalcitrant Chinese factions."[26] Naturally, the CCP stood foremost among the recalcitrant groups.

Ambassador Hurley reported in December 1944 that Chiang Kai-shek had once seen the Chinese Communist Party as an instrument of the Soviet government, but no longer held this view and felt that a settlement could be reached. He also hinted that the impending Chinese civil war was not inevitable, and that Chiang was convinced that by signing an agreement with the Communists he could unite the military forces and avoid civil strife.[27]

The new ambassador, however, was overly optimistic. On the one hand, of all the titles Chiang held, the one he treasured most was Commandant of the Whampoa Military Academy. In fact, Chiang was also Commandant of all military academies and schools under the Nationalist government. On the other hand, Hurley might not have been fully aware of Mao's famous dictum that "power grows out of the barrel of a gun." Asking both sides to give up control of their armed forces was something "more difficult than climbing up to the sky," as an old Chinese saying goes.

Meanwhile, in February 1945 Roosevelt, Stalin, and Churchill met at Yalta to discuss the last phase of the war and the postwar world. During the Yalta Conference, the leaders of the three powers reached a secret agreement on China without consulting the Chinese government. China was not informed of the agreement until several months later. The agreement cut off Outer Mongolia, then Chinese territory, from China. It restored to the Soviet Union colonial privileges in Manchuria, lost to Japan in the War of 1904-05—privileges including control of "preeminent interests" in the region, a lease on the Lushun [Port Arthur] naval base, and joint ownership of the railroad. It gave to the US "Open Door" rights in Manchuria, including internationalization of the commercial port Dalian [Dairen]. Roosevelt promised that he would collaborate with Stalin in persuading Chiang Kai-shek to accept the agreement. The Soviet Union presented Chiang with a carrot—a pact of friendship and alliance, and in helping China to fight Japan—in hopes of expediting his acceptance.

For over four decades, politicians, diplomats, scholars, and journalists outside China have debated the Yalta Agreement. Some feel that Roosevelt handed out too many concessions to Stalin; on the other hand, Dean Acheson once stated that the agreement was not so bad, because it gave the Russians much less than they could have taken by force.[28] Few have questioned, however, whether the items the Americans promised the Soviets were ever in the possession of the United States, or tried to justify brutally violating the sovereignty of a major ally after a great victory. It is obvious that without some common ground, the Yalta Agreement could not have been reached; without any agreement, Roosevelt could not have made concessions to Stalin. What was the common ground regarding American and Soviet policies on China? What were the reasons for Roosevelt's "concessions"? To answer these questions, we must realize that Roosevelt's

China Policy was really twofold. FDR aimed not just to defeat Japan, but also to curb Soviet influence. The closer he came to victory, the larger the second aim loomed—and the more his China Policy became a part of his Soviet Policy.

Roosevelt's postwar design was based upon rivalry with the Soviet Union—recognizing this rivalry, but preventing its developing into conflict. This was acceptable to the Soviets, and it was institutionalized in the decisions reached at Yalta. The common ground shared by the US and the USSR in China was that each had a sphere of interest or influence, and both believed that Chiang Kai-shek was the only person qualified to rule China. Roosevelt's concessions, apart from serving as bargaining chips to exchange for Soviet participation in the war in Asia, were meant to enlist Soviet support for the Nationalists and opposition toward the Communists.

BETTING ON THE WRONG HORSE

To make China an Asian bulwark protecting American interests, Roosevelt secured Four-Power status for her. Rather than securing Chiang's cooperation, however, this development encouraged his intransigence. On 1 March 1945, shortly after the Yalta Conference, Chiang Kai-shek made a speech in which he said that he would not change one-party rule into a coalition government and that he planned to open a National Congress the following November. Chiang continued to offer the Communist Party legal recognition if it agreed to incorporate its army and local governments into the Nationalist government. In Zhou Enlai's letter of 9 March to Hurley, the Communists responded that Chiang's speech had rendered discussion of coalition unnecessary. The Communists also repeated their demand that the Chinese delegation to the United Nations Conference in San Francisco in April include three Communist members.[29]

Chiang Kai-shek's intransigence over collaboration with the Communists was similar to Roosevelt's practice. The FDR administration had never aided the Chinese Communists. No matter how eloquent the speeches or how sound the judgments of second and third secretaries in the Chongqing embassy, the top echelon of foreign policy makers in FDR's administration never agreed to help the CCP's war effort. Roosevelt agreed to incorporate Chinese Communists into Chiang's government only on condition that they could never come to power, as their doing so would enhance Soviet influence and jeopardize American interests. (One report has it that the only US Army equipment given to the Communists during the war was a pair of binoculars.[30]) FDR did not choose to slight the CCP because he had no knowledge of its war effort; his impatient demands to dispatch observers to Communist areas is proof of that. Furthermore, the US military negotiated with the Communists (about coordination of commands) when the US Marines were about to land on the China coast—a landing that never occurred. FDR's administration simply did not have sufficient insight to realize that, after the war, the Chiang regime would meet its end and that no foreign influence, be it American, Soviet, or British, would be able to control China.

Patrick Hurley returned to Washington in February 1945 for consultation. He remained optimistic about the China situation but admitted that there was still a long way to go. The CCP got one full membership in China's delegation to the inaugural conference of the UN in April. Meanwhile, the negotiation for unifying China's military forces was shelved, and on 3 April Hurley left for China, again via London and Moscow. While in London, he told the Imperial Chief-of-Staff, General Ismay, that the chief American aim in China was unification against the Japanese,[31] and said that one of the major difficulties blocking a Nationalist-Communist compromise was Chiang's refusal to deal with a CCP that received foreign assistance. In Moscow, Hurley was told that the Soviets were not aiding the CCP. He was unable to convince Chiang of this; had he succeeded, "there would be little difficulty in bringing about a compromise as a result of which the Communist and National forces would unite to fight the Japanese."

On his way to China, Hurley learned that President Roosevelt had died and that Harry S. Truman had assumed the presidency.

2
Eastern Europe and Yalta

When Truman became President, one of his most urgent concerns was the inauguration of the United Nations. It was no coincidence that the first decision he made was to proceed as planned with the UN inaugural conference in San Francisco on 25 April 1945.

THE US-SOVIET RELATIONSHIP

At this time, the US-Soviet relationship was experiencing some difficulty. In March and April, Allen Dulles, the OSS Chief in Bern, Switzerland, conducted secret negotiations with Nazi SS General Karl Wolff concerning the surrender of German troops in Northern Italy. The Soviets were bitter that this negotiation had started without their knowledge, even after President Roosevelt personally cabled Stalin to explain the situation leading to the negotiations. Another point of disagreement between the US and the Soviet Union was the composition of Poland's provisional government. As an expression of displeasure, the Soviets said that they would not send Foreign Minister V.M. Molotov to head their delegation to the UN conference. Truman urged Stalin, on 13 April, to send Molotov; he also invited Molotov to visit Washington. In Truman's words, this "would be welcome as an expression of earnest cooperation." Stalin was persuaded, and Molotov was scheduled to visit Washington on his way to the conference.

Molotov's name, like Stalin's, was a revolutionary pseudonym. While Stalin's name meant steel, Molotov's meant hammer. Looking back on their life histories of prison, exile, seizure of power, civil war, throat-cutting inner-party struggles and international conflict, one must conclude that these names were aptly chosen. Whether the man from Independence, whose life had been relatively quiet and secure, could successfully deal with these two remained to be seen. Truman himself seemed quite confident. When asked whether he expected to see Molotov when the latter passed through the capital en route to San Francisco, he replied: "Yes. He is going to stop by and pay respects to the President of the United States. He should."[1]

In the agreement on Poland reached in Yalta, there were articles pertaining to the composition of the future government and to "free and unfettered elections." But after the summit the three participants began to argue: Should the new Polish government be completely reorganized, or should it be based on the existing government, with the incorporation of some new elements? The US and UK insisted upon the "reorganization" formula, whereas the Soviet Union insisted on doing it the other way. The different interpretations brought the issue to a deadlock. On 1 April 1945, Roosevelt sent his last message to Stalin urging him to solve the Polish problem along the lines agreed upon at Yalta. Stalin replied on the 7th that the present provisional government was to be the "kernel of the future Polish Government" and subject to reconstruction by way of broadening it. Consultation should be carried out first with representatives of the provisional government, with the other parties consulted individually later on—on condition that they recognize the Yalta decisions concerning Poland.[2] Roosevelt did not live long enough to reply.

After Truman took office, he read the past two months' exchanges between Stalin and FDR. "If the messages Stalin sent to Roosevelt just before I went into the White House were made public, it would cause a complete break with Russia," he later said.[3] More than likely, Truman was referring not only to the specifics of the exchanges, but to the fact that the Polish issue to which they pertained was the most acute issue of the day. Scholars have repeatedly argued that disagreement over Poland was an important contributing factor in the origin of the Cold War. But was it really an issue of great significance, with such far-reaching consequences?

Since Yalta, the US Ambassador in Moscow, Averell W. Harriman, had been sending back messages to the Secretary of State concerning the Polish question. On 14 April, he sent a long cable from Moscow advising the new President how to deal with Stalin's message of 7 April. In Harriman's view, Stalin's proposal that the Polish provisional government serve as the "kernel" was unacceptable; rather, the US must be adamant that five Poles from London, independent of the Warsaw government, also be included, since that government did not enjoy tremendous influence and the US could not accept a "mere whitewash" of it. Harriman also said that if the US were not to "recede from the basic positions suggested above, I do not feel that we should insist upon Stalin's full acceptance of our interpretation of the Crimea Conference."[4] On 17 April, Harriman reported that the Soviet government and the Polish provisional government were preparing a treaty of mutual assistance. After reading Harriman's telegram, Truman decided that he "would lay it on the line with Molotov."[5]

Harriman rushed back to Washington before Molotov's arrival; Truman presided over a meeting in the White House on 20 April. The exchange between the two is of considerable interest. Harriman reported that the Soviets had "two policies which they thought they could successfully pursue." One was the policy of cooperation with the US and Britain, the other was "the extension of Soviet control over neighboring states through unilateral action." According to Harriman, Soviet control meant "extension of the Soviet system." He requested a reconsideration of US policy and abandonment of the illusion that the Soviets would quickly act in international affairs in accordance with the principles held by the rest of the world. Harriman said that the Soviets believed American business needed, as a matter of life and death, the export trade with the Soviet Union, but also said that "give and take negotiation would have to be made." Truman said that he "was not in any sense afraid of the Russians," believing that the Soviets needed the US more than the US needed them; he intended "to be firm with the Russians and make no concessions from American principles or traditions for the purpose of winning their favor." When Harriman asked whether he should go ahead with the UN plan if Russia dropped out, Truman replied very cautiously that "without Russia, there would not be much of a world organization." But, in the give and take negotiations, the US "could not expect 100% of what we wanted, but on important matters should be able to get 85%."[6] By setting such high and unbalanced expectations for bargaining with a supposedly equal partner, and with his advisors not only failing to object but actually giving support, the new President was bound to get into trouble.

Molotov arrived in Washington late on the afternoon of 22 April. He greeted the crowd at the airport with a broad smile and waved his hat, but did not make any statement. That evening, he was received by Truman at the White House. The conversation was generally ceremonial, and each reassured the other that he would honor the agreements reached at Yalta. Later that evening and the following day, Molotov met with his US and UK counterparts, Edward Stettinius and Anthony Eden; all sides refused to budge from their original positions on the Polish question. News soon trickled out that on 22 April the Soviet Union and the Polish provisional government had signed a Treaty of Mutual Assistance.

The Americans were frustrated, and on 23 April President Truman called a meeting of his senior associates. Truman said: "Our agreement with the Soviet Union so far had been a one-way street and that cannot continue; it is now or never." As to the United Nations, he said that he intended "to go on with the plans for San Francisco, and if the Russians do not wish to join us they can go to hell."

The views of his associates varied. Forrestal, Harriman and General Deane were hardliners; Stimson, Leahy and Marshall were more cautious. Stimson said that the Russians were perhaps more realistic than the US in regard to their own security. They would not yield on the question of Poland, and that, without understanding how seriously the Russians took the Polish question, the US was heading into very dangerous waters. As to the election in Poland, Stimson said he believed from his own experience, that no one except the US and Britain understood free elections. Leahy said he would have been surprised had the Soviet government behaved any differently than it did. He believed that a break with the Russians would be very serious, and that the Yalta Agreement was susceptible to two interpretations. Marshall added that difficulties like the flap over Dulles' secret negotiating could be straightened out. Stettinius, on the other hand, held that the text of the Yalta Agreement on Poland was susceptible to only one interpretation. At the end of the meeting Truman thanked his aides for the views expressed and said the US should stand up for its understanding of the Yalta Agreements. He had "no intention to deliver an ultimatum, but only a clear position."[7]

After these exchanges, President Truman received Molotov for the second time—early on the evening of 23 April. Before the meeting, Stettinius submitted a six-point memorandum in which he crystallized the line the President would follow when speaking to Molotov.[8]

At this point, Truman and Churchill had already had some cable exchanges with Stalin on the Polish question. The last cable had been sent jointly by the two Western leaders on 18 April, and at the time of his meeting with Molotov, Truman was waiting for a reply. He emphasized to Molotov that "no policy in the US, whether domestic or foreign, could succeed unless it enjoyed public confidence and support." And he said that "friendship could only be on the basis of mutual observation of agreements and not on the basis of a one-way street." Molotov started to argue; Truman remarked that he wished Molotov would report to Marshal Stalin, and Molotov's face turned ashy.[9] Truman's associates were delighted with this tongue-lashing. Bohlen, for example, wrote in his memoirs: "How I enjoyed translating Truman's sentences! They were probably the first sharp words uttered during the war by an American President to a high Soviet official."[10] The next morning Truman told his staff that he was "hopeful of good effects from the meeting."[11]

Late on the evening of 23 April, Molotov met with his American and British colleagues again, all sides holding firmly to their positions. Eden urged Molotov to draft Stalin's reply on the spot, but Molotov declined on the grounds that it should be done by the Soviet leader himself. Stalin's reply came the next day. He maintained his previous position, supported

Molotov's attitude unswervingly, and charged that the US and UK had conspired to put the Soviet Union—which had the most immediate interests in Poland—in "an unbearable position by trying to dictate to it their demands." According to Stalin, the US and UK demanded "too much," and the only way to solve the Polish question was to take Yugoslavia as a model.[12]

On 24 April, Molotov met with Stettinius in San Francisco. Encouraged by Stalin's message to Truman, he told Stettinius:

> Now attempts are being made to speak to the Soviet Union in the language of a dictator. The Soviet Union is in the first rank of powers and will not be pushed back into the second rank. If the Soviet Union were to be treated as a partner, it would react as a cooperative partner along the lines of the Crimea Conference. But if attempts were made using the Polish situation as an excuse to dictate to the Soviet Union, no good would come out of it.[13]

In his address at the signing of the Soviet-Polish Treaty on 22 April, Stalin had strongly defended his position on Poland, hailing the Treaty as one "of great international importance" and great "historical significance" and saying that "it puts an end to the old relations between our countries, burying them and erecting in their place a real basis for a friendly and allied relationship." He emphasized that if such a treaty existed before the war, it would have rendered German aggression untenable.

Truman's highhanded diplomacy did not pay off. Obviously, Stalin had sent Molotov to Washington to fathom the waters around the new President. After the visit, the Soviets became even more uncompromising on the Polish question. After Truman had returned to civilian life in Missouri, he would say that "Roosevelt had the attitude that he could manage to get along with Russia just like he managed to get along with Churchill. Roosevelt thought his influence with Stalin would be the same as with Churchill. But I had a notion Roosevelt was right."[14] When someone mentioned that Roosevelt might have been able to move them because he had an advantage on the propaganda front, Truman said "that was the thing that worried me more than anything else."[15]

DESIGNS FOR THE POST-WAR WORLD

On 8 May 1945, the Allied Nations announced the unconditional surrender of the Third Reich and, thus, the end of WWII in Europe. Meanwhile, the UN Conference continued in San Francisco. The foreign ministers of the US, UK, and USSR proceeded with negotiations concerning Poland at the conference, and the leaders of the Big Three also continued to exchange messages on this issue. But these efforts did not produce a solution. The Polish question continued to erode relations with the Soviet Union, even as Soviet participation was needed in the war in Asia.

Another issue provoking the Soviets was the Truman administration's decision, after the surrender of Germany, to cut off Lend-Lease aid to the Soviet Union and to recall ships already en route. Later, the US government would claim that this action was taken by a junior official. In fact, a statement stopping Lend-Lease was first drafted by an FEA official, Crowley, with the approval of Will Clayton and Joseph Grew of the State Department. The statement was not released because White House aide Eben Ayers was against it. But in May, Elmer Davis, Crowley, Clayton, and Matthew Connelly (the President's secretary) discussed a statement drafted for Crowley; they consulted Grew and Steve Early, the White House Press Secretary. Grew "showed the customary State Department caution." Connelly phoned the President and got approval for the statement.[16] Crowley later said that the Lend-Lease incident was "the most dishonest action in the history of the Government."[17]

Truman had discussed with Harry Hopkins the possibility of Hopkins' seeing Stalin on Truman's behalf. In fact, Hopkins suggested Harriman for the task, but Harriman proposed sending Hopkins, who had liaisoned between FDR and Stalin. On 4 May, Truman again discussed the mission with Hopkins, who promised to go even though he was ill.

Churchill and Truman agreed on 9 May that it was necessary to hold a summit meeting of the US, UK, and USSR, to address impending issues. On 15 May, Deputy Secretary of State Joseph Grew, Harriman, and Bohlen went to the White House. Grew told Truman that the Big Three Meeting should not be postponed until July, and Harriman added that Stalin was not getting accurate reports from any of his people and had grown deeply and unjustifiably suspicious that the West would deprive him of the fruits of victory. Bohlen suggested that the meeting place had better be on Soviet territory, so Stalin could consult with his Politburo; even in Yalta, the Soviets' failure to carry out the agreement was due largely to internal opposition Stalin encountered upon his return. Truman expressed his wish that Harriman return to Moscow immediately.[18]

In the meantime, Truman continued to study US-USSR relations, consulting frequently with knowledgeable advisors. Stimson, who Truman believed to have "a very sound viewpoint on the subject," came to the White House on 16 May "to discuss his viewpoints on the Russian situation." Elliot Roosevelt and Anna Boettiger came on the same day to tell Truman their impressions of the Russians, British, and French, impressions formed on various trips with their father, FDR. Anna came back two days later "to give further information on Roosevelt's dealings with Russia." Harriman came on 16 May and 18 May "for final discussion before he left for Russia" and to discuss the "Russian situation and trip of Hopkins." Byrnes came on 18 May, to tell Truman that he "should not send Hopkins to Russia"—to which Truman replied, "I thought I would send him. No need for anyone else to get any credit but the President."[19] During his visit to Cordell Hull at the hospital the previous day, Truman had asked the former Secretary of State for "his viewpoints on Harry Hopkins." Hull's answer was positive.

On 19 May, Truman formally assigned Hopkins the mission, and made a note that he told Hopkins of the "very strained relations with Russia over the interpretation of Yalta." He asked Hopkins to tell Stalin what the US intended to do by way of carrying out the Yalta agreements. He was anxious to have a fair understanding with the Russian Government and said that he wanted Stalin to "carry his agreements out to the letter, and we intend to see that he does." Hopkins "could use diplomatic language, or use a baseball bat if he thought it was the proper approach to Stalin." Truman invited Stalin to come to the US, reciprocating Roosevelt's visit to the Soviet Union, and promised that Stalin would be royally entertained. The only difficulty was that Stalin might be nominated as President of the US if he came![20]

Hopkins arrived in Moscow on 25 May and left on 7 June. He made it clear to Stalin that the "US was not only not interested in the establishment of a *cordon sanitaire* around Russia but, on the contrary, was aggressively opposed to it." Stalin did not comment on this. Stalin did finally agree to discuss the names of Poles outside the provisional government with whom consultations might be undertaken; he emphasized the importance of not bringing in too many conservatives, because the consulting body would decide the fate of the provisional government. Truman indicated to Churchill that Hopkins reported "a most encouraging measure in the Polish situation.... Stalin has agreed to invite to Moscow for consultation in conformity with our interpretation of the Yalta Agreement the following Poles from London...." He also informed the nation that "there has been a very pleasant yielding on the part of the Russians to some of the things in which we are interested."[21] One White House insider found the President "happy at the results of Hopkins' mission to Moscow....In fact, he was so pleased and excited that he could not refrain from telling us of the good word from Hopkins."[22]

Since Roosevelt's death, Churchill had been urging Truman to take a strong and firm position vis-a-vis the Soviets. Churchill pointed out that an iron curtain had been drawn down by the Soviets across their front from North Cape in Norway to east of Luebeck and halfway across the Isonzo River. He advised that Western troops should not retreat to the line formerly agreed upon by the Allies until affairs in Soviet-occupied countries satisfied the West: "all matters can only be settled before U.S. armies in Europe are weakened."[23] Truman was very much aware that Churchill would use the US to achieve British goals—and he also wanted to show the British that he was no less worthy of respect than his predecessor. When Eden came to see him to discuss the world situation, Truman would not discuss the UN Conference, telling Eden to "get it from my own Secretary of State."[24]

While sending Hopkins to Moscow, Truman also sent Joseph Davies to London as his emissary to Churchill. Davies was to tell Churchill that, if there were going to be any cat's paw to pull the chestnut out of the fire, "I [Truman] am going to be the paw and not the cat." Churchill was also to understand that Truman was not acting for Great Britain in any capacity, though he wanted the support of Great Britain so far as peace was concerned.[25]

Subsequent to Hopkins' departure from Moscow on 7 June, the Polish question proceeded toward settlement, and the Three Powers finally reached a compromise on the issue of the Polish government. The governments of the US, UK, and USSR announced that on 28 June a Polish Provisional Government of National Unity had been established in conformity with the Yalta agreements, and that all three countries had extended diplomatic recognition to it. As to the *quo vadis* of Poland, that would be another story. At the moment, the Big Three had many important matters at hand, and a face-saving solution of this prolonged issue would evidently be desirable to all parties. But divergent interpretations of the Yalta agreements remained a stumbling block. Truman himself told the White House staff in late May that he "sat up last night reading the Yalta agreements again" and that every time he went over them he found "new meanings in them."[26]

The Research & Analysis Branch of the OSS had produced, in September 1943, a document entitled "The Basis of Soviet Foreign Policy" discussing whether the Soviet Union would cooperate with the Western nations. The OSS branch concluded that the Soviet Union might not do so unless the West recognized the inviolability of its 1941 borders, permitted the existence of friendly governments on its periphery, and made a suitable place for it in the Three-Power scheme of world control. In addition, the Allies should open a "Second Front" in the near future. The document further stated that, judging from the Soviets' inviting the Allies to fight on the continent and appealing for collaboration, it seemed that the Soviets were not irrevocably non-collaborative and would not predominate over all of Europe. The OSS branch believed that the Soviets were then carefully avoiding or postponing the choice between cooperation and independent action, pending a clearer indication by the Allies of their own intentions, but that they might sovietize parts of Eastern and Central Europe. The document concluded that mutual effort toward cooperation would stabilize Europe, while independent policies on both sides would lead to Soviet pursuit of predominance.[27]

A year later, the State Department sent Roosevelt a memorandum in which it said that "postwar Poland will be under strong Russian influence. In this situation, the US can hope to make its influence felt only if some degree of equal opportunity in trade, investment and access to sources of information is preserved....The Soviet Union will probably insist on a Polish Government sympathetic to itself."[28] Then in early 1945 the Joint Intelligence Committee of the JCS made an "estimate of Soviet postwar capabilities and intentions," which the JCS circulated as a memorandum for information. The authors of the document believed that the Soviet Union would be influenced by an ideology of "ultimate inevitable conflict between Soviet and non-Soviet states," but they also admitted the "advisability of compromise to postpone or avoid open and serious conflict." The estimate asserted that:

> in order to accomplish maximum economic recovery, the Soviet Union must avoid conflict with Great Britain and the US, or even such tension as would lead to an armaments race, at least until after 1952....[I]n carrying out its national security policies the Soviet Union will rely heavily upon the development of its own influence upon other nations. In peripheral areas, such as Eastern Europe, the USSR will insist upon control or predominant influence. In Central Europe, China, and perhaps Japan, it will insist upon an influence at least equal to that of the Western Powers. In Western Europe and the Mediterranean, it will attempt to make British influence less than Soviet influence in Eastern Europe.[29]

The estimate pointed out that the Soviet Union would not dogmatically base its policies on the inevitability of war between countries of different social systems but would rather make compromises. It also correctly described the sorts of influence to be imposed by the Soviet Union. This JCS estimate must have had some impact on Roosevelt when he went to Yalta for the summit.

The results of wartime summits among the major powers and the progress of the war itself show that the Western allies agreed to the alleged Soviet demands in the above-mentioned documents. What emerged from these summits was the blueprint of a postwar world comprising, on the one hand, the cooperation of the Allies in the UN and especially their unanimity in the Security Council, and on the other hand, a clear division with both the USSR and the US (and its Western allies) protecting their own spheres of influence and further enhancing their own interests. These two basic features of the postwar world were contradictory in nature. The inability of a world organization to overrule the conflicting interests of the great powers was very similar to the situation after World War I—and would once again lead the world to a new war. But after World War I there were several concentrations of strength and power, whereas immediately after World War II the world was polarized around only two centers, the US and the USSR.

Stalin and Churchill reached an agreement in Moscow on 22 October 1944, incorporating some Balkan countries into their spheres of influence. This deal was commonly called the "percentage agreement." Ambassador Harriman served as an observer during Churchill's visit to Moscow. He looked favorably on both Churchill's visit to Moscow and Soviet foreign policy in general, later remarking before the State Department's Policy Committee that the "Churchill-Stalin meeting had been very successful. Nothing had occurred there which [I] felt to be adverse to our interest....Stalin was very cordial to Churchill and there was an earnest attempt on both sides to come to agreement."[30] Harriman's reports to the President at the time of the talks must have been similar in substance.

In an exchange of messages between Churchill and FDR, the former first advised that the division of spheres of influence in Romania and Greece was made for military reasons. FDR replied that the State Department opposed this arrangement and suggested that there might be consultative bodies to limit the tendency towards spheres of influence. Churchill countered by conceding that continuation of these spheres was not good and suggesting that they be allowed a trial period of three months. FDR agreed, saying that this was not to lead to postwar spheres of influence. In fact, though, he was signalling a green light for such practices.[31] FDR well understood that this was alien to the traditional US policy of an Open Door outside the western hemisphere, but the reality of world power politics told him that dividing the world into spheres of influence was in the interest of the United States.

The presence of the Red Army in Eastern Europe and its political consequences were already irreversible when the Big Three met at Yalta in February 1945. At Yalta they finally agreed upon a Declaration of Liberated Areas, which covered the postwar treatment of the Eastern European countries, Poland included. The US State Department worked out a sentence for the draft Declaration by which the ambassadors of the US, Britain, and the Soviet Union in Warsaw would observe and report on the carrying out of free and unfettered elections. But Roosevelt—more realistic and sophisticated—deleted this sentence.[32] Admiral Leahy was apprehensive. "Mr. President, this document is so elastic that you can stretch it from here to Washington and back again. These Russians are going to interpret it in their own way and will take over Poland." The President replied, "Yes, Bill, you may be right, but I am too tired to fight."[33] Stettinius later explained: "By February 1945, therefore, Poland and all of Eastern Europe, except for most of Czechoslovakia, was in the hands of the Red Army. As a result of this military situation, it was not a question of what Great Britain and the US would permit the Russians to do in Poland but what the two countries could persuade the Soviet Union to accept."[34] Nevertheless, when Roosevelt reported to the Congress after returning from Yalta, he said that the notion of the sphere of influence was no more. He cited the Polish solution as one outstanding example of joint action in the liberated areas. And he said that the Allies had been determined to find a common ground, and "we did."[35]

President Truman might have been a knowledgeable domestic politician, but he was not sufficiently knowledgeable in foreign policy when he took office in the spring of 1945. Able and vocal advisors in foreign affairs undoubtedly had great influence when the new president was forming his perspective on world affairs. Harriman was a loyal Democrat, a former governor of New York, a multi-millionaire, world traveller, and veteran diplomat—and last but not least, an insider in the Roosevelt-Stalin-Churchill relationship. The new President respected the ambassador, and Harriman considered himself a mentor. After the meeting of 20 April, he took Truman aside and told him that he had rushed back "for fear that you did not understand that Stalin is breaking his agreements." It was Harriman who told the President—not the other way around—that "I am greatly relieved that we see eye to eye on the situation."[36] It is no wonder that Harriman became one of Truman's most frequently consulted associates during his first month in office, even though Harriman did not hold a post in the Cabinet or White House. He met with Truman nine times in about a month, five of these times privately.

Just six months before, when Harriman had spoken to the Policy Committee after the "percentage agreement," he had declared that "the Soviets consider a close association with us and the British to be their first line of defense. Through such an association they believe they can best pursue their principal objective, which is to rebuild and develop their economy." He said that the Soviets also had a second line of defense: bordering states "should not unite with foreign aggressors." Harriman saw that "such a policy can of course easily become imperialistic," but predicted that if the US had sufficient interest it could "probably prevent its [the Soviet policy toward contiguous countries] being carried to extremes." Harriman felt the US should immediately approach the Soviets "from the standpoint of friendliness and understanding but with complete firmness" and "take issue with the Soviets on all matters in which they contravene our basic policies." He recommended that the "basic weapon" of the US "should not be the threat to withhold economic assistance but the threat to refrain from cooperation in the maintenance of general security," believing that if the United States followed this line it would "meet with unexpected success."[37]

It turned out that by the spring of 1945 Harriman had already altered half of his original view. He continued to recommend a firm stand toward the Soviets to prevent them from going to extremes in Eastern Europe but no longer advocated a friendly and understanding approach. He would give them no loans, and no longer saw economic development as their principal objective. To Truman, Harriman likened Soviet control of Eastern Europe to "barbarian invasion of Europe."[38] Interestingly, one of Jay Franklin's informants commented, after meeting Harriman in Moscow, that Harriman had no idea of what Truman planned for the future; he was of a "ruminative type, and did not fully understand the reasons for Russian suspicion and secretiveness, which is a very interesting and sociological study, much more of a problem than seemed to me Harriman was aware of."[39]

Harriman's deputy and the charge d'affairs in the Moscow Embassy, George F. Kennan, sent back from Moscow a long memorandum sometime between the end of April and early May, discussing in detail the Soviet Union's international position at the close of the war with Germany. Kennan's view resembled Harriman's of that time. Kennan wrote that it must be Russian policy in the coming period to persuade the West, particularly the US, to give blessing to its domination of Eastern Europe and extensive aid to make good its economic damages. The Soviets thought the American public had been taught to believe that: (1) collaboration with Russia was entirely possible; (2) it depended only upon setting up a proper relationship of cordiality and confidence with Russian leaders; and (3) if the US did not find means to insure this collaboration, then a future war was inevitable.

Kennan said that throughout the eleven years of diplomatic relations between the two countries it had been the US, in at least 99 cases out of 100, taking the initiative to try to establish a relationship of confidence and cordiality, and that these efforts had met almost invariably with suspicion, discourtesy and rebuff; in the future it would not be otherwise. Kennan predicted that if the West denied support for the consolidation of Soviet power over Eastern and Central Europe, the Soviets would probably not be able to maintain their hold there. If the West stood firm, Moscow would have played its last real card—but no one in Moscow believed the West would stand firm. It was on this disbelief that Soviet global policy was based.[40] Kennan's attitude was consistent: he had wanted a showdown with the Soviets on Poland as early as June 1944, and he "never doubted" that the Yalta decision on Poland "was a lost cause."[41]

A third person in the Moscow Embassy, General John Deane, Chief of the U.S. Military Mission, held views similar to those of Kennan and Harriman. Deane sent back a memo immediately after Roosevelt's death that "a new and serious situation has arisen. Not only have we a Russia that is victorious over the Germans but one that is so sure of her strength as to assume an attitude of dominance with respect to her Allies." Deane said that "none of the political or military decisions reached at the Crimea Conference have been implemented." He believed that at this stage, military collaboration with the Soviet Union was not vital to the US, and that Soviet participation in the Far East was assured, in furtherance of the Soviets' own interests. The essence of Deane's recommendations was to cut back or cut off military projects in collaboration with the Soviets.[42] Recall that, during the meeting of 23 April 1945 concerning Molotov's visit, Deane had already been among the hardliners. General Wilson, Deane's British counterpart in Moscow, said Deane told him that the phase where "we must always be conciliatory" had now passed, and now "we could afford to be more tough."[43]

Thus, the senior American diplomats in Moscow had in fact formed a group advocating a line tantamount to reversal of the Yalta Agreements. These frontline diplomats were confident that if the US refused to recognize Soviet access to a sphere of influence in Eastern Europe, regardless of what Roosevelt had assented to or connived at, the Soviets would ultimately yield. Though the military brass in Washington held a different view, probably because of war needs, the position of these diplomats strongly affected—and coincided with—the thinking of their new President.

It is necessary to examine what the Soviets had in mind before we can know whether Truman's policy could work. One day before the death of President Roosevelt, Stalin and Tito signed a Soviet-Yugoslav Treaty of Mutual Assistance. After the signing, Stalin expanded upon his view of the postwar world: "This war is not as in the past. Whoever occupies a territory also imposes on it his own social system. Everyone imposes his own system as far as his army can reach. It cannot be otherwise."[44] This view has been implicit in Soviet conduct ever since. What Stalin needed was not merely the cessation of *cordon sanitaire* but also a group of friendly countries who had social systems similar to that of the Soviet Union. In his view, this was entirely reasonable, because he had strong security concerns and because he had reached an agreement with Churchill and Roosevelt. Any Western change on the question of the spheres, if not strictly for face-saving purposes, would be interpreted by the Soviets as a breach of promise. People in the Kremlin must have reviewed the hostile attitude of the West since the Soviets had come to power; the conclusion drawn from past lessons could only be: never count on the imperialists.

The case of the Polish government clearly shows how fragile the postwar structures designed by the Big Three really were. The two conflicting structures, cooperation in the UN and the spheres of influence, were in need of a strong coordinating mechanism—perhaps a UN remade as a supranational power so it could bang a gavel over disputes between member countries. But no such mechanism existed. There was only a gentlemens' agreement, what in Chinese is called "the speechless echoing of hearts." The effectiveness of a gentlemens' agreement is based upon mutual understanding and a willingness to make necessary concessions. When these bases are shaken, the agreement can easily become a point of controversy. This is what happened in the case of Poland. The Polish issue was not an important origin of the Cold War. It, and other disputes over Eastern Europe, were simply outcomes driven by the contradictory structures of the postwar world.

The untimely death of Roosevelt made matters worse. President Truman thought that a gentlemens' agreement with Stalin would never work and did not believe such an agreement ever existed, while Stalin was convinced that an agreement had been reached but was not being honored—since the other "gentleman" had passed away. Some believed that one root of the entire problem was a rather careless approach toward the making of agreements with potentially momentous consequences. In 1946 Bernard Baruch emphatically advised Truman that American leaders should do their "homework before going to conferences so that agreements are free of ambiguity and so that we have concise grasp of policies we wish pursued."[45]

Clearly, there were second thoughts. On the eve of the UN conference in April 1945, Stettinius, in reply to charges from Molotov, said "there had been no change in our attitude since Crimea." But Molotov insisted that "at the Crimea Conference the atmosphere had been satisfactory but since then they had noticed a definite change and that obstacles were being placed in the way of formation of a Polish government friendly to the Soviet Union." Truman himself, just before meeting Molotov in Washington, expressed regret to Stettinius that the agreement was not more clear cut.[46] After his first-round encounter with Stalin and Molotov in the spring of 1945, Truman even admitted that the Soviet Union had a right to form a belt of security around itself. He told a press conference on 9 June: "I don't blame them for wanting to have these states around them just as we wanted Mexico and Canada to be friendly to us.... I don't feel like falling out with Russia over the fact that they want friendly people around them.

You know they've had that *cordon sanitaire.*" He further said that he did not agree with their form of government and their methods—but if they wanted it, let them have it.[47]

Evidently, issues surrounding the composition of a government or the nature of an election, insofar as they pertained to the sphere of influence of the other power, could be used to one's own advantage or could simply be dismissed. In the late spring and early summer of 1945, Germany had surrendered but Japan was still engaged in fierce fighting. Though Truman decided to be firm with the Soviets, the relationship basically remained one of war allies and remained within the framework of the Yalta Agreement. He had sent Hopkins to "shoot" the Polish trouble, and a summit was on the horizon. Discretion was necessary. Deputy Secretary of State Grew said the State Department "had been meticulous in keeping Moscow informed of every step which was of interest to the Soviet Union." The unfortunate party in all of this was Poland. Prior to the war Poland was a victim of rivalry between Nazi Germany and the Anglo-French alliance. The war in Europe had broken out in Poland when the Nazis attacked a German town at the border with commandos disguised as Polish troops, and Poland continued to be sacrificed in the conflict between the Soviet Union and Nazi Germany. By war's end, Poland was being victimized once again, this time by rivalry between the Western Allies and the Soviet Union. The West wanted to interfere in the name of democracy and justice, the Soviets in the name of revolution. Neither cared about the aspirations of the Polish people!

3

The Road To Civil War In China

President Truman began dealing with Chinese affairs soon after taking office. China's Premier, T.V. Soong, visited him on 19 April and 14 May, urging him to release to China an outstanding loan balance of $200 million. The President responded by granting the request.[1]

Three months had passed since Yalta, yet the China agreement reached by the Big Three was still being kept secret from the Chinese Government. Ambassador Hurley reported to Truman on 10 May that Chiang was not informed of the Prelude to the Yalta Agreements. He believed that Chiang would oppose the terms 'preeminent' and 'lease' in the agreement, because the words connoted extraterritoriality—infringement upon the territorial integrity and sovereignty of China. Hurley said that Chiang had been receiving information regarding the Yalta decisions from his own sources (in Washington and Switzerland) and he advised that Chiang be formally informed of these decisions.[2] On 9 June 1945, Truman sent Hurley the text of the Yalta Agreement on China, for presentation to Chiang on the 15th.[3] Truman showed the Agreement to T.V.Soong on the same day. Hurley had already informed Chiang of the main points in the agreement on 21 May, and asked Chiang not to discuss the agreement with Stalin or Truman on his own initiative.[4]

Truman continued to discuss the China Policy with some old China hands, including John Carter Vincent, Owen Lattimore and Edwin Locke, Jr.[5] Meanwhile, the relationship between the Nationalists and the Communists was deteriorating rapidly.

THE NATIONALISTS AND COMMUNISTS

The Nationalist Party (or KMT) was established—by Dr. Sun Yat-sen—in 1905; the Communist Party (CCP), in 1921. Before his death in 1925, Sun decided to reform the KMT on the basis of the "Three Policies": in coalition with Russia, in coalition with the Communists, and help the workers and the peasants. Thus, he inaugurated the first period of

KMT-CCP cooperation, 1924-1927. General Chiang Kai-shek, one of Dr. Sun's key associates, launched a coup in April 1927, split with the CCP, set aside the Three Policies, and seized national power. The Russian advisors to the KMT went home, and the Communists were purged. From 1927 on, the CCP and the KMT were engaged in a bitter civil war. Only after the War of Resistance against Japan broke out in July 1937 did the two parties cooperate again, but this cooperation was never to be a smooth one.

In one of the resolutions at its 6th Congress in May 1945, the KMT charged the CCP with persistent "armed insubordination." The Congress expressly reaffirmed Chiang's decision to convene a National Assembly, which would make possible the establishment of a constitutional government. The CCP held its own Congress, the 7th, from 23 April through 11 July 1945. The Chairman of the Party, Mao Zedong, predicted in his political report to the Congress, entitled *On the Coalition Government*, that Chiang would start a civil war after the Japanese were driven out of a good portion of China. Mao requested that the British and US governments heed the voice of the Chinese majority and take care that their foreign policy did not run counter to the people's wishes, thereby impairing the international friendship. According to Mao, it would be a grievous error for a foreign government to support Chiang. For the moment, the Communists were discreet enough not to point a finger at the US—when finger-pointing was unavoidable, they would first name the British.

In his report, Mao also called for a coalition government with the Nationalists and other parties and outlined policies for the proposed government. Of course, there was not the slightest possibility that Chiang would accept the proposal, but the plan was appealing to the nation and it was in fact the first design for the future People's Republic.[6] At the time, the People's Political Council, a national political organ, was serving as a forum for exchange of views—no matter how diverse—among the KMT, the CCP, and the smaller parties. Interestingly, when the KMT convened a Council meeting on 7 July 1945, the CCP boycotted it.

The Council meeting in July marked the end of Hurley's first-round effort to bring the two rival Parties to terms. Three days after the opening of the meeting, Mao wrote a commentary for Xinhua (the Communists' official news agency) entitled "The Hurley-Chiang Duet Is a Flop," in which he openly charged that Hurley's support played a decisive role in encouraging Chiang's audacity in demanding that the CCP hand over its army in exchange for "legal status."[7] Two days later, Mao wrote another commentary entitled "On the Danger of the Hurley Policy," claiming that US policy, as represented by Hurley, was "leading China to a crisis of civil war." He remarked that when Hurley went to Yanan in November 1944 he agreed to the Five-Point draft agreement proposed by the CCP but that he later changed his tune and even bluntly declared that the US would cooperate only with Chiang and not with the CCP. Mao warned that if Hurley's policy continued, the US Government would "fall hopelessly into the deep, stinking cesspool of Chinese reaction," and would place itself in opposition to the hundreds of millions of Chinese people.[8] In Mao's view, Hurley represented a group of people in the US Government. Specifically, "[when] Roosevelt died...Hurley, beside himself with jubilation, returned to the Embassy in Chongqing." Mao was intent on extending a warning to the new administration in Washington.

The Hurley statement to which Mao repeatedly referred was made on 2 April, in a Washington press conference. Hurley remarked at the conference that the CCP "supports three principles, and the three principles are government of the people, by the people, and for the people," but the greater part of his statement actually supported Chiang and denounced the Communists. He said that "there can be no political unification in China as long as there are armed political parties and warlords who are still strong enough to defy the National Government," that "the military strength of the armed political parties and the warlords has been overestimated in the United States," and that Chiang "is not fascist-minded...[but aims rather] to relinquish all the power he possesses to a government of the people,...by the people, and for the people." On the role of the US, Hurley said that "we do recognize the National Government of China and not any armed warlords or armed political parties in China."[9] What makes these sentences especially noteworthy is that they were uttered by the US Ambassador to China while Roosevelt was still the President.

On 10 August, the Japanese government requested the Allies' permission to surrender; on the 14th, Japan formally announced surrender. Though the Chinese exulted over this long-sought victory, it immediately intensified the serious strains in the KMT-CCP relationship. The principal issue concerned how to accept the surrender of Japanese forces in China. In Northeastern China (Manchuria), the Japanese Kwantung Army would surrender to Soviet forces, but south of the Great Wall the Communists were, in many places, closer to the Japanese troops than were the Nationalists because the Communist areas were often situated at the enemy rear while the Nationalist forces were usually deployed along an open front line.

Zhu De, Commander-in-Chief of the 18th Group Army (the official umbrella designation for all Communist regulars), on 10 August ordered all troops under his command to accept the surrender of those Japanese troops within their reach on the basis of the Potsdam Declaration. The Nationalists charged that Zhu's order was "a presumptuous and illegal act." The unspoken concern of the KMT was that Zhu's action would render it impossible for the Nationalists to accept the surrender of troops far from Nationalist positions. Chiang dispatched to the Communists an order that "all units of the 18th Group Army should stay where they are, pending further orders." Mao responded in two telegrams. Besides reaffirming the right of forces under the CCP to accept the surrender, he demanded that Chiang immediately abolish the "one-party dictatorship, and call a conference of all parties to set up a democratic coalition government."[10] Chiang, of course, did not accept Mao's proposal. In a commentary for Xinhua, Mao openly asserted that "Chiang Kai-shek is provoking civil war."[11]

After being informed about the Yalta secret agreement on China, Chiang instructed T.V. Soong to proceed from San Francisco to Moscow. Soong was to negotiate a friendship treaty, which Stalin agreed to sign. At the same time, Truman asked Harriman to return to his Moscow post; Truman was eager to enlist the assistance of the Soviets in settling problems in the Far East. Soong arrived in Moscow in late June and returned to Chongqing to confer with Chiang during the second half of July. After hard bargaining, the Sino-Soviet Treaty was signed on 14 August 1945—further increasing Chiang's confidence in dealing with the CCP.[12]

Believing that he had the backing of both the US and the USSR, Chiang thought that he might be able to make new gains through negotiation with the CCP. And the US was strongly urging him to negotiate. Although he doubted that Mao would come, he sent Mao three telegrams in August inviting him to Chongqing for peace talks. To Chiang's surprise, the CCP decided that they should send Mao, Zhou Enlai, and Wang Ruofei. Many Communist officials believed that once Mao arrived in Chongqing, Chiang would never allow him to return. Mao himself sent out a party circular outlining the situation: "At present the Soviet Union, the United States, and Britain all disapprove of civil war in China," and there is some possibility of bringing about a new stage of cooperation between the two parties [KMT and CCP] and of peaceful development. To achieve this, however, the CCP would have to make concessions. If Chiang wanted a civil war after the Communists had made concessions, the latter could justifiably fight in defense.[13]

To show that the US government had a spirit of goodwill and that Mao's safety was assured, Hurley flew to Yanan on 27 August to accompany Mao and his entourage to Chongqing. Mao and Chiang discussed the formation of governments at all levels, the principles of peace, democracy, solidarity, and unity, and freedoms of person, speech, belief, and assembly. But the major item of discussion was unification of KMT and CCP troops and governments. The Communists demanded that CCP troop strength remain at 20-24 divisions, while the Nationalists were willing to settle for an even 20—not much of a difference. The Nationalists wanted unification of government carried out first, while the Communists insisted that until the constitutional provision for popular election of provincial governments had been adopted and put into effect, the status quo of the areas under their control should be maintained. Both sides agreed to discuss this question further.[14]

After six weeks of heavy bargaining in Chongqing, Mao returned to Yanan on October 11. On the eve of his departure, he and Chiang signed a document commonly known as the Double Tenth Agreement, as it was signed on the 10th of October 1945.[15] The negotiations and the resulting agreement gave hope to the Chinese people and the world that civil strife might be avoided. This was not to be the case.

US AID TO THE NATIONALISTS

T.V. Soong approached the State Department in early September, urging the US government to live up to Roosevelt's promise to equip 120 Chinese divisions. Neither the State Department nor the White House could find records of this promise; later it was discovered that in Cairo FDR did promise to equip 90 divisions, including 30 divisions previously promised. Soong knowingly excluded these 30, making his total 120. In any case, even the promise to equip 90 divisions had not been recorded in writing.

When asked by the White House, Harry Hopkins testified that there was a verbal agreement between FDR and Chiang in Cairo.[16] According to Hopkins, FDR had said that Chiang could "buy the stuff" after the war ended. Hopkins believed that FDR was trying to insure that China remained in the war, strengthen Chiang's hand in dealing with "recalcitrant Chinese factions," and fulfill his wish that China ultimately become a great power. Hopkins observed that, at the time, FDR was using every means at his command to prevent Chiang's government from collapsing. Hopkins now suggested that the White House should say that they could not find a record of the promise.[17] But on 4 September 1945, the President's Naval Aide, Captain Vardaman, said that Truman believed "we are 'hooked' for the 90 division figure."[18]

Mao Zedong addressed a meeting of Communist cadres in Yanan on 17 October 1945, reporting on his mission to Chongqing. Mao said that, although agreement had been reached on some principles, other points had not been resolved. The question of the Communist-controlled Liberated Areas had not been solved, and that of the armed forces had not really been solved either. Mao noted that KMT forces were attacking the Communists at the time of the negotiations and that the CCP's answer was to be "tit for tat." As to what this might mean, he remarked that it depended on the situation; sometimes refusing to negotiate was "tit for tat"—but sometimes negotiating was, too. As for the weapons under Communist control, Mao said that "every gun and every bullet, must all be kept, must not be handed over." Mao had not the slightest illusion about Chiang Kai-shek's intentions.[19] KMT and CCP forces had not, in fact, ceased fighting before, during, or after the negotiations in Chongqing.

The US military was already deeply involved in the China Theater by the end of the war, with (1) the Headquarters of the US Army, China, under General Wedemeyer, (2) the 14th Air Force and the 10th Air Force, both under the command of General Stratemeyer, (3) US Army personnel serving as instructors for KMT military forces, (4) various US military units transporting military equipment and supplies for KMT forces, (5) the OSS parachuting commandos and intelligence teams into China, (6) the Navy Group, China, under US Navy officer Mills Miles, working closely with the KMT secret police chief Dai Li, and (7) US Army generals moved into the China Theater to command KMT forces after the war in Europe ended. The JCS instructed Wedemeyer on 1 August 1945 that the purpose of his mission was twofold: to advise and assist Chiang, and to refuse to support Chiang "in fratricidal war." These two conflicting charges "confronted Wedemeyer with a dilemma the general quickly recognized."[20]

In the spring of 1945, Wedemeyer had discussed with the Chiang government his plan for reducing the number of divisions in the KMT forces, to make them more effective in combat. He said that among 327 divisions, only the 5 in India were effective. He believed that 45 divisions would be enough for local security missions; along with the 39 already under the US-KMT aid program, the total of 84 would be sufficient, and the remaining 200-odd divisions should be deactivated. Chiang's Minister of War had claimed that 35 divisions had already been deactivated, but Wedemeyer found that, on the contrary, one army had been added to the original number in early May.[21] Wedemeyer's comment that all but 5 divisions—all trained and equipped by the US—were ineffective was, of course, an exaggeration, and was unfair to troops who had been fighting valiantly. Wedemeyer's proposal, if implemented, would have reduced Chiang's strength, internationally and domestically, and also infringed upon China's sovereignty. In any case, Chiang would never agree to deactivate troops unless he considered it absolutely necessary. He did not want to challenge Wedemeyer directly, so he invented the "reduction" reported by his Minister of War.

Wedemeyer received data from the US War Production Mission in China revealing that China's economic capacities had been seriously underestimated. The Mission concluded that, from current stocks and 1945 production, China could equip and maintain 80 divisions. Wedemeyer, accepting this view, now suggested adding 40 US-sponsored divisions for a total of 120 divisions of KMT forces.[22]

On 30 July, the JCS advised Wedemeyer that it would be highly desirable to occupy key ports in Asia—in this order: Shanghai, Pusan, Yantai [Chefoo], and Qinhuangdao [Chinhuangtao]—"in order to better facilitate the reoccupation of the country by Chinese forces." Wedemeyer conferred with Chiang and T.V. Soong the next day, and they agreed to the landing of US forces in the Chinese ports.[23] When Japan was about to surrender, Wedemeyer cabled Army Chief of Staff General George C. Marshall, recommending that he send US troops and that the Japanese be instructed to surrender only to the Chinese Nationalists, never to the Communists. Informed of this recommendation, President Truman agreed and stipulated that the Japanese emperor order all Imperial Armed Forces in China (excluding Manchuria) to surrender to Chiang Kai-shek.[24] Then, in August and September, US forces moved 140,000 KMT troops to Manchuria. Before the end of September, all the important cities along the China coast, including Nanjing and Beijing, had been occupied by KMT forces. In addition, the US Marines' Sixth Division had arrived in Qingdao, and troops of the US Marines First Division (Reinforced) were fanning out along the railroads in Tianjin, Beijing, Tangshan and Qinhuangdao. The headquarters of the Marines' Third Amphibious Corps was set up in Tianjin in early October. Ahead of the American and KMT troops, OSS daredevils parachuted in, to set up intelligence outfits in northern China's big cities.

Despite Wedemeyer's deactivation proposal, Lend-Lease equipment and supplies for the KMT government continued to arrive—even after the end of the war. On 5 September, Truman approved a JCS memo suggesting that, after Japan's defeat, all Lend-Lease supplies be stopped "except for Allied forces engaged against Japanese forces which have not surrendered." The Lend-Lease to China would be in accordance with a recent directive to the Commanding General of US Forces, China Theater, which included the provision that "the US will not support the Central Government of China in fratricidal war."[25] On the grounds that the Japanese forces had yet to surrender in China and that the equipment was not to be used in China's civil strife, the US military Lend-Lease to Chiang in the first two months after the war reached some $430 million, more than half the value of wartime arms aid. In all, Lend-Lease to China after the Japanese surrender was $700 million. This sum included a West China stockpile of ammunition, sufficient to supply the 39 divisions of the US-KMT aid program for 120 days, and nominally priced at just $20 million. As a matter of fact, by 23 August 1945, all 39 divisions had enough ordnance to make them completely operable in combat, with the exception of two items.[26]

DIVERGENT VIEWS OF THE CHINA SITUATION

Americans from all walks of life wrote to the White House airing their views on China. In October, Roland B. Parker, Field Director of American Red Cross in China, sent the White House a memo in which he noted that "when I came overseas I was pro-Chiang and pro-Churchill" but that an American officer had recently told him "I hate Chancre Jack (Chiang Kai-shek) and the whole Chiang gang." In Parker's words:

> Two others [American officers in China] stated that they and their fathers always voted the Democratic ticket but that they certainly would not do so next time as they blamed the present administration either for inexcusable ignorance of the situation here or for inexcusable policy if it knows the facts. Since then I have heard similar comments from many enlisted men as well as officers. I have heard only one man state that he felt that we were right in aiding Chiang—and he has a desk job....Hatred of the Chiang Government [is] almost universal....[I] fear that deploying Chinese troops and supplies will result in clashes with Communists and see no need of our taking that chance. Some fear that Chiang's emissaries will shoot down some American planes and with help of their American publicists, hang the label on the Communists.

Parker then directly challenged the basic China Policy:

> I don't think the US has the right to try to divide China..., but if the Chinese wish to divide themselves, that is their business. And I think any possible danger of undue Russian influence in China is accentuated by every move we make to support a government which cannot possibly claim to be the government of, for, and by the people of China.[27]

J. Spencer Kennard, a Protestant missionary who taught history at West China University in Chengdu for seven years during the war, wrote to a State Department official in September. He said that his experience in China led him "to the conviction that America's own interests call for a policy of strict military neutrality....The Communists will not lay down their arms till those armies lay down theirs also....[T]he wise policy is for America to leave solutions to the Chinese themselves. No people have greater capacities for shrewd common sense in their compromises."[28]

American people who might not have been to China also expressed their views to representatives in Congress. G.R. Williams of Denison, Texas, for instance, telegraphed Senator Tom Connally on 6 November 1945: "Respectfully urge you to use your great influence with our State Dept to prevent further use of our armed forces ammunition and transportation facilities in China civil strife. Other nations have no right to intervene in our internal affairs we have no right interfere with theirs." Senator Connally's reply is interesting: "Retel (Regarding your telegram) agree with your view and have expressed that view to high authorities."[29]

The President's secretary, Charles Ross, received a letter in August from Chien Tuansheng (Qian Duansheng), a prominent Chinese law professor and a member of the China Democratic League. In this letter, Chien observed that the KMT "seems to be sure of American material support and consequently considers itself no longer obliged to bow to the demands of public opinion....I believe the good policy of Mr. Roosevelt and presumably of Mr. Truman is being badly carried here on the spot because Chungking [Chongqing] has been led to believe that right or wrong it could count on American support." The letter was forwarded to Ross by a State Department official, Arthur Ringwalt. In his cover letter to Ross, Ringwalt wrote that "In view of present developments in China, the content of Mr. Chien's letter is, perhaps, particularly timely."[30]

The President did not agree with the view expressed by Mr. Ringwalt and much of the American public—and he did not like the people in the State Department. As early as May 1945, he said that the Department was in awful condition.[31] When Byrnes returned from the CFM London meeting in late September, Truman repeated this complaint. He and Admiral Leahy were of the opinion that there were quite a few "pinkies" in State, and Truman reportedly said that now he knew why Roosevelt did not trust it.[32]

But there were people in the State Department whose views were even more extreme than that of the President. One was Under (sometimes Acting) Secretary Joseph C. Grew. Grew sent Secretary of War Henry Stimson a memo in June 1945 citing a memo submitted to the department in 1935 by John MacMurray, a former Minister to China and senior official in the State Department and the Foreign Service, in charge of Far Eastern affairs. MacMurray was once Assistant Secretary of State when Grew was Under Secretary. Grew remarked that MacMurray was generally recognized as an expert in Far Eastern affairs and that his memo was based on direct and intimate observation of China. MacMurray wrote:

> Patient efforts of Japan for nearly ten years tried to preserve the
> letter and spirit of the Washington Treaties in the face of Chinese

intransigence....Japanese forces had then done in good faith only what had been forced upon them to do in fulfillment of the mission to protect the lives and property of their nationals. The effect of our own attitude was to condone the high-handed behavior of the Chinese and to encouraged them to a course to recalcitrance. The Chinese had been willful in their scorn of their legal obligations, reckless in their resort to violence for the accomplishment of their ends, and provocative in their methods."

MacMurray predicted that Japan would be "persuaded" by the conduct of China, the US, and Britain to believe "that it could depend only on its own strong arm to vindicate its rightful legal position in eastern Asia."[33]

After reading this passage, one has no difficulty understanding how the US "persuaded" Japan to invade China when Mr. Grew and Mr. MacMurray were taking care of Uncle Sam's China Policy. Mr. Grew continued to work in the State Department in the Truman administration.

FIGHTING INTENSIFIES IN CHINA

After Chiang and Mao signed the Double Tenth Agreement in Chongqing, the military picture in China became even darker as the forces of the two sides clashed more often and more fiercely. In some areas the Communists retreated, especially in areas near big cities and communication lines. But the Nationalists also sustained more losses than before; in October, they suffered two major setbacks in the North. KMT troops attacked the Communist base area in the southern part of Shanxi province in September. The Communists counter-attacked in October, destroying 35,000 KMT troops and capturing several generals, including army and division commanders. Another KMT contingent of three armies launched an attack on the Communist area in southern Hebei Province. After one army commander led his troops in going over to the Communists, the other two armies were surrounded and disarmed as they tried to retreat.

Faced with the unpleasant military situation and public opposition to an American military presence in China, in mid-November Truman defended the necessity of keeping American troops there. He wrote: "We should make it plain that...there are more than 1,000,000 Jap soldiers in Central China, that Russia, Britain and the US have recognized the Central Government under Chiang Kai-shek....We are neatly winding up the war."[34] The new Secretary of War, Robert P. Patterson, made a statement for the media along the same lines. He said that the US was only concerned militarily with completion of the surrender and evacuation of Japanese forces, and that there were still "more than a million armed Japanese" in the China Theater. He asserted that the U.S. troops in China would not be used for the suppression of civil strife, but would protect

American lives and property; if they were attacked, he expected them to react with "vigor and success."[35]

The main reason for keeping US forces in China was of highly questionable validity. There were not one million armed Japanese in China by November 1945. The total under General Okamura, who surrendered in the China Theater (excluding the Kwantung Army in Manchuria, which surrendered to the Soviet Red Army) was 1,090,000, including combat, supply, medical, transportation, and communications people.[36] This number was larger than the total surrendering in Southeast Asia and the Pacific Islands. The surrender in China had started with V-J; even if the Japanese had not all surrendered by November 1945, the KMT and CCP troops had sufficient strength to deal with them. The Americans knew very well from their own experience that Japanese soldiers would strictly obey the surrender decree of the emperor. General MacArthur remarked after two months of occupation in Japan that "there has not been a single untoward incident between the Japanese and American Forces of Occupation."[37] The unsolved problem in China was repatriation to Japan, which at the time was proceeding very slowly—at 20,000 a month. If the US government was eager to solve the problem of Japanese troops in China, it should have sent more ships, not US troops.

The War Secretary noted that US troops were in China to protect American lives and property, and that when they were attacked they were to react with "vigor and success." This was also untenable. China was not a defeated country. Sending troops in the name of protecting lives and property was an obsolete pretext often used previously by the Japanese in their invasion of China.

In the first draft of his statement, sent to the White House for clearance, Secretary Patterson said that the KMT government had been deeply and helpfully involved in the common cause against Japan, both inside and outside China, while the Communist forces contributed nothing. Later, he sent a second draft to the White House, asking Sam Rosenman to clear it with the President. He wrote Rosenman a cover note describing his "revised statement on US military policy in China. The revision is in the interest of accuracy, and you will note that the statement about Chinese Communist forces contributing nothing has been omitted." Obviously it was Rosenman who had asked him to have the draft revised.[38]

When Hurley cabled Byrnes on 12 September 1945, he once again reviewed the tasks Roosevelt had assigned him when he went to China in 1944. He said he had accomplished all the assignments except one: unification of the anti-Japanese forces in China. Hurley was not sure of Truman's China policy; he said in the telegram that perhaps the US would not continue a long-range policy to establish a unified democratic government in China. At Hurley's suggestion, he and Wedemeyer returned to Washington in October for consultations.[39] Under Secretary of State Dean Acheson called the White House on 11 October to make an appointment for them, saying that, "quite contrary to expectations, Ambassador Hurley is quite willing and eager to return to China." Hurley and Wedemeyer went to the White House on 19 October 1945. After meeting with them, Truman recorded in longhand: "I told them my policy is to support Chiang, K.S."[40]

But as early as three months after the war, Truman was already very concerned about the possible collapse of the Chiang government. In fact, this might be a major reason for his sending Marshall to China. White House aide Eben Ayers remarked in November 1945 that the USSR-US-China situation still seemed to be receiving a great deal of attention from the President and he talked at length about it, beginning with the situation in China proper, where he said the U.S. was "in the middle." He felt that if the US were to "pull out" of China, the KMT government would not be able to carry on.[41]

Hurley repeatedly asked for permission to resign, but Byrnes would not agree. Abruptly, Hurley resigned anyway. His letter of resignation to the President was dated 26 November, and Truman accepted the next day. On that day, the 27th, Truman announced that General George C. Marshall would go to China as his special representative, but the Ambassadorship remained vacant until the next summer, when Leighton Stuart was appointed.

In fact, Hurley had done a credible job in trying circumstances. When he first went to China as FDR's personal representative, his mission was to keep the Chiang government from collapsing, to harmonize relations between Chiang and Stilwell, and to unify the anti-Japanese forces in China—the KMT and CCP—in the war effort. Hurley fulfilled the major requirement of his mission during wartime by keeping Chiang's government functioning, but Roosevelt paid a heavy price in yielding to Chiang's demand for Stilwell's removal. Regarding unification of the anti-Japanese forces, Hurley was rebuffed. He did, however, play a significant role in bringing the two rivals to the negotiating table, and they signed an agreement of sorts. Henry Wallace later wrote to Truman about his 1944 mission to Chongqing, remarking that "Roosevelt talked to me before I left, not about political coalition in China but about 'getting the two groups together to fight the war'." Chiang having told Wallace that talks with the CCP had no prospect of success, Wallace suggested to Roosevelt a coalition not with the CCP but with "progressive banking and commercial leaders," those who formed "the large group of Western-trained men." In short, Wallace admitted that none of the three—Chiang, Roosevelt, and himself—recommended a long-term political settlement between the KMT and the CCP.[42]

Controversy swirls around the figure of Patrick J. Hurley. According to some people, he was instrumental in the removal of Stilwell. It is true that he did not support Stilwell, but Chiang's intransigence over the Stilwell issue was based on his own judgment of the situation, not Hurley's opinion. Chiang had great skill in creating a sort of Collapse Syndrome. He understood that the Americans needed him no less than he needed them, so the collapse of his government during the war became a sword of Damocles he hung over the head of the US. When faced with a clear choice between Chiang and Stilwell, Roosevelt chose the former. One of the tactics of Chinese monarchs was "containing alien barbarians with alien barbarians"; Chiang had considerable personal experience in putting this tactic to use. He had used the Western Allies to contain Japan; now, why couldn't he use the Japanese invasion to contain the US?

The US was susceptible to the Collapse Syndrome. Apart from Chiang, the possibility of a Soviet-Nazi separate peace had always been a threat to the US in the course of the war. Churchill complained before the summit in Potsdam that Britain had not been rewarded for what she had done by a show of US gratitude; Britain could have had a separate peace with Hitler at any time. Others could threaten the US, but the US would not reciprocate. It may not be polite to ask this sensitive question, but was Uncle Sam a sucker?

Although Hurley may not have played much of a role in the Stilwell affair, he did blunder in consenting to the CCP's proposed draft of the Five-Point Agreement; Chiang Kai-shek would never agree to it. Hurley's position was bound to change later, and making a promise that cannot be fulfilled is worse than no promise at all. His change of position would be interpreted by the CCP as a change in America's China Policy, and precipitated fierce attacks from the Communists, aggravating an already difficult situation. Hurley's advisors were either ignorant or idealistic; otherwise, they would have advised strongly against the CCP proposal.

Hurley has also been accused of being overly optimistic about the attitudes of Stalin and Molotov toward Chiang when he passed through Moscow en route to Chongqing in 1944 and 1945, and of having blindly believed the contemptuous statements made by the Soviet leaders about the CCP. These accusations are probably true to an extent, but surely are not matters of great import. The basis of the FDR administration's China Policy during the closing stage of the war was the US-Soviet rivalry. The secret agreement about China reached at Yalta was iron-clad evidence. Hurley's judgment and what he advocated were within the bounds of US policy.

Some say that Hurley's objection to the CCP's proposal of January 1945 that Mao Zedong and Zhou Enlai visit President Roosevelt lost the US a good opportunity in China. But Hurley's objection conformed to the administration's policy. Given that FDR could remove Stilwell to placate Chiang, that the US gave the CCP no military aid during the war, and that even the Soviet leaders said they would not be associated with the CCP, how could Hurley be expected to act other than he did? In any case, Hurley was not FDR's sole source of information in China, and FDR always took China Policy into his own hands. It was certainly a presidential decision not to invite the CCP leaders to visit Washington, and it is too flattering to say that Hurley was pivotal in Roosevelt's calculating attitude toward the Communists before Yalta.

When Truman became President, he inherited most of the ingredients of FDR's China Policy, and emphasized that his policy was to support Chiang. He believed that the CCP had not fought the Japanese but, on the contrary, were helping them.[43] Some low- and medium-level officers in the State Department and the Foreign Service suggested that the China Policy of "leaning to one side" was neither advisable nor feasible, but they were not decision-makers and few of them had any profound understanding of the issue. Hurley's own reported differences with the Truman administration concerned its persistence in carrying out the Yalta Agreement on China; he was becoming disillusioned with the Soviet Union and its lack of influence over the CCP. He was also at odds with some State Department officials and China career officers, including Dean Acheson. Hurley's own position at the time was in flux: in the spring of 1945, he was exulting over Stalin's cooperative attitude towards the China issue, but by the fall he was attacking the Yalta Conference for selling out China to Soviet domination.

Yet another controversy involving Hurley centered upon attitudes toward the colonial powers in Southeast Asia. Hurley was critical of the US policy of supporting the colonial interests of Britain, France, and the Netherlands in Asia, and expressed this criticism repeatedly. In a telegram to Truman on 10 May 1945, Hurley said the policy of the imperialist governments was to keep China divided against herself. In a message to Truman on 29 May, he noted that Roosevelt had told him and Wedemeyer on 8 March, and later repeated to him alone, that Hong Kong should be returned to China. Although Churchill himself told Hurley that would only occur "over my dead body," Hurley still believed that if the US had a firm policy on Hong Kong, the British would yield. Hence, he suggested that a strong Lend-Lease measure be used as leverage, to bring the UK "to its knees" in Hong Kong, adding that in San Francisco the US delegation stood with the imperialists.[44] Hurley reiterated in a telegram to Byrnes on 12

September that the US vote with the UK and France and against Russia and China on the issue of colonial independence was a reversal of the Atlantic Charter policy.[45]   Hurley's view was sensible, but the Truman administration could not have turned this view into a policy, for Truman had to strike compromises with Britain, France, and the Netherlands in Asia in the interest of global alignments.   Of course, Hurley's criticism of colonialism was by no means altruistic.   On 21 May 1945, he cabled Truman that "Mountbattan and representatives of other nations with colonial interests in China wanted to make Mountbattan commander, under Chiang, of all Allied forces in China." Hurley recommended that the American government oppose the appointment of a Commander-in-Chief from any country other than the US and ask Chiang to appoint an American general as Commander-in-Chief of the China Theater.[46]

On other fundamental issues such as support of Chiang at any cost, non-recognition of the CCP, and the forced incorporation of the CCP into the Chiang government, Hurley had no disagreement with Washington. As for the Soviet role in China, the US China Policy's ultimate purpose was to set up a unified pro-US government that would serve as a tool to offset Soviet influence; this was also Hurley's wish. All considered, Hurley and the Truman administration did not have differences over aims. The disputes between them over China Policy were essentially tactical and peripheral, partisan and personal.

The resignation of Ambassador Hurley reflected the larger predicament of the US in China. Keeping the Republican Hurley in the administration, if possible, would give the impression that the China Policy had a certain bipartisan cast. But in his heart, Truman did not object to Hurley's departure. Hurley had treated him with contempt, in the manner of an Oklahoma cowboy; this was simply unacceptable to the straight-talking President from Independence. But while Truman preferred that Hurley fade away quietly, the ambassador chose to raise hell. In the meantime, the situation in China was developing toward all-out civil war.

4

Debut of Atomic Diplomacy

On the 6th and 9th of August 1945, the US Army Air Force, as authorized by the President, dropped atomic bombs on the Japanese cities of Hiroshima and Nagasaki. Evaluations of the role these bombs played in forcing Japan to surrender are very diverse. In President Truman's view, the atomic bomb did not win the war, but certainly shortened it.[1] In fact, the significance of the bomb for American foreign policy in general and policy toward the Soviet Union in particular is greater than its significance for the war itself. Japan was very close to surrender by early August, and the bombings and the entrance of the Soviets into the war, were the straws that broke the camel's back.

DELIBERATIONS ON THE A-BOMB

Even before the successful explosion of an atomic device, the bomb had become an issue of dispute among the well informed in Truman's administration. Truman himself had not been briefed on the Manhattan Project when he was Vice President. Roosevelt did not consider him an insider and did not even show him the White House Map Room. Truman officially learned about the atomic project from War Secretary Henry L. Stimson, almost immediately after his swearing-in ceremony. About two weeks later, Stimson and Vannevar Bush, the scientist-administrator of the project, briefed Truman on the bomb and told him that it would be ready within four months.

At Stimson's suggestion, the President formed an Interim Committee, chaired by the War Secretary, to study the implications of the atomic bomb and especially the question of its use on Japan; James Byrnes served as Truman's own representative on this committee. A panel of four scientists, headed by Robert Oppenheimer, assisted the committee. The committee and its panel came to serve as a channel for forwarding suggestions from other scientists to Stimson and Truman.

49

With the bomb on the agenda and victory in Europe at hand, some informed people, especially the scientists, were very much concerned about both the moral feasibility of using the bomb and its implications for the future of mankind. Particularly concerned was a Hungarian physicist, Leo Szilard. Szilard, along with his colleague Eugene Wigner, had visited Albert Einstein at his home in Peconic, New York, in 1939, initiating the bomb project. In March 1945, Szilard visited Einstein again, this time urging him to introduce Szilard to Roosevelt for the purpose of expressing apprehension about the bomb.[2] Since Roosevelt died shortly afterwards, Einstein's letter introducing Szilard never reached him. Truman, however, read the letter and asked Byrnes to handle it; Szilard went to Spartenbury, North Carolina, to see Byrnes on 25 May 1945.

After several meetings, the Interim Committee reached some important conclusions on 1 June 1945. Stimson went to Truman's office on the 6th to report that the Committee recommended using the atomic bomb against Japan. The major part of his report, however, concerned the implications of the bomb for the Soviet Union:

(1) No revelation should be made to the Soviets until the bomb was successfully dropped on Japan.

(2) If the matter came up at the forthcoming Big Three summit before the bomb was tested, the US should say that "we are not ready."

(3) Future control of atomic power could be based upon each country's promising to make public all work done, and upon an international committee with full power of inspection.

(4) The *quid pro quo* for a Soviet partnership would be a solution to present troubles—like Poland, Rumania, Yugoslavia, and northeastern China.

Truman agreed, and said that, in order to give the scientists more time to finish the bomb, he had delayed the meeting of the Big Three until 15 July.

Stimson also reported that he had been trying to hold the Air Force to precision bombing; he felt "a little fearful that before we could get ready the Air Force might have Japan so thoroughly bombed out that the new weapon would not have a fair background to show its strength." Truman "laughed and said he understood."[3]

On 11 June a group of scientists, headed by James Franck and including Szilard, submitted a report to the panel. The report said that the importance of nuclear weaponry lay in "the possibility of its use as a means of political pressure in peace and sudden destruction in war." There were only two ways to minimize the danger of destruction—keep the discoveries secret for an indefinite period of time, or speed production so no one dared to attack for fear of retaliation. But the first option was not feasible, since the Soviets would be able to reconstruct the US program within a few years. Furthermore, monopolizing the necessary materials was not possible, since there were uranium deposits in Czechoslovakia and the Soviet Union. An armaments race would be unavoidable, even if the US kept its atomic secret. As to the second option, stockpiling could invite a potential enemy to attempt a sudden unprovoked blow, while the enemy's industry and population might be dispersed over a large territory, offering it some hope of surviving an attack. The report called for an international agreement on atomic weaponry, but argued that using the bomb on Japan without warning could easily destroy all chances of reaching such an agreement. "Russia, even allied countries..., as well as neutral countries, may be deeply shocked," and would not trust a US proclamation that the weapon should be abolished. The report suggested first demonstrating the bomb in a desert or on a barren island before using it against Japan, or keeping the secret as long as possible. The authors of the report warned that decisions concerning the bomb must not be left to the military alone.[4]

The Panel overruled the Franck report and other views opposing military use of the bomb on 16 June, saying that they "can propose no technical demonstration likely to bring an end to the war; we see no acceptable alternative to direct military use."[5] Two days later, a meeting was held in Truman's office, attended by his key associates. They decided to use the bomb. After the decision had been made, John McCloy, who was accompanying Stimson, inquired as to whether it was possible to give Japan a warning prior to the bombing. Truman encouraged him to elaborate. Under Secretary of the Navy Bard then suggested in a memo that Japan be warned three days in advance, offering a chance to surrender.[6] But in the process of discussion, the suggestion was rejected by the Chiefs and Secretaries of the Services, on the grounds that it was not yet certain whether the bomb would explode.[7]

This uncertainty was not unfounded. The nominal capacity of the test bomb was 20,000 tons of TNT, but the scientists in the Los Alamos Laboratory were not confident it would have such power. They talked about a "dud" that wouldn't explode at all, and about a "fizzle" that would explode—but just barely. In the Laboratory's betting pool, Oppenheimer himself put his money on 300 tons of TNT.[8] Admiral Leahy, who was present when Truman first learned about the bomb from Stimson, said then that, as an explosive expert, he did not think it would explode. In a meeting in the White House Projection Room chaired by Forrestal on 17 May and in a special meeting of the Joint Chiefs of Staff on 10 June, details of a plan for invasion of Japan were still being discussed, since at the time no one was certain about the bomb's real potential.[9]

Some scientists were so concerned about the future of the bomb that they petitioned that it not be used at all in WWII. (Another group counter-petitioned.) A poll taken in the Chicago lab of the Manhattan Project showed most people favored direct military use. The Interim Committee reported on 21 June that all scientists were concerned about the future control of atomic power, and that one approach to such control was international exchange of scientific knowledge.[10]

On 18 April Truman had "authorized State, War, and Navy to confer on matters affecting political and military problems in the war areas." This initiated the Committee of Three, which took a hard line on the issue of bombing. The three Secretaries met on June 19 and suggested that, to avoid cave-to-cave fighting, Japanese moderates should be exploited; the bomb would provoke the moderates to take action.[11] When the Committee of Three met again on the 26th, Stimson felt the country would not be satisfied unless S-1 (the atomic bomb) was used to weaken Japan and to show that every effort was being made to shorten the war.[12]

THE BOMB, THE SOVIETS, AND THE BRITISH

As the Committee of Three was meeting on 26 April, George L. Harrison, Stimson's deputy on the Interim Committee, sent Stimson a memo suggesting that the Soviets be informed of the bomb during the "Big Three" summit to avoid embarrassing them. Truman and Stimson met on the 2nd and 3rd of July. A draft statement, to be released by the President after the bombing of Japan, was submitted for approval, and the two discussed how Truman would inform Stalin of the bombing during the upcoming Potsdam summit. Hence, the policy of not informing the Soviets beforehand was reversed.[13] The US-Britain-Canada Combined Committee on S-1 met on 4 July, completing the decision-making and consultation process—though final authorization to the military was yet to be issued.[14] When the bomb test in New Mexico turned out to be a success, Truman was already in Potsdam.

The code name of the Big Three's last wartime conference, 16 July through to 2 August in Potsdam, was *Terminal*—an end to one journey, but the start of another. The questions addressed did not live up to the billing as an epochal event. Truman himself later commented that "Potsdam was just a rehash. It was a conference to implement the agreements made at Yalta."[15] White House aide Eben Ayers commented before the conference that the Secretary of State was only in for a few days. Leahy, on the military side, was "tops." The American delegation lacked plans. The President's spokesman Charles Ross made no preparations for the conference and knew very little, if anything, about what he was likely to be up against.[16] If anything new was discussed in Potsdam, it was the atomic bomb.

Though the bombs were to be dropped on Japan, Truman and his associates were more concerned about the USSR whenever the bomb question was discussed. Following the success of the test, the final decision to drop the bomb was made in Potsdam on 23 July in a session attended by Stimson, Eisenhower, Marshall, Byrnes, Leahy, and another naval officer, probably King. Pros and cons were discussed one more time, and all present favored bombing.[17] As Byrnes later remarked, using the bomb could end the war before the Soviets got in.[18]

The success of the test had great impact on American decision-makers. As Leahy wrote in his memoirs, "One factor that was to change a lot of ideas, including my own, was the atom bomb which was tested successfully in New Mexico on the day when we arrived at Potsdam."[19] Stimson wrote a document during the Potsdam conference entitled *Reflections on the Basic Problems Which Confront the US*, which clearly reflects his state of mind at the moment. Before sharing the atomic secret with the Soviet Union, he felt that the Soviets must adopt in their social structure the Western concept of democracy, and effectively put it into action.[20] Truman himself probably now felt freer to talk to Stalin like a Missouri horse trader. When the Soviets argued over the number of American troops in Potsdam during the summit meeting, Truman said that if they "didn't want to go on with the conference as it had been set up, my plane is ready to take me back home."[21] On the other hand, Truman was shocked by the formidable performance of the test device. Leahy recalled later that after the test Truman did not like the idea of using such monstrous destructive power; Truman wrote on 25 July that the bomb "may be the fire destruction prophesied in the Euphrates Valley Era, after Noah and his fabulous Ark."[22] The power of the bomb was still a topic to which Truman often returned in his post-presidential years: someday this demon might backfire. Possibly this consideration was in his mind when he spoke with Stalin.

Truman had lunch with Churchill on 18 July; they discussed the bomb, and decided to tell Stalin about it. Truman and Churchill believed at the time that Japan would "fold up before Russia comes in, with the Emperor asking for peace." Truman said, "I am sure they will when *Manhattan* appears over their homeland."[23] On 26 July, the British leaders would return home for the election, with the summit meeting adjourning until their return. Truman chose a break during the session of 24 July to speak with Stalin, informing him that the US had a bomb equal in power to 20,000 tons of TNT and that it would be dropped on Japan in a week; he did not, however, tell Stalin the nature of the bomb. Stalin politely thanked him.[24]

Stimson informed Truman, in a memo of 30 July, that the atomic project "is progressing so rapidly that it is now essential that statement for release by you be available not later than Wednesday, 1 August." Stimson apologized that the "circumstances seem to require this emergency action." Although Stimson did not specify what these the circumstances were, from the context of events it appears likely that both the Soviet Union and Japan figured into Stimson's considerations. Truman replied: "[A]pproved. Release when ready but not sooner than August 2."[25]

Churchill was defeated in the election. Truman told his staff, "Churchill did not expect [the defeat], when he returned to Britain he was entirely confident."[26] Clement Attlee and Ernest Bevin, the new Prime Minister and Foreign Secretary, returned to Potsdam to continue the conference. Only one of the three long-time Allied war leaders now remained on the scene, further eroding the import of the proceedings; the Potsdam Conference ended on 2 August without much achievement. But the decision of the US and Britain to give Japan an ultimatum urging its surrender and the events that were to follow were so closely connected in the minds of people all over the world as to cast a false halo over the summit.

Leahy later said that the conference was frustrating for both the Soviets and the Americans. Will Clayton added that the frustrations arose from two sources: Russia insisted on putting the western boundary of Poland on the Oder-Nesse line, and Russia demanded $10 billion in reparations from Germany.[27] Nevertheless, the conference did give Truman an important opportunity to scrutinize his major opponent. His impression of Stalin was by no means unfavorable. On one occasion, Stalin felt ill and did not come to a session. Truman's reaction is revealing: "If Stalin suddenly cashes in..., I wonder if there is a man with the necessary strength and following to step into Stalin's place and maintain peace and solidarity at home." He worried that a "demagogue" who "could play havoc with European peace for a while" might replace Stalin.[28] "Stalin was one who said something one time, and would say the same thing the next time—in other words, he could be depended upon." (He did not feel the same way about Molotov and Vyshinsky.[29]) Truman seems to have viewed Stalin almost as a friend. When he learned from Defense Secretary Forrestal that Stalin didn't like him, Truman said, "That I can't believe. Stalin and I were able to get along all right. We had no disagreements whatever except over the treatment of our people in Bulgaria and in Romania. That was the first of all the broken agreements."[30] In another instance, Truman defended Stalin, saying that the Soviets had reasons not to "stand by their agreements [since] they were having trouble getting their soldiers back into civilian life....And when Stalin got back from Potsdam he found a turmoil....And that's the reason for the upsets." Truman believed that Stalin was justified in his fears: "I am sure he was a very good historian, and he was very much afraid that the U.S. would join France and England in another *cordon sanitaire.*" And Truman did not think Stalin was "a real dictator;" "Stalin would stand by his agreements, and he had a Politburo on his hands like the 80th Congress." Interestingly, Truman's overall impression was "that Stalin is as near like Tom Pendergast as any man I know." Truman's advisors were similarly impressed. Will Clayton, for example, said of him: "Stalin is broad-gauged, dignified, knows how to give in when it suits him; speak clearly and briefly without notes, well ordered mind--things stored there in proper sequence and order. He always spoke with no show of feeling."[31]

On the other hand, Truman mentioned that, when the US Ambassador to France, Caffery, came to see him in Potsdam, he was "scared stiff of Communism." The vision of a Western Europe lying in ruins and Communism rising from the ashes must have constantly flashed through Truman's mind as he returned home from Europe.

The President learned about the bombing of Hiroshima on his way home. As he had predicted, Japan would not surrender until the Soviet Union came into the war. The Soviet government declared war the day after the Hiroshima bombing, on 7 August. On the 9th, as another atomic bomb was dropped on Nagasaki, Soviet troops were sweeping across Manchuria. The Empire of Japan surrendered on the 15th.

Truman addressed the nation on the results of the Potsdam Conference on 9 August, saying that the Eastern European countries "are not to be spheres of influence of any power." He knew this was not true. As for the atomic bomb, he said, "we thank God that it has come to us, instead of our enemies; and we pray that He may guide us to use it in His ways and for His purposes."[32] But when Japan claimed that it was knocked out of the war by the bomb, Byrnes cited "Russian proof" that the Japanese knew they were beaten before the first bomb was dropped.[33]

The Americans did not rest on their laurels, but rather pressed forward with the atomic project immediately after Potsdam. The President instructed the Director of the Office of War Mobilization and Reconversion that continuance of outstanding contracts of the Manhattan and related agencies would benefit the government and was essential to national defense. He authorized the War Department to arrange for the placement of new contracts, even without the approval of the Mobilization Office.[34] During the Cabinet meeting of 31 August, Truman stressed the necessity for a sound military policy, calling for the US to continue as a military power so as to maintain leadership among nations. Byrnes made similar points.[35]

At the same time, in the top echelons of the Truman administration there was much concern about dealing with the Soviet Union on the matter of the atomic bomb. Stimson, about to retire, wrote the President on 11 September 1945 that the bomb could not serve "as a direct lever" to change "Russian attitudes toward individual liberty." Any demand for such changes "as a condition of sharing in the atomic weapon" would be resented; "the change is more likely to be expedited by a closer relationship in the matter of the atomic bomb." Apparently, by September Stimson had reversed the view he held at the time of the Potsdam conference. He also sent Truman an important memo in which he said that unless the Soviets were "voluntarily invited into partnership on a basis of cooperation and trust," Anglo-Saxon possession of the bomb "will stimulate in effect a secret armament race of rather desperate character." Stimson believed that relations with the Soviets were "dominated by the problem of the atomic bomb," and suggested approaching them directly and immediately rather than "merely continu[ing] to negotiate with them, having this weapon rather ostentatiously on our hip."[36]

On 20 September Truman told his secretary that he would bring up the matter of the bomb in a Cabinet meeting the next day. Earlier on the 20th, Senators Arthur Vandenberg, Tom Connally, and Scott Lucas had visited Truman on behalf of the Senate Foreign Relations Committee to discuss the bomb. Vandenberg wanted to form a single Joint Congressional Committee, instead of having several committees in both houses take jurisdiction over the development, control, and use of atomic energy. Vandenberg thought that Truman agreed with him—but Truman's private comment was that the senators were seeking publicity.[37]

After Truman awarded Stimson the Distinguished Service Medal on 21 September, the Cabinet discussed the bomb in a meeting that Truman found "most interesting."[38] Stimson, in the last proposal of his career, proposed that since Russia had been a steadfast friend, the US should not hesitate to give Russia the secret of the bomb. He suggested that this be done in two steps: first in a scientific exchange, and then via the industrial establishment. The Cabinet split over the Stimson proposal. Patterson, and Hannegan sided with Stimson. Krug also sided with Stimson, but suggested a six-month freeze to see how the situation would evolve; McKellar seconded Krug. On the other side, Fred Vinson said if the atomic secret were given out, the US would have to give out all other weapons as well. "Shall we give all and receive nothing?" Tom Clark agreed that the US should carry a big stick. Vannevar Bush and Acheson made no comment. Truman himself was thinking of exchanging with the Soviets scientific knowledge of atomic energy without giving away industrial knowledge. He asked the Secretaries to think the problem over and inform him of their views.[39]

These views continued to diverge. Secretary of Agriculture Anderson responded in a letter to Truman, coming down strongly against divulging the atomic secret. But Patterson, the new War Secretary, wrote Truman in support of Stimson's memo of 11 September. Philips B. Fleming, Administrator-General of the Federal Works Agency, wrote that he favored giving the secret to Russia so as to promote trade between the two countries: "By sharing, we may acquire a trustworthy reliable friend." Based upon six weeks of travel in Russia during 1944, he believed that "the Russian people desired only friendship and peace with us." Acting Secretary of the Interior Fortas wrote that "American scientific isolation--or an Anglo-American-Canadian scientific bloc--is an invitation to World War III."[40]

Truman explained his view clearly and emphatically during one of his daily meetings with close White House staff:

> There was general misunderstanding of the situation. Some people have been urging that the US keep control. The whole question really was one of making scientific information available to all....Other nations might have the scientific information--in fact, our own experiments developed largely from what some German scientists already had--but they could hardly develop the bomb itself, that we would not turn over the plants and equipment to do it. Other nations had made automobiles and planes but they had not been able to make them equal to the US, although they had the knowledge and had seen how they were made.

One staff member remarked that an attempt on the part of the US to keep the bomb to itself would spell the end of the United Nations organization. Truman agreed.[41]

About two weeks before the 21 September Cabinet meeting, a surprising event occurred in Ottawa, Canada. A code clerk in the Soviet Embassy defected to the Canadian Mounties. Igor Gouzenko was allegedly an officer of the GRU, the Soviet Military Intelligence Service. Norman Robertson, the Canadian Under Secretary of State for External Affairs, reported to Prime Minister Mackenzie King on 6 September that "a most terrible thing had happened. It was like a bomb on top of everything and one could not say how serious it might be or to what it might lead."[42]

From the secret documents and information Gouzenko carried, it could be concluded that an extensive Soviet espionage network existed in Canada and the US. This network included A.N. May, a British scientist working in the research laboratory at McGill University; May ranked among the foremost Western atomic experts. The Canadians were stunned. At first they did not inform the US and British governments of the Gouzenko case, as they were afraid that doing so might jeopardize their relationship with the Soviet Union. When they realized the implications of the case, they reversed this initial position. MacKenzie King decided to visit London, to consult with Attlee in person. Prior to the London trip, he made a secret trip to Washington and met with President Truman on 30 September 1945.[43]

MacKenzie King informed Truman of the information the Canadians had secured from Gouzenko, to which Truman replied that every effort must be made to get full information before anything at all was disclosed. He thought the matter should be discussed by Attlee, Mackenzie King and himself: he repeated two or three times that nothing should be done without agreement among the three. He also repeated several times that he was especially interested in any information or evidence concerning espionage in the US. MacKenzie King produced a reference implicating a staff member under an Assistant Secretary of State; Truman, turning to Acting Secretary Dean Acheson, remarked that this would not be surprising.[44] Truman was very secretive about this conversation with MacKenzie King; he did not reveal its substance even to his close staff in the White House.[45]

After meeting with Truman, MacKenzie King talked with Acheson. In the latter's view, the British Government was pressing for immediate arrests and for disclosure of Gouzenko's information because "they've gotten fed up with the Russians and are prepared to take any chance," but "we are in the Western Hemisphere and we have to consider our position." The US and Canada would be more immediately affected than Britain if relations with the USSR were severed and, if war came out of it, Canada would certainly become a battle ground. King concurred with Acheson's view. Acheson and King agreed that Canada and Britain should have the same types of weapon as the US.[46]

Years later, when Truman spoke of how he informed Stalin of the bomb in Potsdam, he still believed that Stalin did not understand what he was talking about. In reply to the observation that the Russians had been getting information about the bomb through their espionage network, Truman said, "I don't think Stalin had it at all. I think the Russian scientists were getting it."[47] However, as Marshal Zhukov wrote in his memoirs, after having been informed by Truman of the bomb, Stalin immediately ordered Soviet scientists to make headway on their own atomic bomb project. Harriman reported to Truman on 9 August 1945 that Stalin showed great interest in the atomic bomb and said that it could mean the end of war and aggression, but that the secret would have to be well kept. They had found the Berlin Laboratories in which the Germans were working on the breaking of the atom but he did not find that they had come to any results. Soviet scientists had also been working on the problem but had not been able to solve it.[48]

There were also secret intelligence reports concerning the Soviets' knowledge of the bomb before Truman's revelation to Stalin. President Roosevelt hired John Franklin Carter (Jay Franklin) in 1940 to set up a small intelligence organization, which would carry out missions to be reported directly to Roosevelt. Carter continued working for Truman until the liquidation of his organization in November 1945. From 15 June to 6 July 1945, a group of 16 American scientists attended the 220th anniversary celebration of the Soviet Academy of Sciences. Among them was Henry Field, an anthropologist who worked secretly for Carter's outfit. Field recruited two other scientists to work for Carter; they reported in September that they could find no traces of a Soviet atomic project. "If Russia has had anything like *Manhattan*, many of her most important scientists would have been 'out of town' or would not have shown their research work." But the *Time* correspondent could not find any physicists in Moscow on July 27—three days after Truman informed Stalin of the bomb.[49]

The Soviets were not the only ones who were troubling Truman in connection with the atomic bomb issue. British Prime Minister Clement R. Attlee wrote Truman after the first bomb was dropped on Hiroshima: "There must be a reevaluation of policies and a readjustment of international relations. There is widespread anxiety as to whether the new power will be used to serve or to destroy civilization....Its influence on international relations is immediate." Attlee went on to say something not very appealing to Truman: "You and I, as heads of the governments which have control of this great force, should without delay make a joint declaration of our intentions to utilize [it] as trustees for humanity."[50] Attlee was demanding an equal status in the question of atomic energy, which Truman would not accept. Truman replied to Attlee on the same day when he addressed the nation concerning Potsdam—9 August. He declined to make the joint declaration suggested by Attlee. The following week, Attlee cabled Truman urging continued collaboration in research and development in the defense field; on 25 September, he wrote Truman a long letter, saying that "the emergence of this new weapon has meant...a qualitative change in the nature of warfare...I have to consider the defense forces required in the future in the light of San Francisco [the UN], but San Francisco did not envisage the atomic bomb. Its conceptions of security are based on appreciation of a situation existing in June this year." Truman remained cautious of the British throughout: after Acheson and Clayton visited him on 18 September 1945, Truman noted in longhand that he "told them to take everything into consideration in talking to British."[51]

Attlee had urged international arrangements in the area of atomic energy.[52] On 3 October, Truman sent a special message to the Congress, in which he urged the setting up of an Atomic Energy Commission to control everything connected with atomic activities in the US. He emphasized that the atomic power developed during the war was "due in large measure to American science and American industry." But he also said there was "substantial agreement that foreign research can come abreast of our present theoretical knowledge in time." He believed that the only hope for international arrangements concerning the atomic problem would be renunciation of the development and use of atomic bombs. He proposed first to start discussions with "our associates in this discovery, Great Britain and Canada, and then with other nations"—but he set a condition for the discussions: "I desire to emphasize that these discussions will not be concerned with disclosures relating to the manufacturing processes leading to the production of the atomic bomb itself."[53]

The follow-up after Truman's statement on international discussions was slow. As a matter of fact, Truman had other plans. When replying to Attlee's letter of 25 September, Truman merely said, "Later I shall of course be pleased to discuss the question with you," at some unspecified time.[54] In Truman's mind the final commitment to international discussions was yet to be made. He said on 12 September that there should be a program "on the highest moral plane," and offered two options: the US could keep the secret entirely to itself, or "all cards [could] be laid on the table and we'd say 'here it is' for everyone."[55]

THE COUNCIL OF FOREIGN MINISTERS: LONDON

In Potsdam it was decided that a Council of Foreign Ministers, composed of representatives from the US, USSR, Britain, China, and France, would convene every three months. The initial task of the CFM was to prepare the peace treaties. Byrnes proposed at the start that all Foreign Ministers would attend all meetings, while only the relevant signatories of the peace treaties would have the right to vote.

When Byrnes went to London for the CFM Meeting in September 1945, he was convinced that the Russians would now be easier to deal with; this was the first meeting of the wartime allies since Potsdam and since the atomic bombing of Japan. As Stimson recorded in July 1945, Byrnes "told me that the United States was standing firm and he was apparently relying greatly upon the information as to S-1 [the atomic bomb]."[56]   Indeed, Byrnes went to the CFM meeting with a bomb ostentatiously in his hip pocket (though atomic diplomacy had already been initiated by Truman at Potsdam). Molotov reiterated in London the Soviets' claim to a base in the Black Sea Straits, a claim rejected by Byrnes and British Foreign Minister Bevin. He also reiterated another claim, to Soviet access to Tripolitania, and this too was rejected. When he asked the US and Britain to recognize the governments of Romania and Bulgaria, they refused to extend recognition until free elections were assured and they questioned the extent of individual liberties in the two countries.[57]

Frustrated, Molotov withdrew his consent to Byrnes' formula for attendance and voting at the CFM meetings, and threatened to leave. Byrnes, aghast, called Leahy from London on the morning of 22 September. Truman was not in Washington. Byrnes strongly advised that Leahy, before securing Truman's approval, send a telegram to Stalin in Truman's name. Leahy did as Byrnes asked. The message said that Truman had been informed of Molotov's possible withdrawal from the London meeting, and that the dispute concerned the question of whether France and China should attend discussions on the Balkans. Leahy (in Truman's name) urged Stalin to tell Molotov not to disrupt the Council, as doing so would have an adverse effect on world peace. Three hours later, Byrnes sent the draft of a more detailed telegram from London; Leahy sent it to Stalin. In Truman's name, this second message conceded that, in Potsdam, it was agreed that only signatories would attend meetings discussing peace treaties—but claimed there was also a verbal understanding that the other members of the Big Five could participate in such discussions without voting rights. Stalin replied that it was agreed in Potsdam that peace treaties should only be discussed by future signatories.[58]

The London meeting proceeded, without settling the question of participation. Byrnes made a new proposal that France and China join the discussion of peace treaties, along with all European members of the United Nations and non-European members who took an active part in the European military campaign. Molotov rejected this, requesting instead discussion of the occupation of Japan, which was not on the original agenda. Byrnes, taken by surprise, declined to discuss the occupation issue formally at the September meeting, but he could not avoid discussing it when delegates met outside the conference room. About a month earlier, the US government had proposed setting up a Far Eastern Commission, to advise on the occupation of Japan. This would not satisfy the demands of other countries, since the proposed Commission would have only an advisory capacity. The Soviet Foreign Minister, during the 26 September session, criticized the American occupation policy in Japan and requested that an Allied Control Commission be set up in Tokyo. The Soviets ganged up with Britain, France, China and the British Dominions, all of whom wanted some kind of commission in Tokyo, after the example of Germany. Byrnes reluctantly agreed; however, the US—represented by General Douglas MacArthur—would play the leading role.[59] The agreement to organize some kind of Control Commission in Tokyo looked to be the only solid result of this otherwise almost futile meeting.[60]

The participants at London did put forward various proposals and demands, on the table and off the record; however, in an atmosphere of mutual suspicion, no compromises could be reached. In the end, the London CFM meeting wound up without a joint communique. The Russians were blamed. Winant, the US Ambassador to the UK, forwarded to Byrnes on 5 October the comment of Sir Orme Sargent, Under Foreign Secretary in charge of Soviet affairs: (1) Sargent personally believed that the Soviets still wanted to cooperate with the West on their own terms; (2) in discussing the Romanian and Bulgarian treaties, the Soviets really had France in mind; they wanted to see France a second- or third-rate nation, enmeshed in discord with the US and UK; and (3) the Soviets wanted to drive hard bargains while they were still strong militarily in Europe.[61] On the same day, Caffery, the US Ambassador to France, cabled Byrnes that Foreign Minister Bidault was very upset with the Russian attitude and very worried about its possible effect on France. Tindall, US Military Attache in the London Embassy, reported to the War Department on 2 October that, according to one Foreign Office official, "the Russians will never consent to a meeting of the Big Five, basing their refusal on extreme difficulties experienced at the current meeting." Tindall also reported the view of *The Times* that "the real issue is the question of zones of influence," and compared the US attitude toward Japan with the Russian attitude toward the Balkans and the British attitude toward the Western European Bloc.[62] Clearly, atomic diplomacy at the CFM meeting did not work out as anticipated by Secretary Byrnes.[63] Molotov aptly observed of Byrnes that "he doesn't need to persuade anyone. He just has to hold up a little bomb."

On 25 September 1945, Acting Secretary of State Dean Acheson sent Truman an important State Department policy statement reflecting the President's thinking. Acheson, in his memo to Truman, said:

> [A] policy of secrecy is both futile and dangerous, and the real issue involves the method and conditions which should govern interchange of scientific knowledge....[The US-UK joint discovery] must appear to the Soviet Union to be unanswerable evidence of an Anglo-American combination against them. It is

impossible that...the Soviet Government could fail to react vigorously to this situation....Over-all disagreement with the Soviet Union seems to be increasing. Yet I cannot see why the basic interests of the two nations should conflict....[But if Russian aims are not understood] there will be no organized peace but only an armed truce.

Acheson suggested approaching the Russians after discussions with the British, while at the same time trying to prepare public opinion at home for such an interchange.[64]

Truman delivered a special message to the Congress on 3 October 1945. He said that knowledge of atomic energy should be used "not for the devastation of war, but for future welfare of humanity." On the domestic front, the Congress should enact legislation for overall control of all atomic activities in the United States and set up an Atomic Energy Commission for this purpose. On the international front, since the essential theoretical knowledge was already widely known and foreign research could catch up with that of the US in time, Truman asserted that international discussion "cannot be safely delayed until the UN is functioning and in a position adequately to deal with it." He proposed discussions first with Britain and Canada and then with other countries "in an effort to effect agreement on the conditions under which cooperation might replace rivalry in the field of atomic power." This was the first comprehensive atomic policy statement of an American President.

Truman did not specify in his special message when the international discussions would begin. Nor did he do so in his message to Attlee on 5 October. In view of the lack of progress at the London CFM Meeting, Attlee was shaken by Truman's noncommittal stance. He wrote Truman on 17 October that "I am now also being subjected to heavy parliamentary pressure from both parties to make a statement on the government's policy. I have to reply to a question tomorrow....It is our view that the meeting of Foreign Ministers was overshadowed by the problem, and that the prospective conference of the UN will be jeopardized unless we have some clearness on our attitude to the problem." Attlee—and Mackenzie King—thought that the three of them [Attlee, King, and Truman] should meet as soon as possible. Truman agreed to a meeting, scheduled for 11 November in Washington, but suggested that, to avoid publicity about *Manhattan*, they should identify other issues as the reasons for meeting. Attlee would not go along with this, replying that the matter could not be contained any more.[65]

Truman, of course, worried about the outcome of the London CFM Meeting, but he did not give up hope. He commented on 24 September that the Russians "are direct action fellows and know what they want....If we do too, we would get along all right with them."[66] In his press conference of 8 October, he added that Russia was misrepresented in America and vice versa: "The difficulty, I think, is a matter of understanding between us and Russia. There has always been a difficulty, principally because we don't speak the same language."[67] Some of his senior associates held the same view. James Forrestal, Secretary of the Navy, said on 1 November that "Everybody wants peace but everybody would like the other fellow to strip himself first to demonstrate his goodwill....The nub of the problem is that we have to find some way to break the wall of non-communication now existing." Forrestal was convinced that Byrnes' "non-roll-over tactics" in London would not bring good results.[68]

Truman had already been in office for half a year, but some people still saw him as that obscure Vice-President from Missouri and tried to tell him how to do his job. Byrnes offered frequent wisdom. William Donovan, while still OSS Chief, told Truman "how much he could do to run the government on an even basis"; Rear Admiral R.E. Byrd came to the White House to tell the President "how to settle world peace";[69] W.Randolph Hearst, Jr, told Truman what "Papa thought"—to which Truman explained diplomatically, "I don't give a damn"; Messersmith, Ambassador to Mexico, told Truman "how to run the Government, including Germany, Japan, South America, OPA, etc." Even Ely Culbertson, the contract bridge wizard, told Truman that, "[I] have a way to save the world," but Truman "doubted its efficacy."[70] Under a deluge of unsolicited advice and in the face of vociferous criticism in the press, Truman decided that in future "I will decide, and discuss afterward."[71] White House staff members observed that the President had been trying to delegate authority, but every attempt to do so failed.

In his speech in New York on Navy Day, the President said that the basis of US foreign policy was military strength, and the fundamental principles of US foreign policy were righteousness and justice. Americans must firmly adhere to what they believed right, and should never compromise with evil. The US should progress steadily toward international cooperation, but only within the framework of righteousness and justice. The President also said that the world could not afford to let the cooperative spirit of the war allies disintegrate. A common danger had united them in the war; now, let a common hope draw them together in peace. The atomic bombs already dropped must be a call to ever-closer unity. As to the free exchange of fundamental scientific information on the bomb, it could not wait upon formal organization of the UN, but would begin in the near future. This was, according to Thomas Dewey, the Republican Governor of New York, "the greatest speech on foreign policy that had ever been made. "[72] It was, according to former Secretary of State Cordell Hull, "a magnificent presentation of foreign policy. "[73]

Byrnes suggested in a memo of 29 October 1945, per advice of the War Department, that the two US Army divisions stationed in Czechoslovakia should be completely withdrawn by 15 November. Byrnes wrote that the two divisions were needed to police the border between US and the Soviet forces in Europe. In fact, Eisenhower estimated that there were 300,000 Soviet troops in Czechoslovakia, that the number would be increased to 500,000 in winter, and that the Soviets had asked Czechoslovakia for supplies for this force. Efforts made by Czech President Benes to secure a Soviet withdrawal had been unsuccessful and a Soviet commitment to reduce its garrison in Czechoslovakia to eight divisions had not been carried out. Byrnes attached to his memo the State Department's draft of a telegram to Stalin, for approval by the President. Byrnes said this message to Stalin was proposed by Benes and US Ambassador Lawrence Steinhardt, as a means of achieving Soviet withdrawal: the US and the Soviet Union would withdraw their troops simultaneously. If the Soviets refused to withdraw, or used delaying tactics, then their intransigence should be widely publicized. Truman carefully considered this suggestion. He first wrote, "Committing us to withdraw sounds reasonable. But I doubt if the Ruskies listen to us." Later: "Our withdrawal should be done only on condition the Russians leave at same time." Finally: "OK. HST." After being cleared by Leahy, State's message was sent to Stalin, noting that the stationing of US and Soviet troops in Czechoslovakia—an Allied state that suffered Nazi domination longer than any other member of the UN—had been draining that country's resources. On 2 November, a cable in the President's name was sent to Ambassador Harriman in Moscow, changing the withdrawal date from 15 November to 1 December. [74] The Soviet government agreed to simultaneous withdrawal of its forces. [75] This was, of course, a well calculated action on the part of the Soviets.

During this period, most of the flash points on the international scene—notably Iran and China—were related to the Soviet Union. Truman complained that, throughout the war, the Americans never had any information "as to what was being done by the Russians—in production, manufacturing, arms, etc." He now felt ill-informed about the Soviets international intentions, and considered sending a special envoy to talk with Stalin. Hopkins and Leahy were mentioned as possibilities. Truman saw no reason for a new Big Three summit—or at least had no expectation that anything could be accomplished by one. [76]

Truman was especially concerned about the situation around the Black Sea Straits. On 1 November he showed his staff a map of Turkey, marked with a large number of colored tabs. Truman explained that the tabs represented Russian divisions.[77] On the 19th, he said to his staff that the international situation was regressing and the Russians were attempting to "grab control of Black Sea Straits." Turkey would fight, but it would be like the Russian-Finnish War.[78]

Ambassador Harriman reported, on 22 November, a conversation he had with veteran Soviet diplomat Litvinov. Litvinov reportedly said that neither side knew how to behave towards the other, and this was the underlying reason for the breakdown of the London CFM meeting and for subsequent difficulties. When asked what the Americans should do, Litvinov said "nothing." When asked what he could do personally, he again said "nothing;" he believed he knew what should be done, but was powerless to do it—and was extremely pessimistic. Harriman called for careful attention to Litvinov's comments, but pointed out that Litvinov's views might be colored by the fact that he had long been out of favor.[79]

In a change from his attitude earlier in the year, Ambassador Harriman was now attempting to appreciate the Soviet point of view. He observed that the Soviet leaders had lived their entire lives in an almost constant state of fear. Victory in Europe gave them for the first time a sense of security—but then the atomic bomb came along. So Molotov turned aggressive in London, and in his speech on 7 November bragged about bigger and better weapons. Harriman now believed that the Soviets saw American imperialism as a threat to the Soviet Union.[80]

THE COUNCIL OF FOREIGN MINISTERS: MOSCOW

On the atomic front, the Truman administration faced three big issues. First, Attlee, supported by Mackenzie King, was to come to Washington to discuss the international arrangements, at the core of which was Britain's intention to share in all components of the atomic project now in American hands. Second, it still had not been decided whether to share atomic information with the Soviet Union. Third, the dispute over domestic control—whether by the military or by civilians—was reaching a crescendo.

The Secretaries of State, War, and Navy met three times in October to discuss the atomic question, insofar as it concerned the UK and the USSR. It was decided that scientific information would be exchanged with the British, but industrial exchange would not be initiated unless the US was granted access to inspect British atomic-related plants.[81] In a memo of 5 November, Vannevar Bush, Director of the Office of Scientific Research and Development, told Byrnes that since the Quebec Conference of 1944 the British had not been given much in the way of American manufacturing information.[82] With regard to the USSR, the Secretaries resolved that scientific information must be released only in exchange for inspection rights. They believed that the Russians were not reliable, and that Stalin had been preparing for war with Japan in Yalta, in violation of his Soviet Japanese Non-Aggression Treaty, and that he could easily repeat the same sort of treachery now.[83]

Attlee and Mackenzie King came to Washington on 11 November to discuss international control of atomic energy and US-UK-Canada cooperation in this field; after an announcement and a memorandum were signed, Attlee returned home on the 16th, apparently content.[84] But meeting with only the Western allies could not solve the major problems—the US-Soviet relationship, and the conclusion of peace treaties with Germany, Italy, and the satellites. However unpleasant, the US would have to sit down again with the Soviets to address these problems. According to Byrnes, it was he who proposed convening a new meeting with the Soviets; the President consented. In view of the failure in London in September, this would not be a full CFM meeting, but would be limited to the Big Three. On 23 November, Byrnes sent his proposal to Molotov by way of Harriman, suggesting that the meeting convene in Moscow.[85]

Upon receiving the proposal, Molotov responded favorably, but wanted to know what subjects would be discussed. Harriman said they could take up all open questions between US and the USSR, including the possibility of another CFM meeting, the civil strife in China and other issues in the Far East, and the disturbing developments in Iran. Harriman suggested that all three Secretaries place issues on the agenda and that the meeting should be informal. Harriman expressed in his cable to Byrnes that, personally, he was pleased by the proposal and felt that it would assist in allaying the Soviets' "unfounded" suspicions.[86]

The Moscow meeting convened on 16 December. Stalin returned to the Soviet capital from vacation to speak with the American and British foreign ministers. A *Time* correspondent reported, after the meeting concluded, that "a room that held both Bevin and Molotov would never be mistaken for a college reunion. But after the table-thumping display of hard manners at London, the air of sober, workmanlike cordiality at Moscow seemed reassuring."[87] Truman observed, on the 17th, that the Soviets were confronting the US with "accomplished facts," citing the situation in Poland, the 500,000 troops in Bulgaria, and the prospect of a move down the Black Sea Straits: "we can't send any divisions to prevent them moving from Bulgaria. I don't know what we are going to do."[88]

After much hard bargaining, the Moscow meeting produced agreement on several issues.[89] It was resolved that the satellite peace treaties should be ready before 1 May 1946. (This was to prove feasible.) An Allied Far East Commission in Washington and an Allied Control Commission in Tokyo would be set up for the occupation of Japan. (With the US still exercising effective control, these were little more than farce.) In Korea, there would be a provisional government and a five-year four-power trusteeship. (This was never realized.) In Romania and Bulgaria, some face-saving actions for the West would be taken, to pave the way for granting the governments of the two countries diplomatic recognition. The only reported decision concerning China was that both the USSR and the West would support Chiang Kai-shek. On the matter of Iran, nothing was agreed upon, Molotov remarking that nothing with regard to Iran was suitable for mention in the meeting's communique.[90]

As to the single most important issue, international control of atomic energy, an Atomic Control Commission was to formed, to report to the UN Security Council. The discussion focused on the relationship between the Commission and the Council. The West naturally insisted on relative independence for the Commission since they would have a majority, while the Soviets insisted that the Security Council should have authority over the Commission, since they would be then able to exercise their veto. Whatever the decision, only Heaven knew how either the Commission or the Security Council would control the atomic activities of individual nations. Exchange of information was not even mentioned in the meeting's communique. Judging from later events, the effectiveness of the Moscow decision on atomic energy was nil.[91]

The US top echelon clearly considered the Moscow meeting a failure. Leahy, for example, commented that the Moscow communique was "an appeasement document which gives to the Soviets everything they want and preserves to America nothing....Byrnes was not immune to the communistically inclined advisors in the State Department."[92] Such evaluations were too pessimistic, since the Soviets had held out only on their vested interests. Nevertheless, what those people in power thought at the moment decided courses of action for the future.

Truman was extremely unhappy about the results of the Moscow meeting and the behavior of James Byrnes during it. After leaving office, Truman said: "Late in 1945 and early in 1946 and when Byrnes went to Moscow and didn't report to me and didn't accomplish anything either, I came to the conclusion that Russia was not going to go along with us."[93]

The behavior of Secretary Byrnes, from his "walking with an atomic bomb in his hip pocket" during the London meeting in September to his "softness" toward the Soviets during the Moscow meeting in December, reflected the limitations of atomic diplomacy. Possessing a stockpile of atomic bombs was one thing; using that stockpile as a means to difficult ends was quite another. The Truman administration, frustrated by the end of 1945, considered getting tough with the Soviets—not as a tactical reaction but as basic policy. The shift from allies to enemies occurred in 1946.

5
1946—Prelude to the Cold War

The year 1946 marked a turning point in the Truman administration's stance toward the Yalta framework. The parallel structures of the UN and the spheres of influence, as agreed upon in Yalta, had not functioned well in 1945. But resolving the issue of confrontation vs. containment would require the impetus of events making for increased tensions, reforms in the machinery of the US government, and theories to rationalize new policies. All this would take time.

INCREASING INTERNATIONAL TENSIONS

The atomic bomb continued to be a central issue in US-Soviet relations—an issue played out largely in the United Nations. At the beginning of 1946 the Truman administration set up a committee to formulate a plan for the international control of atomic energy. Truman planned to release in the near future a considerable amount of scientific and technical information related to atomic energy, but not of direct military importance. A statement to this effect, drafted by the President, was approved by the War Department. The Cabinet, however, decided not to issue the statement. That was on 8 March, right after Churchill's Iron Curtain speech at Fulton (discussed later in this chapter).[1]

At about the same time, the US chose veteran Democrat Bernard Baruch as its representative to the newly established UN Atomic Commission. After a long interview with Baruch on 16 March, Truman made a note that Baruch "wants to run the world, the moon and maybe Jupiter—but will see."[2] Truman's instructions to Baruch grew out of three basic conclusions. (1) Leaving atomic development in national hands and relying solely on the existing international system would not provide security. (2) An international atomic development authority should be set up, and given adequate powers. The consequences of violating the authority's orders should be clearly stated. (3) The international authority must have managerial control of all atomic energy activities intrinsically dangerous to world security, with power to control, inspect, and license all other related activities.[3]

Truman also faced demands from the British. Attlee told him they wanted full interchange of information and a fair division of materials.[4] Then Harriman reported, in June 1946, that the British were very concerned over the McMahon Bill on atomic energy, which treated Britain no differently from all other nations. Attlee had told Harriman that "the British Government will be compelled to undertake the development of production of atomic energy." Harriman himself observed that the British "would much prefer to work with the US but are confused and concerned over how best to proceed and want us to clarify the situation which has developed."[5]

In March 1946, Truman approved a test of the effects of atomic explosives, as requested by the JCS. An early determination of their effectiveness against naval vessels was thought essential in evaluating strategic implications of the atomic bomb. Truman's approval carried a proviso: "that an equal number of the members of Congress [observing the test] shall come from the Military, Navy and Appropriations Committees of each House."[6] By way of preparation for the test, a review of US strategic bombing was undertaken, eventually leading to the *Report of US Strategic Bombing Survey*—which the War Department had hoped would be released prior to the test.[7]

Foreign observers were invited to the test, code-named Crossroad and conducted at Bikini Island. Molotov told the US Ambassador that two Soviet observers would attend. He thought that Soviet observers would not have the same facilities as the others, but was corrected on this point by the Ambassador, who informed him that they would be treated equally.[8] In the event, Crossroad was not spectacular; the US Charge in Stockholm reported in July that the test had lessened US influence.[9]

Baruch, meanwhile, was preparing to present a plan before the UN Atomic Commission. He wrote to Admiral Ernest J. King in late May, inquiring how to create a desire to comply with the future treaty for control of atomic energy and how to set up automatic punishment of violators. The Admiral recommended that steps be taken "to create a *fear*," causing people to comply with the treaty as a matter of self-preservation.[10] Eisenhower, as Army Chief-of-Staff presented his view in reply to another inquiry, sent by Baruch to the JCS. Eisenhower maintained that the US should not give up its advantage any faster than other powerful nations made concessions. By way of preventive measures, he insisted upon provisions for retaliation and the possibility of employing atomic weapons against recalcitrants.[11] Truman instructed Baruch on 10 July that atomic raw materials must be controlled at the source and that the US should not throw down its gun until it was sure the rest of the world could not take up arms against the US.[12]

The essence of the Baruch Plan was international control and inspection of material and plants, with no veto power on the atomic issue in the Security Council and with the US enjoying a monopoly in atomic weapons. Baruch wanted provisions to sanction violators, but Acheson disagreed. In the UN Commission, the Baruch Plan was rejected by the Soviet Union—and it also displeased the British. The intent of the US was clear: using its possession of bombs, the US would force the Soviet Union to either yield to international control and inspection or forgo acquisition of scientific and technical information. Obviously, the Truman administration did not expect the Soviets to accept the plan.

In September, Baruch already expected the UN Atomic Commission to fail. He told his staff that, looking forward to the day when negotiations might break down, efforts should be redoubled to accumulate stockpiles of raw materials and atomic weapons. He believed at the time that other delegations would not go along with the US if he attempted to force the issue with the Soviets. The US had lost the initiative.[13] One Soviet official in the UN commented privately that the US plan for international atomic control was in essence a plan for world government—and the world was not ready for it. The notion of world government had been rejected in Dumbarton Oaks in 1944 and again in San Francisco in 1945.[14]

The U.S. lost no time in collecting intelligence in the realm of atomic energy. The National Intelligence Authority in August 1946 authorized and directed the Director of Central Intelligence to coordinate the collection of all intelligence related to foreign atomic energy developments and potentialities and to transfer all personnel and working files of the Foreign Intelligence Branch of the Manhattan Project to the Central Intelligence Group at the earliest practicable date.[15]

On 30 December 1946, the UN·Atomic Commission decided to vote on the Baruch Plan. According to Baruch, at first the British did not support it, but at his insistence the British representative yielded. In the end, the Commission voted, with the Soviet Union and Poland abstaining, to put the issue on the agenda of the Security Council.[16] The US could never again whet the Soviet appetite for sharing of knowledge about atomic energy: the issue had come to a deadlock. The Soviets' effort to produce their own weapons shifted into high gear. So did Britain's. As a matter of fact, the Baruch Plan did not add strength to US atomic diplomacy. Rather, it weakened the leverage of that diplomacy.

During 1946, apart from the Chinese civil war, another explosive situation existed in Iran—a manifestation of deterioration in the relationship between the Soviet Union and the West. The Iran situation also revealed the delicate chemistry between the US and UK.

The dispute over affairs in Eastern Europe in 1945 and later, was one in which the US could afford to give in, if it so chose; the dispute did not bear directly on the well-being of the United States. The Soviet demands for control of the Black Sea Straits and for a bridgehead in Tripolitania immediately threatened the security of the sea avenue via Gibraltar and Suez, which Britain considered the life line of its empire. And the dispute over the Iranian question related directly to oil and to the British sphere of influence in the Middle East. These factors made for greater tension in UK-USSR relations than in US-USSR relations during the immediate post-war period. Bevin testified in a Cabinet meeting in early 1946 that the Soviet "attitude towards Turkey and Persia, their claims to former Italian colonies in North Africa, and their attempt to secure the intervention of the Security Council in Greece all pointed to a desire to reduce British influence in the Mediterranean."[17] At the time, Brazilian statesman Arhana believed that the Soviets were building a machine specifically designed to crush the British Empire—and that, because of Britain's weakness, the empire was being forced into the US orbit.[18] Hence, the weakening of the British position did not necessarily harm US interests.

A report dated 7 February, from the US Embassy in London, cited a British Foreign Office official as commenting that the Soviet interest in backward areas like Tripoli, the Near East, Indonesia and Southeast Asia reflected an adulteration of Communist doctrine. The Soviets were trying to create unrest among the underprivileged, enhance Soviet prestige and influence, and embarrass the British. Indeed, they wanted to replace Britain in the backward areas and to increase their influence in neighboring countries.[19]

The US State Department believed in May 1946 that the Soviet Union expected the conflicts supposedly inherent in the capitalist system to erupt between the US and Britain, and that the Soviets were trying to provoke such conflicts. The Soviets were in fact pressing the British on a number of vital points where the two countries' interests clashed. The State Department characterized Soviet pressures in terms of (1) threatening British security in the Far East, Tripolitania, France, Greece and Syria, the Black Sea Straits, and Iran; and (2) gnawing away at the British Empire by way of the "Fifth Column" and in a propaganda war.[20]

Earlier, in September 1945, the British government had convened a two-week conference of its representatives in the Middle East to discuss British policy, as well as Soviet and American activities, in the region. The UK and the USSR both stationed troops in Iran, but were obliged by treaty to withdraw six months after the war; at the conference, Iran became the focus of UK-USSR relations in the near term. The conferees were also apprehensive of Soviet penetration throughout the Middle East, fearing that the people of the region, given their lot under the existing social system, were a ready audience for Communist propaganda. Aside from the Communist threat, the Americans were launching a commercial offensive in the region, and the UK and the US were about to enter a period of commercial rivalry. Hence, Britain should not make any concession that would assist American commercial penetration of an established British market.[21]

During the Moscow CFM meeting of December 1945, Bevin informally suggested to Stalin that a tripartite commission be established to accelerate the withdrawal of Allied troops from Iran and to advise and assist the Iranian Government in establishing provincial councils in accordance with the Iranian constitution. Stalin indicated that these proposals might form the basis of a settlement, but Molotov said subsequently that the Soviet government was not prepared to continue discussing the matter on this basis and the discussions were broken off.[22] Meanwhile, the Soviets supported a separatist movement in Iranian Azerbaijan and the establishment of a government independent of Tehran.

The West wanted Iran to make an issue of the Soviets' refusal to withdraw their troops at the UN, but Iran was too afraid of antagonizing the Soviets. The Iranian Ambassador had been pressing for several days in January 1946 for an interview with Truman. The State Department told him that until Iran decided whether to place its case before the UN, the President would not meet with him. On the 23rd, State recommended to the President that he receive the Ambassador, since Iran had made its decision. Truman saw no point in doing so, but said he would do as State wished.[23]

Iran moved forward on two fronts. First, Qavam, the new Iranian Prime Minister, worked to have Iran's case considered by the UN. Stettinius, the US Ambassador to the UN, turned down a suggestion by the Chinese Ambassador that the Security Council take no action on the Iran case but permit bilateral negotiations to take place.[24] The Security Council eventually agreed to such negotiations between Iran and the USSR, but reserved the right to request reports at any time regarding the progress of the talks. If these reports were deemed unsatisfactory, the Security Council could call the matter back.[25] Second, Qavam attempted a direct settlement with Vyshinsky on 29 January, and visited Moscow for negotiations in late February. The Shah of Iran, worried about this visit, said to the US Ambassador that Qavam was a Persian Kerensky who paved the way for Soviet domination and that Iran was the first victim of Middle East oil.[26]

While in Moscow, Qavam told Kennan that he was unable to reach an understanding with the Soviets and planned to leave on 5 March. Asked whether the US would support Iran, Kennan replied that the US would do everything in its power—if the matter were returned to the Security

Council.[27] The Shah observed on the following day that the Soviets would withdraw from the UN if vigorously opposed. In his view, Britain no longer had sufficient power; the US was Iran's only hope.[28] But Stalin and Molotov told Qavam that Soviet interests required troops in Iran and that "we do not care what the US and Britain think and we are not afraid of them." "Soviet honor," according to Stalin, was involved in the Iran question.

Qavam further said that when he went through Baku, in Azerbaijan, the city was surrounded by antiaircraft guns. His consul in Baku informed him that this was the product of an order for general mobilization.[29] Hence, the Soviet Union appeared ready to use force. The US Ambassador reported Soviet troops along the Turkish border—an estimated 7-12 divisions—and said that troops might be deployed to surround Tehran from the west, north and east. The Shah feared a Soviet blitzkrieg.[30]

The Soviets feared that Iran would complain to the Security Council, as Qavam had told the US Ambassador he would do.[31] Qavam sent an emissary to inform the US and UK Ambassadors that the Soviets viewed bringing the Iran matter before the Council as a "hostile act [which] would have unfortunate results for Iran." The Soviet Charge modified this position: Iran should take no initiative, but rather wait for the Security Council to ask for a report. Qavam, afraid he would be overthrown, asked the advice of the US and the UK.[32] At the time, the US consul was reporting heavy Soviet troop movements southward from Tabriz toward Maragheh; the consul himself was ordered at gunpoint to leave a railroad station outside Tabriz. Iran decided that the Foreign Minister should present Iran's case before the Security Council—but should do so in a moderate fashion, to avoid provoking the Soviets.

Meanwhile, the US embassy in Moscow reported that the Soviet Union wanted to bring about an Iranian government that would allow Soviet troops to remain and grant oil concessions. The embassy believed that Soviet policy in the Middle East was to avoid withdrawal at all costs short of a complete diplomatic break with Britain.[33] Bevin felt strongly that there should be no postponement of the Security Council meeting, and advised that yielding to the Soviet Union on the Iran issue would seriously jeopardize the future of the UN.[34]

The Soviet Union eventually proposed withdrawing its troops from Iran in exchange for an agreement on joint exploitation of oil deposits in the northern part of the country. Iran was notified that: (1) the Soviets would evacuate completely within five or six weeks, "if nothing further happened"; (2) an Iran-USSR joint company would be set up in the oil industry, with Iran having a 49 percent share; and (3) the title of the Soviet-supported "Prime Minister of Azerbaijan" would be changed to "Governor-General," and the local legislature would become a provincial council. Qavam told the UK and the US that he would ask for the Soviet evacuation within four weeks, forward the Soviet decision on this point to the Security Council, make a counterproposal on the matter of oil, and decline action on the Soviet suggestion regarding Azerbaijan.

The US Ambassador reported on 28 March that British prestige in Iran had seriously declined; many Iranians believed that Britain was no longer interested in Iran.[35] In fact, the British desired withdrawal of Soviet troops unconditionally. Kennan, however, observed that troop withdrawal would certainly encounter opposition in influential Soviet circles; the US should ask for arrangements to ensure that a Soviet-Iranian agreement would be fairly executed.[36] Stalin and Gromyko claimed that the USSR and Iran had reached such an agreement, which Qavam promptly denied, saying that the crux of the crisis was the Russian desire for Iran's oil.

The Iranian government did reach an agreement with the Soviets in April 1946: Soviet troops would withdraw, and Iran would not present its case to the Security Council. Iran also agreed to form a joint oil company with the Soviets pending approval of the parliament. (The Iranian parliament actually declined to set up the joint oil company, in October 1947.) The US pressed Qavam not to drop Iran's case, but Qavam—under pressure from the Soviets—had already committed to dropping it. Antagonizing the Soviets might result in loss of all he had gained. Iran's representative was instructed to make a statement simply leaving the matter in the hands of the Security Council for whatever action it might choose to take.[37]

In April 1946, Soviet troops began to withdraw from Iran (excepting Azerbaijan); the withdrawal was still in progress as of early May. The Shah of Iran was concerned that, in talks with the Azerbaijan delegation, Qavam might consent to an Azerbaijan Army. There was indeed some cause for concern about the talks: in mid-May the Azerbaijan delegation angrily left Tehran, and the Soviet Ambassador pointedly told Qavam that this might result in "iron and blood."[38]

During this period the Qavam Government was walking a fine line. On the one hand, it needed Western help as a counterweight to Soviet pressure. On the other hand, it had to make concessions to avoid infuriating the Soviets. In a call to US Ambassador Stettinius on 20 May 1946, UN Secretary General Lie said that the whole Iranian question was very difficult, especially since the civil war had broken out, and that he had no idea where it would end.[39] In early June, the US Ambassador reported from Tehran that the situation in Iran was explosive; a coup d'etat, by the right or the left, might well occur.[40]

At this point the British Ambassador in Tehran decided to take a more active role, in the belief that the UK could not sit by and as its position eroded and—and its oil interests in southern Iran were lost.[41] The Soviets, however, believed at the moment that they should act slowly; the US Ambassador reported from Moscow on 10 June that the Soviets thought time was on their side in Iran. The interplay of the US and the UK at this point is interesting. On 11 June, an Iranian Foreign Office official stated that the Azerbaijan question would be settled shortly; then, three days later, the Shah informed the US Ambassador that he had received indications of a desire on the part of the Soviets to improve relations with him.[42] On the 18th, the US Ambassador reported that Qavam had gone so far over to the pro-Soviet camp that he could not retract.[43] The British wanted to issue, jointly with the US, a warning to Qavam—but the US thought this action inadvisable.[44] The Truman administration apparently did not want to act so as to benefit Britain, and tried to turn the Iran situation to its own advantage: on 25 June the US replied to Qavam's expressed desire to visit America, telling him that he would be welcome.[45]

The Soviets, not to be outdone, invited the Iranian princess to visit the USSR. The State Department believed this was a part of a Soviet plan to support the Shah, thus showing Qavam that he was not indispensable.

In late November 1946, the US government authorized the Ambassador to tell Iran that the US would support Iran's sovereignty not only in rhetoric but also by appropriate action.[46] Informed by Qavam that the Soviets viewed Iran's sending troops to Azerbaijan as undesirable, the US Ambassador replied that sending troops was justified and that the US supported doing so; furthermore, Qavam would be justified in bringing the matter to the Security Council, where the US would support Iran energetically.[47] Ambassador Smith reported from Moscow that the Soviets were following a policy of political, rather than military, subjugation in Azerbaijan and were using the region as an instrument to disrupt and ultimately capture the central government. This was a policy readily adapted to China, Iraq, Afghanistan and, before long, India.[48]

Britain would not tolerate its influence being weakened in Iran. The importance of Iran's oil for the British is apparent. At the prices prevailing as of January 1947, the British-controlled share of Middle Eastern crude oil was predicted to be worth around 164 million pounds Sterling in 1950 and 226 million pounds in 1955. The replacement value, at 1946 prices, of Britain's major assets in the Middle East oil industry was substantial: for the Iran-Abadan Refinery, 120-150 million pounds Sterling; for the Palestine-Haifa Refinery, 25 million pounds; and for trunk pipe lines, 20-plus million pounds. In January 1947 the Middle East was supplying 60 percent of the oil required for British use. This share would rise to 70 percent by 1955.[49]

No wonder the Soviets wanted to drive the British away! And the Americans wanted to assume Britain's role in Middle East, although they already had 40 percent of all known oil reserves in the region. By end of 1946 the Americans were taking in hand the Iranian affair, which until then had fallen within the British sphere of influence.

A JCS memo on *US Strategic Interest in Iran*, dated 12 October 1946, explained the importance of Iranian oil and the geopolitical importance of Iran. During the Fourth Five-Year Plan, 70 percent of the Soviets' oil came from the Baku oilfield, and 84 percent of the Soviet Union's refining capacity was located in the Caucasus. These areas fell within the effective range of bombers taking off from Iran, as did many Soviet military factories. Should the US and its allies ever attack the Soviet Union from the south, they would encounter massive logistics problems if the Middle East—and Iranian oil—were in the hands of the Soviets.

The JCS memo also expressed suspicion of the Soviets' intentions in forming a joint oil company in northern Iran, since the oil reserves there were marginal. The Soviets might be seeking to generate rifts within Iran as a prelude to dragging Iran into the Soviet sphere of influence. The JCS believed that dividing Soviet influence (to the north of Iran) and British influence (to the south) would enhance the Soviets' capacity to pursue security aims by political means and would suggest to other countries that the West was unable to protect interests in the region. It would also consolidate a Soviet base in Iran, from which the Soviets would push further southward.[50] Of course, it would be naive to believe that the Soviet Union would happily take a hands-off stance in Iran or the whole of the Middle East, or that the British would welcome an American intrusion into a traditional sphere of influence.

Problems in the Black Sea Straits and in Greece and Turkey had been hot topics in Potsdam and at the CFM London meeting of September 1945. Truman said at Potsdam that "the question of territorial concessions was a Turkish and Russian dispute which they would have to settle themselves, but the question of the Black Sea Straits concerned the US and the whole world." Stalin compared the Black Sea Straits with Panama, Suez, and Gibraltar—all of which had military protection.[51] The Soviet Union wanted to revise the Montreux Convention on the Black Sea Straits to its advantage; from Turkey they wanted a base in the Straits and the return of Kars and Ardahan Provinces, which at one time belonged to Russia. In Greece, the British-backed government was being threatened by an armed liberation movement, which the Soviet-backed governments in the Balkans supported. As of early 1946, the situation in the region was tense: the

Soviets continued to apply pressure on Turkey, and fighting in Greece was escalating.

US Ambassador Wilson reported from Ankara in March 1946 that the movement of Soviet troops into Bulgaria and through Iran toward the Turkish frontier meant the use of force after mid April (when roads would be dry enough) could not be ruled out. The Soviets' objective of installing a "friendly" Turkish government would give them control over the Straits and fill the remaining gap in a belt from the Baltic to the Black Sea.[52]

The US sent the USS Missouri for a show of force in Turkey in the spring of 1946. Ambassador Wilson reported that the visit of the American battleship was a complete success; the Turks had cooperated in making it so.[53] The matter of warships—this time, the Soviets'—arose again shortly later, when the State Department briefed Truman on 11 June 1946. Stalin had reportedly told the British ambassador in Moscow that the USSR needed complete freedom for its ships to move to and from the Black Sea, but that freedom of passage alone was of little value unless the USSR had a base somewhere in the Mediterranean.[54] On 27 June the Prime Minister of Turkey informed the US ambassador that the Soviet ambassador was urging Turkey to recognize that the USSR had more immediate interests in the Straits than any other power, because it would need a base there in time of war. If Turkey would discuss this matter, Soviet demands on Kars and Ardahan could be disregarded. The Turkish Prime Minister replied that before the Soviet Union withdrew its territorial demands, such discussions could not begin.[55]

On 9 August, the Soviet Union informed the US that it had proposed to Turkey defense of the Straits by "joint means."[56] On the 12th, the Turkish Foreign Minister informed the US that the Soviet proposal in regard to the Black Sea Straits was contrary to the spirit of Potsdam Conference, which had undertaken only to revise the Montreux Convention;[57] reports on the 13th had Stalin stating repeatedly and incongruously in a meeting with Massaryk, Czechoslovakia's Foreign Minister, that the Soviet Union had no intention of attacking Turkey.[58] Had Stalin perhaps changed his position as a result of Turkey's firm stance—and the backing Turkey received from the US?

Kennan commented at the time that "I doubt that the opening of the Black Sea Straits is Russia's main objective in the present war of nerves against Turkey. The real objective is to crush the independence of the Turkish government, and to make Turkey a puppet state which would serve as a springboard for domination of the eastern Mediterranean."[59] The US informed Turkey on 19 August that it would not agree to the Soviet proposal concerning the Straits, but would be glad to meet in regard to the Montreux Convention. The Soviet Union was similarly informed.[60] Thus, the Straits issue went directly to the two future superpowers. Several years later, Acheson told the Turkish Prime Minister that "the President considered this [rejection of the Soviet proposal] the most important decision he had made subsequent to the bombing of Hiroshima. "[61]

Secretary Byrnes was convinced that the time had come when the US must help its friends in every way possible and refrain from assisting those that might oppose American principles. He believed, in particular, that the US must assist Greece and Turkey; he had suggested to Bevin that Britain might furnish military equipment while the US rendered economic assistance.[62] In fact, by early December, the military situation in Greece was deteriorating rapidly. The US Embassy in Ankara reported that Turkey had granted the Greeks' request for arms and would also sell Greece a large quantity of wheat.[63] But Greek finances were reaching the crisis stage. In mid-December, US Ambassador McVeagh reported that equipping the Greek Army at the earliest possible date was critically important.[64] The State Department anxiously inquired the extent to which Britain was able to supply Greece with the arms necessary for peace and stability.[65]

Insofar as the world situation is concerned, then, the year 1946 closed on a troubled note.

US GOVERNMENT REFORMS

The American experience in WWII and America's position in the postwar world order necessitated reform of the US security apparatus. The year 1946 was critical for the planning and preparation of this reform. Its would ultimately result in establishment of the National Security Council; creation of a single Defense Department, to serve as an umbrella over three services, each remaining intact; institutionalization of the Joint Chiefs of Staff; and the birth of an unprecedented Central Intelligence Agency. As the legislative foundation of these reforms, there was first the National Security Act in 1947, then an amended version of the Act in 1949.

During the Truman years, the NSC was still in its infancy, and was greatly influenced by the Secretaries of State and Defense. The NSC's budget for the year 1947-48 was only $110,000; for the next year, it would ask for $200,000, enough to permit employment of only 31 staff members.[66] The Executive Secretary of the NSC did not yet have the status that future National Security Advisors would enjoy. When he resigned after serving as the first Secretary, Sidney Souers suggested to Truman that the Secretary should be a non-political confidant of the President, so as to be objective, able to subordinate his own personal views in coordinating those of all responsible officials, and willing to forgo publicity and personal aggrandizement.[67] The Special Assistant for National Security Affairs was not installed until the Eisenhower administration, to recast the NSC as a formal mechanism for long-range planning and decision-making in foreign and defense policy.[68]

The other three components of the Truman reform built upon familiar ideas. Merger of the military services was not a new concept; the debate on this subject can be traced back long before the war. The birth of the CIA reflected, on one hand, lessons learned during the war and, on the other, Truman's own perspective on the intelligence community.

Because Truman dissolved the Office of Strategic Services within weeks of Japan's formal surrender, it has been said that he was contemptuous of intelligence. This is not true. Truman did understand the importance of intelligence, but he was wary of operations like the OSS and, to some extent, the FBI. Early in May 1945, he told Harold Smith, the Budget chief, that he was having a study made of intelligence services and that he was against building up a Gestapo.[69] In August, he said that "there should be a good intelligence service for the President and the State Department."[70]

Smith sent a report to the Secretary of State on 15 August concerning establishment of an Office of Intelligence and Research, to have a planning staff, divisions for research, analysis, and dissemination, a library, and its own files. Through this new Office, the State Department should assume leadership in developing an integrated program of foreign intelligence and research for the government as a whole, under the chairmanship of the Under Secretary of State. On 20 September 1945, Smith gave Truman the order dissolving OSS. Truman signed it, saying that he now had in mind an Intelligence Service different from what countries had in the past—a broad intelligence service attached to the President's office.[71] And the FBI should be cut back to its prewar size, and confine its operations to the US.[72]

Truman's perspective on intelligence can also be seen in his treatment of Franklin Carter's unit, the small intelligence outfit set up by President Roosevelt to carry out secret missions. According to Carter, the outfit existed for 57 months and carried out 26 operations; he reported to FDR even on Harriman, with whom one of his informants met while visiting Moscow in June and July 1945. When Truman assumed the Presidency, he retained the Carter organization, which continued to operate until two months after termination of the OSS. Truman wrote Carter a letter of thanks on 11 December 1945, upon termination of Carter's outfit, and continued to seek Carter's advice thereafter. For example, Carter and Truman corresponded in January 1946, concerning the establishment of a national intelligence authority, and in April 1946, concerning American propaganda within the Soviet Union and a plan to combat Soviet influence in the Near East.[73] Clearly, Truman's attitudes toward the OSS and the

Carter outfit were quite different. Presumably, Truman wanted an intelligence service over which he would have complete control.

Truman convened a meeting to address intelligence matters on 9 January 1946; Leahy, Rosenman, Harold Smith, Vaughan, Vardaman, and several others from the Navy Department participated. Smith reported that during the war, people from various US intelligence organizations had been falling all over themselves in South America; Leahy said intelligence had been handled poorly and that during the war he could not get any intelligence out of Army, Navy, or State.[74] Truman clearly believed that the previous, segmented intelligence set-up would not suffice in the postwar era. The National Intelligence Authority was set up at this time, reflecting his belief that it was essential to combine the intelligence services of State and other departments and to make information available to those needing it in implementing foreign policy.[75]

A Central Intelligence Group (CIG) was established in the spring of 1946. Truman told a group of newspaper editors that the US, on the one hand, needed a central intelligence organization encompassing everyone in the field, FBI included, and, on the other hand, needed to guard against a Gestapo and other accoutrements of a military dictatorship. Hence, the Central Intelligence Group should be under civilian control—and under the control of officers elected by the people: "then you won't have any trouble in the future."[76]

As a matter of fact, the most important intelligence arms had never ceased to function; the wartime Anglo-American collaboration in electronic surveillance of Soviet transmissions continued, with presidential authorization, after the war ended. The Combined Chiefs of Staff sent an order to all British and American "Ultra" recipients on 16 September 1945, stating that "the termination of hostilities in no way affects the necessity for maintaining the security of Ultra....[Threats] may arise in the future and knowledge of what has been achieved by Ultra in this war can only serve to put our future enemies on their guard."[77] It is clear who the "threats" and "future enemies" were.

In the final analysis, Truman understood that he needed effective intelligence to cope with the postwar situation, but he did not want to have the FBI casting a wide net at home or an OSS roving the world out of his control. Some others did not share his plans. William Donovan's followers had never given up hope of forming a central intelligence organization after their own design. David Bruce, former OSS European chief, writing to Allen Dulles in December 1945, said it would be desirable for the *New York Times* and *New York Herald Tribune* to comment in editorials that the Pearl Harbor investigation pointed up once again the need for a CIA.[78] People say in Washington that there are two groups of government bureaucrats, one that comes and goes with the President, one that stays on indefinitely. In this case, the second group was to get its way. In 1946, it became clear that the newly established CIG could not deal with the situation, and that a large and strong CIA was bound to emerge. What this CIA would do in the future would dwarf the adventures of the OSS.

RATIONALIZING NEW POLICIES

In 1946, the USSR and the West took pains to justify their conduct. In addition to such luminaries as Joseph Stalin and Winston S. Churchill, lesser lights also did their parts in explaining the East-West relationship. In January, US Army lieutenant colonel Edward F. Willet, presented a paper on *Dialectical Materialism and Russian Objectives*. This paper was the Truman administration's first study of the Soviet state and Soviet communism. The Willet paper came in the nick of time: the US would soon need the a new theoretical basis for its policies and actions. Not intended for public consumption, the paper earned the praise of high officials in the Truman administration, especially James Forrestal. It was also read by Admiral Leahy. Willet believed that if communist doctrines were strictly applied in the contemporary world, it followed logically that violent conflict between Soviet communism and capitalist democracy was inevitable. At the moment, both the Soviet Union and the United States were war-weary. But Willet went on that it was not clear whether Eastern Europe would ultimately serve as a *cordon sanitaire* or as a springboard for Soviet invasion of other countries. Communism was messianic and driven, whereas capitalism was passive and lacked spiritual drive. The US should take no economic action from which Russia would benefit, and should keep herself in a strong defensive position.[79]

In his State of the Union Address on 21 January 1946, Truman reaffirmed as foreign policy his twelve-point statement of Navy Day the previous year. He stressed the theme of peace. The Soviet press gave the address 22-inch coverage, but failed to mention a number of important points, such as those dealing with destructive use of atomic energy, China, the Control Council in Germany, and Korean sovereignty.

The US embassy in Moscow reported ten days later that the Soviets' own approach to international affairs embodied two basic beliefs. First, the Soviets were certain that the employment problem in America could not be solved and that efforts would be made to address it by exporting on credit. Secondly, the Soviets believed that economic tensions between the US and Britain would inevitably lead to acute political tensions. The embassy also reported that one Soviet economist had mentioned in the newspaper a 1928 speech, in which Stalin predicted that the US and Britain would fight a war over economic differences. The embassy believed that mention of the Stalin speech might have special significance at this moment.[80] Analysis of other Soviet press reports in January found that two-thirds of the items on the US related to reconversion difficulties, industrial strife, unemployment, and impending economic crisis; racial and political discrimination were mentioned, too.[81] Also in January, the Soviet press carried a list of scientists receiving awards from the government. Among them: Konstantin Petrzhak and Georgi Flerov, awarded a Stalin Prize for their discovery of "spontaneous disintegration of uranium," a step on the path to Soviet atomic capability.[82]

Stalin's famous speech of 8 February was his first important policy statement after the war ended, and it became the theoretical basis of future Soviet foreign policy. Stalin claimed that capitalism was responsible for the world wars. War did not arise accidentally or from the faults of statesmen but was, rather, inherent in monopoly capitalism; the uneven development of world capitalism and its catastrophes and crises sent the capitalist world into two hostile camps. The two world wars had both resulted from crises of capitalism, but differed radically in character. The second war was forced upon the people of the world by Fascism, took on an anti-Fascist and liberating character, and had as one of its aims the reestablishment of democratic liberties. The Soviet victory showed not only that the Soviet system was truly popular, but also that it was superior to any other social system. Stalin also praised the Red Army and the Soviets' preparations for war—obviously a defense against criticism within the party with reference to his own negligence in the face of the threat of war.

Stalin then set out tasks for the future. He hinted at Soviet efforts in atomic energy, saying that Soviet scientists would soon be able to surpass foreign scientific achievements. He described the fundamental aims of the new five-year plan as restoring war-torn areas, surpassing prewar levels of industrial and agricultural production, abolishing the rationing system, and raising the standard of living. In the longer run, over three or more five-year plans, a mighty upsurge would propel output to three times the prewar level, with Soviet industry producing 60 million tons of steel and 500 million tons of coal per year. Only under such conditions would the security of the Soviet Union be assured in any eventuality.[83]

Reactions to Stalin's speech, though diverse, centered upon the question as to whether he was advocating war. For example, the *Intelligence Review* of 21 February 1946 held that the longer-term program alluded to by Stalin could be interpreted only as a program for strengthening Soviet war potential. But the review also noted that the speech emphasized defense rather than aggression.[84] The British Foreign Office emphasized that Stalin saw rivalries among capitalist countries—that is, between the US and Britain—as the cause of war.[85] US Ambassador Adolf Berle reported that Brazilian President Arhana interpreted Stalin's speech as an indication of Soviet determination to take a hard line.[86]

The popular press naturally accorded the speech extensive coverage. The *New York Times* initially (1) highlighted Stalin's emphasis on the economy rather than the military, in "Stalin Sets a Huge Output Near Ours in 5-Year Plan; Expects to Lead in Science"; and (2) suggested that he was sounding a clarion call against future emergency, in "Seeks Production Rise to 'Guarantee Against Any Eventuality'" and "Lays War to Capitalism". But several days later a *Times* editorial commented that Stalin's economic plan was in fact a war plan, and a report from its London bureau, headlined "Aims of Russian Communists again likened to a mystery in an enigma," said the speech "reopened many questions." Hence, in about a week, the *Times'* interpretation of Stalin's speech ran the gamut from economic through military to enigmatic. *Time* observed that "Stalin's speech contained no threats [and] was dry in tone, defensive in content," but that "its truculent exaggeration of the danger of attack from the capitalist world was the most warlike pronouncement uttered by any top-rank statesman since V-J Day." In its previous issue, *Time* had reported from Moscow that "the war has cost Russian production a decade of progress....Whatever their long-term aim might be, Soviet leaders wanted peace long enough to put more food in Russian bellies, more clothes on Russian backs....One major bottleneck is trained industrial manpower. Russia lost millions of his best workers in the war...."

In fact, Stalin's speech of 8 February was not about war. It was a sign that Soviet leaders believed there could be no reconciliation with the West over a number of important issues. It was a ploy in the battle of nerves between East and West, already in progress for some time. At the time of the speech the Soviet Union simply did not have the strength to fight a war with the United States and its allies.

Partly as a comment on Stalin's speech and partly as an attempt to present his own views on the Soviet system and Soviet foreign policy, Kennan, then the US Charge in Moscow, sent back a long telegram on 22 February. The essence of this telegram later appeared in an article on "The Origins of the Soviet Conduct," under the pen name "Mr. X." Kennan contended that the Soviet leaders were orthodox Marxists, that their foreign policy was based on the perception that they were under capitalist encirclement, that they would participate in legitimate international activities intended to weaken the West and strengthen themselves, and that unofficially they would make use of all possible vehicles for the same purposes. Kennan's conclusion was that Soviet power was calculated and did not take unnecessary risks; on the whole, the Soviets were weaker than the West, the success of the Soviet system had not yet been proven, and

Soviet propaganda could be easily defeated. He therefore recommended that the US government recognize the nature of Soviet Communism and educate the public as to the realities of the Russian situation, focus on solving America's domestic problems, present to foreign countries a positive and constructive vision of the future, and have self-confidence and courage.[87] Kennan's long telegram stands out as a statement of principles and as the most important American theoretical study of the Soviet Union at the time. Future events would unveil how well the principles were accepted by American decision makers.

The small city of Fulton, Missouri, gained worldwide attention overnight in March 1946, when British opposition leader Winston Churchill delivered a speech there, in the company of President Truman. This was Churchill's famous "Iron Curtain" speech. Churchill, almost evangelically, told the world that the Soviet Union had set up an iron curtain between its sphere of influence and the West. The delicate process leading up to this event in Fulton is of considerable interest, for the light it throws on the Truman administration.

General Harry Vaughan, Military Aide to the President, was an alumnus of Westminster College in Fulton. Some time in September 1945, Vaughan received a letter from Charles F. Lamkin of the Alumni Association of Westminster College, urging that he persuade Truman to accept a Doctor of Law degree from Westminster. Vaughan replied on 27 September that he had told Truman that, if he took a degree from another college, then "he would have to take one from Westminster [in his home state]. Vaughan went on, "I'll continue to work on him and see what can be done."[88]

President Truman had been corresponding with Churchill after Potsdam and the latter had indicated the possibility of paying a visit to the US. In a letter dated 3 October 1945, Westminster invited Churchill to make a speech on world affairs at the college. Truman added, in long hand, "This is a wonderful school in my home state. Hope you can do it. I'll introduce you. Best regards."[89] On 29 October, Vaughan wrote to Eugene Baker of the Westminster Alumni Association of St. Louis that he doubted the President would have time to accept a degree, but that there was a possibility of Churchill's coming to the US and delivering a speech at Westminster. In Vaughan's words, "Of course, this is not all definite, but if this comes about the President will undoubtedly be there also and degrees may be given at that time."[90]

Churchill warmed to the idea, writing Truman on 8 November that "at any rate it is the only public speaking engagement which I have in mind and the explanation for it would be my respect for you and your wishes." He told Truman that he would be making the speech "under your aegis," and "this might be advantageous from several points of view. "[91] Churchill wrote on the 29th that "naturally I would let you know beforehand the line which I propose to talk in my address on world affairs, so that nothing should be said by me on this occasion that could cause you embarrassment. I do not think this is likely to happen, as we are so much in agreement in our general outlook. "[92]

Churchill had been troubled by coughs and colds.[93] While recuperating under the Florida sun as the guest of a Canadian, Colonel Clarke, he learned that Truman might come to Miami. On January 29, he wrote to Truman:

> I need a talk with you a good while before our Fulton date. I have a message to deliver to your country and to the world and I think it very likely that we shall be in full agreement of it. Under your auspices anything I say will command some attention and there is an opportunity for doing some good for this bewildered, baffled and breathless world.[94]

Truman replied, "I know you have a real message to deliver at Fulton and, of course, I shall be most happy to talk with you about it. "[95] He did not, however, make the Florida trip, so Churchill flew into Washington and visited him at the White House on the 10th. Their discussion concerned plans for the trip to Fulton.[96] Churchill came to Washington again in early March, and Truman accompanied him to Fulton by train; en route, the two played poker with their entourage.[97]

Before Churchill delivered his address in Fulton, Truman introduced him, using the following original typescript:

> I have no knowledge what Mr. Churchill may wish to say, but I have assured him that we all hope he will make to us a full and free statement of his thought in regard to what he believes to be advantageous to the prevention of war and to the future welfare of the people of our two countries.

Truman revised this text by pencilling in "do not know" in place of "have no knowledge" and adding at the end "A great Englishman who is half American."[98] When he made the introduction, Truman actually said:

> [I] never met Mr. Churchill personally until the Berlin Conference between Mr. Stalin, Mr. Churchill, and myself. I became very fond of them. They are men, and they are leaders in this world today when we need leadership. It is a pleasure to me to introduce Mr. Churchill. He is one of the great men of the age. He is a great Englishman, but he is half American. Mr. Churchill and I believe in freedom of speech. I understand that

Mr. Churchill is going to talk on 'The Sinews of Peace.' I know
he will have something constructive to say to the world in that
speech.

The President closed by saying that it was one of the great privileges of his
lifetime to present "the great world citizen."[99]
After the speech Churchill told Truman's staff that this was "the most
important speech of his career." Commenting on the Presidential Seal
affixed to the wall of their railroad coach, Truman observed that, since
peace had come, he had the eagle's head turned around to face the olive
branch. To this, Churchill replied that perhaps the eagle's head should be
on a swivel—and that the berries on the olive branch looked suspiciously
like atomic bombs.[100] On the morning of 6 March, Truman finished the
trip to Washington on the "Sacred Cow," while Churchill continued by
train.

An attempt to water down the connection between Truman and
Churchill's Iron Curtain speech is evidence in the prepared text of Truman's
introduction. But that text was so blatantly divorced from the facts that
Truman felt compelled to change it at the last moment, making it more
ambiguous. After the fact, the White House staff persisted in the attempt
to dissociate Truman. Charles Ross wrote in his diary that he "had to deny
again" at a press conference that the President had advance knowledge of
Churchill's speech. Ross told the assembled journalists that although
Churchill came to Washington in February to visit Truman, they did not
discuss the speech.[101] Dean Acheson, scheduled to speak at a dinner for
Churchill in New York on 15 March, cancelled his appearance at the last
moment; the *New York Times* reported that the cancellation led to
speculation about the administration's reluctance to be linked with any
further proposals by Churchill.[102] General Vaughan, who had engineered
the Truman-Churchill visit to Fulton, emphasized that:

we had no idea what plans Mr.Churchill had in America and we
were very agreeably surprised when he came back saying that he
would be glad to accompany the President and make the speech
as required...Contrary to some of the statements in the press, the
President did not discuss with Mr. Churchill the subject of his
speech nor did any of us see the speech until it was released to
the press a few hours before it was delivered.[103]

About the time Churchill came to Washington in February, Truman
himself learned of Churchill's views from the US Ambassador in Havana,
who had entertained Churchill while he was visiting Cuba. The ambassador
reported that Churchill was deeply apprehensive as to the future of the UN.

Churchill had referred to Russia as the ever-threatening "bear who walks like a man," and said that "Russia will not only master the secret of atomic warfare but will not hesitate to employ it for her own ends in this atmosphere of postwar friction and confusion." Should this happen, UNO would mean "United Nations Orphan." "Formal merger or alliance would doubtless be impossible, untimely and unpopular on both sides of the Atlantic [but] the sheer pressure of events will of necessity force our two great commonwealths to come together in some workable manner."[104]

In replying to questions about the Iron Curtain speech on 8 March, President Truman insisted that he "had not seen a copy of the address in advance of delivery as announced by an aide to Churchill," but he did not state that he had no advance knowledge of the content of the address.[105] When reporters asked Byrnes on the same day whether the US "associated itself" with the speech, he replied that the US "had nothing to do with it."[106]

Though Churchill's speech was to be known as the "Iron Curtain" speech, in the beginning people were more concerned with his proposal for an Anglo-American alliance. Truman's aide Eben Ayers wrote in his diary that "Churchill delivered a stirring address, calling for close alliance between the US and Britain."[107] Asked whether he disavowed Churchill's suggested Anglo-American alliance, Truman replied that he did not.[108] Years later, however, Truman's senior aide Clark Clifford said that an "Anglo-American alliance would not be appealing to President Truman. There was no reason why there should be an Anglo-American commitment of some kind; the alliance had to be broader than that."[109]

Naturally the mere presence of Truman on the platform and his introduction of the speaker—let alone their correspondence and consultation prior to the speech—led people to view Churchill's speech as having the formal endorsement of the American President. Whatever effort the administration might make to deny that Truman had read the text beforehand, most people would remained unconvinced. Obviously, Truman, might not be in full accord with everything Churchill planned to say in the speech. But equally clearly, he was not taken completely by surprise. (Nor were the American decision makers unwittingly used by Churchill as a cat's paw.) Truman had commented after meeting Churchill in Potsdam for the first time that Churchill was "a most charming and very clever person—meaning clever in the English, not the Kentucky, sense. He gave me a lot of hooey about how great my country is and how he loved Roosevelt and how he intended to love me, etc....I am sure we can get along if he doesn't try to give me too much soft soap."[110]

Apart from themes the US government might not endorse, the speech at Fulton was potentially advantageous to the US in two aspects. First,

Truman "could gaze on the magnificent balloon and watch the effect as the world, and Russia, reacted."[111] It was high time to teach Uncle Joe a lesson in view of his intransigence over almost everything. And the speech would pump up the morale of the Western allies and other pro-Western countries. Second, the speech could be used as a tool to turn public opinion at home—a potential advantage that is frequently overlooked. Letting Churchill make the speech could be most cost-effective; after all, Churchill was no longer Prime Minister, and it would not be pertinent or necessary for Truman to publicly endorse a policy statement by the leader of the British opposition. Furthermore, Churchill was a commanding figure, who clearly could not be bossed around by the American president.

Britain's Labor Government did not want to be connected to the Fulton speech, either. Attlee said after Fulton that he had no advance knowledge, and Bevin said it was made on Churchill's own responsibility, and that government policy toward Russia was laid out in his own speech in the Commons on 21 February. As an advance copy of the Fulton speech was being distributed by the British Ministry of Information, the Cabinet was considering a directive that, in future, speeches made by persons other than members of government should not be handled in this way. A week later Attlee said it was not appropriate to issue such direction.[112] Bevin told the Cabinet in June 1946 that, in forums such as the CFM, the UK government had encountered more difficulties since failing to dissociate itself from the views expressed in Churchill's speech. He suggested that, in the forthcoming debate in Commons, it should be made clear that these views were not shared by H.M. Government; Attlee concurred.[113]

In March 1946, Truman sent General Bedell Smith, who had served as Eisenhower's Chief-of-Staff in Europe during WWII, to the Soviet Union as his new Ambassador. Before Smith's departure for Moscow, Truman told him "to tell Stalin I had always held him to be a man to keep his word. Troops in Iran after March 2 upset that theory." Truman also told Smith "to urge Stalin to come to U.S.A."[114]

Smith reported on 1 April concerning Molotov's first call on him in Moscow, during which Molotov listed past and present difficulties between the US and USSR, and claimed he saw no reason why the two countries should not resolve that, while permanent prevention of war might be difficult, it was possible. Kennan felt that the atmosphere during the call was somewhat less cordial than on similar previous occasions.[115] But two days later, Smith reported to Byrnes on the presentation of his credentials. During a private interview after the presentation both Vyshinsky and Soviet President Schvernick were very cordial. Smith asked that Byrnes report to Truman concerning Schvernick's interest in the veterans problem in the US and, in particular, questions of absorbing veterans into industry and giving them educational assistance; Soviet veterans wanted a period of rest and freedom from discipline and were not inclined to return to work at once.[116] On April 6, Stalin, in declining for medical reasons Truman's invitation for a visit to the US, mentioned that he had seen Ambassador Smith.[117]

The US State Department looked upon the world situation in spring 1946 as showing no danger of war, and inclined toward following a firm Soviet policy. On 15 May, it issued a document entitled *USSR—Policy and Information Statement*. This statement merits examination, as it sums up the Truman administration's Soviet policy to date.

(1) The primary US foreign policy objective at the time was to convince the Russians of the value of cooperation based on international justice. This was the only way to peace. The obstacles were:

(a) traditional and unfounded Russian suspicions;

(b) exaggerated Soviet views of the antagonism between communism and capitalism;

(c) the Soviets' new pride in military and industrial strength;

(d) the Soviets' inclination to rely only on their own resources; and

(e) the Soviets' confidence in their ability to becloud issues and to attain political aims by way of "fifth columns."

(2) The alleged Soviet objective was security. It was clear that they had no confidence in the West; it was not clear whether Soviet expansion was aimed at security or at aggrandizement. Until the Soviets' true aims were clarified, the US must assume that the Soviet Union might expand by unilateral actions and must formulate a policy applicable in such a contingency.

(3) Before going too far, in terms of international cooperation, the US must see hard evidence from the Soviets in the form of implementation of commitments.

(4) Imposing pressure on the Soviets, other than through diplomatic protests, was difficult. The impact of economic pressure was not necessarily substantial. Mobilizing the public opinion necessary in the US and elsewhere for support of effective pressure would require a considerable period of time. The UN would be a promising agency for rallying public opinion.

(5) In dealing with the Soviets, the US must conduct a global policy, rather than simply judging each issue by its apparent merits in isolation.

(6) American policy should be firm, because the language of power, backed by reason and right, is the only language the Kremlin understands.

(7) The Soviets viewed the UN as an instrument for preventing a Western bloc that could appeal to backward and colonial peoples. If the Soviets did not engage in international cooperation through the UN, one alternative was a return to isolationism—but this had already been rejected by Congress and the American people. A second alternative entailed building a world, outside the Soviet orbit, where Western political and economic values might be preserved; in other words, a group of like-thinking free governments and societies not dependent upon Soviet participation in the UN.

(8) The U.S. was ready to support friends in need, regardless of Soviet criticism or displeasure.

(9) Soviet conceptions of power relationships were extremely elastic; the Russians traditionally would never engage an equal or superior power.

(10) The Soviets deployed a repertoire of nine characteristic techniques in their negotiating and propaganda efforts. [These are listed.]

The State Department's policy paper of 15 May was unquestionably shaped by Kennan's long telegram of 22 February (examined earlier in this chapter). Like the telegram, the policy paper did not characterize Stalin's speech of 8 February as a speech about war; rather, it stressed the economic aspects of the speech, pointed out that special attention was given to expanding the output and lowering the prices of consumer goods, and noted the emphasis on developing scientific research.[118]

The unalarming tone of the State Department paper accorded with the President's views. Though troubled by the inability of the US to react effectively to Soviet moves in bordering areas, Truman did not see any great Soviet war potential. Not only did Truman have a monopoly on the mighty bomb, but he was also convinced that "Russia couldn't turn a wheel in the next ten years without our aid."[119] On 17 July, he told a group of editors and executives from McGraw-Hill Company that he saw "some improvement in world affairs, [with] the world situation slowly and gradually approaching a settlement—able to sign peace treaties,...leaving only Germany and Austria to deal with."[120] He wrote former Vice President John Garner in September that "there is too much loose talk about the Russian situation. We are not going to have any shooting trouble with them but they are tough bargainers and always asked for the whole earth expecting maybe to get an acre."[121]

, however, was more wary of the Soviets. Leahy's memo 26 July 1946 starts: "This memorandum sets forth the plans commanders in case of outbreak of hostilities with the Soviet goes on to report the situation in each area. In Germany there were いー -two Soviet divisions and in Austria, four divisions, plus 4,000 aircraft in Germany and Poland; General McNarney believed the Soviets could make it to the Rhine in one day and sweep across the American zone in five days. In Italy there were American, British, Polish and Italian forces facing the Yugoslavians and the Soviets, with heavy military build-up in the Balkans. In Japan and Korea there were 170,000 American and British troops facing 150,000 Soviet troops and, in all the Far East, Soviet troop strength totalled 625,000; in case of hostilities, the American troops in Korea would evacuate to Japan to defend the Japanese islands at all costs.[122]

At the time, the British thought their relationship with the USSR could be improved. An official in the Foreign Office official informed Harriman that British-Soviet trade negotiations had successfully concluded, and that the UK was very anxious to resolve all outstanding questions with the USSR.[123] The Foreign Office was even seriously considering establishing diplomatic missions to Ukraine and Byelorussia. And the British government had already recognized the incorporation of the three former Baltic republics into the Soviet Union.[124]

In September 1946, Henry Wallace, Vice President in the preceding administration and Commerce Secretary in the Truman Cabinet, made a foreign policy speech, cleared in advance by Truman. Wallace criticized what he saw as an overly rigid attitude toward the Soviet Union, infuriating Secretary of State Byrnes—who, at the time, was attending the CFM meeting in Paris. Byrnes threatened to resign if Wallace was not fired. Bernard Baruch threatened to resign, too. Truman's statement firing Wallace is a masterful piece of correspondence. The first paragraph was drafted by Clark Clifford, the second by Will Clayton, and the third by Charles Ross. After making the statement, Truman turned to Ross and said "Well, the die is cast."[125] He went to the yacht *Williamsburg*, called Harriman in London, and asked him: "How would you like to be the Secretary of Commerce?" Harriman replied, "hell, yes."[126]

Ross told Truman that the break with Wallace was bound to come sooner or later, and that it was impossible for Truman to drive two horses in opposite directions; Truman was "put in the middle" by events over which he had no control. Truman said that a good deal of the tension in Cabinet meetings would now be ended, and that now he could rely on team work from all members of the Cabinet.[127] And he told John Garner, on the day after he fired Wallace, that the situation "is cleared up since yesterday and from now on we will have smooth sailing. I am sure I will."[128] Byrnes phoned back from Paris that he felt the ousting of Wallace and the appointment of Harriman had pleased the Russians; for the first time, Molotov had asked to see him. Truman believed this to be a direct result of "what happened in here."[129] But Wallace was considered a leftist within the Truman administration, and his forced departure was really a signal of Truman's breaking with the Soviet Union.

Studies of the immediate postwar years tend to pay great attention to a White House policy paper entitled *America's Relations with the Soviet Union*. The paper was requested from Special Counsel Clark Clifford by Truman, and was presented to Truman on 24 September 1946. It was written primarily by George Elsey, not Clifford. Clifford did not design the framework, did not do the research, rarely discussed the paper with Elsey, and did not read the proofs. Elsey was a young lieutenant in the Navy Reserve—quick, brilliant, and a good writer. But he was not a profound thinker, was not familiar with Marxist doctrine and practice, and was not experienced in diplomacy.[130]

The Clifford (or Clifford-Elsey) paper was the first comprehensive overview of US-USSR relations in the form of a White House policy document, based upon facts and opinions officially presented to the White House by departments and agencies of the Truman administration. Since Willet's article, Kennan's telegram, and the State Department's policy statement of 15 May all prefigured the Clifford paper, it may be that the importance of the paper has been overemphasized.

The Clifford paper stressed the importance of the US-USSR relationship to world peace. It discussed the necessity for knowledge of Soviet policies and activities on the part of US policy makers; it pointed to the Soviet belief that war with the capitalist states was inevitable and the likelihood that the USSR would increase its power, and weaken that of the potential enemies, by all possible means; it noted Soviet violations of agreements between the US and the USSR; it interpreted the reparation question as a major issue of dispute between the two countries; and it reviewed the construction of Soviet bases, Soviet activities to weaken the US military position and US influence, and Soviet espionage. All of these matters affected the security of the United States. The paper recommended that the primary objective of US policy should be to convince Soviet leaders that it was in the Soviet interest to participate in a system of world cooperation. The US should seek—by cultural, intellectual, and economic exchange—to demonstrate to the Soviets that the US had no aggressive intentions. But on an pivotal issue, the paper differed from the Kennan and State Department positions and seemed more in line with the military: it suggested that, until the Soviets abandoned their belief that war between the two systems was inevitable and ceased to increase their power at the expense of others, the US must assume that the Soviet Union might start a war at any time.[131]

Among the departmental documents for preparation of the Clifford paper was a memorandum from Dean Acheson, officially recognizing that some of the disputes between the two countries originated in different interpretations and conceptions. Acheson wrote on 6 August 1946 that:

> the Soviet Government does not ordinarily deliberately violate the letter of its international agreements....[Difficulty regarding the implementation of agreements] results from the divergence of objectives with which the two countries approach postwar problems....Soviet definitions of terms such as 'democratic', 'friendly', 'fascist', etc. are basically different from the non-communist understanding of these words."

He explained that the Soviets utilized this difference as a way to avoid direct charges of violations of agreements.[132] The Clifford paper incorporated this view.

The Clifford paper marked the climax, on the US side, of the lead-up to a new international setting. In its policy, the US was ready to institutionalize demarcation of spheres of influence, and would respond to any Soviet challenge with a firmer stand. What President Truman needed was an appropriate occasion to make his decision public.

It is universally acknowledged that urging settlement of old accounts leads to a cooler relationship, be it between people or nations. The United States sent the Soviet government a note on 24 September 1946, on the settlement of Lend-Lease—and got no reply. Exactly three months later, the State Department instructed Ambassador Smith to raise the question again with the Soviet authorities, at the earliest possible date.[133] The Soviets must have sensed that an open confrontation was approaching. In September, in answering questions from a British correspondent, Stalin emphasized that there was no real danger of war, that Western capitalism could not encircle the Soviet Union even if it tried, and that the Soviet Union would continue to collaborate with other nations peacefully.

Also in September, the US Embassy reported from London that during the past four weeks there had been a hardening of the British government's attitude toward the USSR, and the US Embassy in Moscow was informed that Stalin's recent statement appeared to contain a maneuver to detach Britain from the US, as expected in some quarters.[134] The following month, Stalin answered questions from the president of United Press: the tension between the USSR and the US was not increasing, the USSR did not have the atomic bomb, the British troops in Greece were "unnecessary," and Germany ought to be a political and economic entity. The US Embassy in Moscow believed Stalin's answers to the UP were intended to deceive the West.[135]   *Time*, however, reported that most people believed Stalin wanted peace, with only a few believing that he was driving a wedge between the US and UK.[136]

Truman was not happy about the results of the mid-term election in November 1946. Molotov passed through Washington on 7 November and paid a courtesy visit to Truman. He expressed to Truman that the results of the elections would not adversely affect the good relations between the two countries. Truman replied that there would be no change as a result of the elections insofar as "our good relations with our neighbors" were concerned, and again invited Stalin to visit the US.[137]   In fact, the election results were so appalling that Senator J. William Fulbright, a Democrat, went so far as to say that "President Truman should appoint a Republican Secretary of State and resign from office."[138]   In order to regain the popularity which the Democrats had previously enjoyed, the President needed something eye-catching. That would be a task for 1947.

Was there really a danger of war? Not at all. By the winter of 1946 it was reported that the USSR had reduced military appropriations by 54 percent in the 1946 budget—from 128 billion rubles in 1945 to 76 billion in 1946. The US said its military appropriations for 1946 were down 73 percent—from $45 billion in fiscal 1946 to $12 billion for 1947.[139] Nevertheless, at the turn of the year, thunderclouds were moving closer and closer.

6
All Quiet on the Western Front

The veiled hostility in Soviet-US relations, after the aggravations of 1946, was close to breaking into the open. Even so, the animosities in Europe in the late 1940s were a sort of "noisy thunder, sparse rain," as the Chinese say. Outwardly, a war seemed imminent, but inwardly both sides knew that war would not come. Nevertheless, the people were being manipulated—or, as they said at the US State Department, "educated"—to overcome their wartime goodwill and to believe that the Communists or, conversely, the imperialists were preparing for war.

Some may question how accurately this characterization reflects reality. To answer this question, this chapter presents four case studies: the Truman Doctrine, the Marshall Plan, the situation in Czechoslovakia in February 1948 and the Berlin blockade.

THE TRUMAN DOCTRINE

The British Government had indicated to the US that, owing to financial difficulties, British troops would be withdrawn from Greece, and had asked for US assistance. In late February 1947, Britain again urged the US to go into Greece. In view of the British withdrawal, the Truman administration decided to provide Greece and Turkey with large amounts of aid. The President addressed a joint session of Congress on 12 March, to request the necessary appropriations. Truman availed himself of the occasion to announce a general policy against Soviet and Communist expansion, in a statement that has since come to be known as the Truman Doctrine.

The Truman Doctrine in itself is not arguable, in that any government can make any statement at its own discretion. But the use of the Greek-Turkish matter as a pretext for formulating and rationalizing the Doctrine merits scrutiny. Was there really such a serious situation in Greece and Turkey at the time?

As a matter of fact, the State Department briefed the President at the end of 1946 that Turkey was ready to meet the USSR halfway, if there was any possibility of a reasonable settlement. The Turkish Foreign Office contemplated a regional agreement, involving the US, UK, USSR and Turkey, for defense of the Straits in time of war. Unless some such settlement could be made soon, Turkey would be obliged to appeal for US economic aid since it could not bear the burden of maintaining a large military against Soviet threats.[1] The Turks believed that the USSR might assume a reasonable stance.[2] The US, however, believed that a regional agreement on the Straits would be unwise, since the USSR would not remain content with any such settlement.[3] In early 1947, the US Ambassador in Ankara, Wilson, believed the Turkish Foreign Office was concerned that a general agreement on world questions might be concluded by the US, UK, and USSR, at the expense of Turkey; the Turks wanted to have a plan of their own ready when the Straits were discussed.[4]

Meanwhile in Greece, Prime Minister Tsaldaris was unable to secure the cooperation of opposition leaders in forming the broadened government needed for dealing with difficult economic and financial conditions. He hoped that prompt US aid would overcome the difficulties. Interestingly, in comments of January 1947, the Prime Minister did not mention the danger of invasion at all. In early February, McVeagh, the US diplomat to Greece, expressed his belief that gradually withdrawing the British forces was safe as well as salutary, now that the UN understood the border problems and Greek forces were being strengthened to handle internal disturbances.[5] McVeagh and US diplomat Ethridge recommended assistance to Greece to prevent an imminent financial collapse, since if Greece fell to the Communists the whole Near East and part of North Africa would be under Soviet influence.[6] The American representative on a UN mission in Greece also reported that the Soviets viewed Greece as a ripe plum; he suggested issuing a warning to the Soviets.[7] The British Foreign Office, however, informed the US Charge in London that the situation in Greece was not as serious as the US representatives had reported—an assessment challenged in turn by the Americans in Greece.[8] The U.S. Embassy in Moscow weighed in with a report that the presence of British troops was the only factor keeping Greece out of the Soviet camp.

Communications concerning the Greek situation continued to fly through late February and into March. The US embassy in London reported that the British were sincere in the matter of withdrawing their troops.[9] On the same day, the Turkish Foreign Minister told US Ambassador Wilson that Soviet policy was aimed at dominating Turkey and that a large Turkish army was necessary—but that, as the Soviets demobilized following conclusion of treaties with former Nazi satellite countries, Turkey was able to reduce its army somewhat, thereby lightening its economic burden.[10] In early March, a British Foreign Office official informed a US diplomat that a few thousand British troops would probably remain in Greece until Soviet troops were removed from Bulgaria as stipulated in the Bulgarian treaty.[11] At the same time, the Greek Charge d'affaires sent the State Department a formal request for "financial and other assistance," to restore domestic order; he did not mention possible attacks by Soviet-camp troops. All of these communications point in one direction: the general tenor of thinking at the time was that the Soviet threat was not so serious as previously thought.

The estimated relief needs of Greece after the end of the UNRRA program were $56 million.[12] Could US aid ameliorate the Greek situation? Perhaps, but not with certainty. Ambassador Porter, for example, believed that assurance of generous unconditional US aid over a long period might result in continued gross misconduct by the Greek government, and that the US should make self-help measures a condition for aid.[13]

US military involvement in Greece was actually not a new consideration. As early as 1 November 1945, White House advisor Sam Rosenman sent Truman a memo concerning an idea put forward by Skouras, a Greek politician. Skouras recommended that one-half of the British troops leave Greece, to be replaced by US troops; the British and Greeks would announce their request for this action, and their intent to have the American and British troops withdrawn simultaneously—say, ninety days after the elections. Truman discussed the idea with Leahy and Byrnes, and said he would talk with Attlee about it.[14]

In the early spring of 1947, the Truman administration considered it necessary to publicly clarify the US-USSR relationship. Apart from long-range considerations, there were also immediate concerns motivating such an action. First, in late January, Ambassador Smith had reported from Moscow his anxiety about confusion in the American media over apparent manifestations of conciliation in Soviet foreign policy. He believed the media had only a limited knowledge of Communist theory and history and did not understand that "Soviet policy is motivated and guided by a well-defined, enduring and fundamentally consistent doctrine sustained over 23 years since Lenin's death."[15] Second, as noted earlier, Ambassador Wilson reported that the Turkish Foreign Office was concerned, in view of recent indications of a more conciliatory Soviet attitude, that the US and UK might attempt to seek a general settlement of world questions with the Soviets and that concessions might be made at Turkey's expense.[16] Third, in early February, British officials in charge of Soviet affairs had repeatedly indicated that, while there was no change in the substance of the UK's policy with regard to the USSR, every move must be carefully considered from the view point of protecting Bevin against "Labor Party rebels." The British public, for the most part, were thought to desire close relations with the Soviets.[17] Incidentally, the US Embassy in London reported a few days later that the Labor government was experiencing its first real loss of public support, due to a coal strike.[18]

In reaction to Truman's address in the Congress, quite a few believed that aid to Greece and Turkey should be channeled through the UN.[19] While the aid appropriations were soon approved, this did not reflect the true sentiment prevailing in the Congress. Francis Case, Chairman of the House Committee for consideration of the aid bill, told Truman:

> the printed record can never convey the intensity of feeling that accompanied the words....Very, very few spoke of the bill with enthusiasm. Support was reluctant....At least 75 members, I judge, would have voted against final passage, myself included, had it not been that we thought it would be like pulling the rug out from you or Secretary of State Marshall, in the positions you had taken in Moscow....[The House passed the bill] in the hope that it might give you a little help and a little time to get that job on its way.

Case pointed out that some House members were impressed by talk about oil reserves in the Middle East, but believed that there were cheaper ways for the US to lick its energy problem than policing the Mediterranean and the Middle East. "The people of the United States are weary of 'government by crisis;'" furthermore, the House "does not want to by-pass or weaken the United Nations."[20]

Some of the views expressed by Congressmen and Senators also reflected the anti-British feeling prevailing at the time. Congressman John B. Bennett wrote to Vandenberg objecting to subsidizing Britain to maintain a Greek government that "they think the Greeks ought to have."[21] Senator Joseph O. O'Mahoney of the Appropriations Committee wrote Truman that "it is easy to see why the government of the British Empire would desire to have the resources of the United States to sustain its policy."[22]

In fact, Britain, a country of limited resources but heavy commitments, had no choice but to change priorities from time to time. The attention of the Labor Government now focused more on Middle Eastern oil than ever before. In early 1947, the Foreign Secretary and the Minister for Fuel and Trade examined trends in oil production, and concluded that the oil resources of the Middle East were of vital importance to Britain and the Empire. The Middle East was expected to contribute a larger share of the increase in world oil output than any other region; US output was likely to fall without the discovery of major new fields. Under the circumstances, it would hardly be surprising if the British left Greece and Turkey to the Americans and concentrated upon the Middle East.

Another factor behind Congressional sentiment was an olive branch offered by Stalin. On 10 January, Marshal Montgomery, then Chief of the Imperial General Staff, visited Moscow. Stalin told him that, since the UN had been established, the position of the Anglo-Soviet Treaty was not clear. (Later, *Pravda* reported Bevin's having mentioned in a radio broadcast that Britain regarded the treaty as "suspended in the air.") Stalin also indicated that he did not oppose an Anglo-American military alliance, provided it was not aimed at the Soviet Union, and referred to the possibility of an Anglo-Soviet alliance without specifying whether it was solely for the purpose of containing Germany.

The Labor Government found Stalin's remarks intimidating, hurriedly informed him that the British attitude had not changed, and indicated a desire to extend the Anglo-Soviet Treaty; Stalin agreed in principle. Bevin reported to the Cabinet in early February that any such negotiation should not estrange the US, because once the Americans withdrew from Europe, Britain would be left in an impossible position. Bevin sent a message to Marshall on the matter, but the Americans did not reply.

During a Cabinet discussion, the British Chiefs of Staff were convinced that alliance with the Soviets would seriously affect exchange of military information with the US. Cabinet members believed that the Soviets wanted to secure their western frontier because they still feared German aggression, and that the Soviets were apprehensive of US economic penetration in Europe and the Middle East. They suggested cooperating with the Soviets in economic undertakings, such as Middle Eastern oil—warning, however, that relations would not improve if simultaneous advances were not made in the political sphere. They ventured that it would allay the Soviets' suspicions if a loan for reconstruction could be given them by the International Bank, of which the USSR was not a member. Some Cabinet officers were of the opinion that any military alliance with the USSR should fall within the framework of the UN, and should include the US, France, and other nations.

The actions decided upon by the Cabinet included a message to Stalin, expressing willingness to update the treaty and asking him to propose revisions. No mention of military alliance was to be made in this message. The Cabinet would take up the matter again after receiving Stalin's reply.[23] On 19 February, the US State Department reported to the President that, according to an officer of the British Foreign Office, a draft revision of the Anglo-Soviet Treaty would follow very closely the text of the Anglo-French treaty: "We cannot offer the Russians less than we do the French and we do not want to offer them more."[24]

Objections to the Truman Doctrine, as expressed by members of the US Congress, were mostly beside the point, reflecting either naivete or ignorance of the facts. What Truman had in mind was not merely aid to Greece and Turkey, or a helping hand for the British. The situation in Greece and Turkey, and the question of aid to them clearly did not warrant a drastic and anti-Soviet statement of general policy by the American president. Rather, Truman chose the occasion of Britain's withdrawal from Greece to launch what he believed to be his own foreign policy. Indeed, Truman told Eben Ayers that his foreign policy started in March 1947.

"Was there really a Soviet threat when the Truman Doctrine was announced?" This question was addressed not long ago to a former British diplomat active in the postwar years. His reply: "It was not a Soviet threat. It was an American perspective, and we British agreed."[25] Nevertheless, it cannot be concluded that Truman was not worried about the Soviets in early 1947. He wrote on 10 May that whereas it used to be from the Log Cabin to the White House, now it could be from the Kremlin to the White House.[26]

The Sung Dynasty author Ouyang Xiu once wrote that "the attention of one who drinks is not on the wine, but on the beautiful around him." As shown by subsequent developments, Truman's attention was not on the wine but on the scenery. The direct result of the Truman Doctrine was not the start of a regular war, but the disclosure of a cold one. The doctrine laid out the central norm in prosecuting this war: the policy of containment. It further institutionalized the demarcation line between Soviet and American spheres of influence. Its nature was both offensive and defensive—politically offensive, while militarily defensive.

THE MARSHALL PLAN

About three months after announcement of the Truman Doctrine, Truman and Secretary Marshall discussed who would head up "relief in Europe." Two days later, Marshall put forth a proposal for European recovery in his Harvard Speech of 6 June. This suggestion eventually evolved into the European Recovery Plan (ERP), or Marshall Plan.[27] Interestingly, many laid claim to initiation of the plan, probably because, as an economic matter, it carried no danger of being branded a warmonger. Kennan said it was he who pressed for containment—and for aid to Europe as a form of containment. Bohlen said the Marshall Plan started in Moscow when he and Marshall attended the CFM. Truman said it was he who let Acheson talk about European aid in Cleveland—but that if the Plan had been named after himself it would not have had the consent of the Congress.

It is well known that Truman himself said the Truman Doctrine and the Marshall Plan were "two halves of a walnut." In 1948, he added a footnote: "This ERP was instituted for the purpose of recovery of Europe and for the purpose of raising the iron curtain peacefully."[28] Hence, the Marshall Plan, like the Truman Doctrine, was also of a dual nature, both defensive and offensive. It served five distinct purposes: (1) rescuing the Western European economy, so as to rehabilitate world capitalism; (2) blocking revolution in the Western European countries, thus offsetting Soviet influence; (3) attracting the Eastern European countries with something the Soviets were unable to offer, and thus encouraging their separatist tendencies; (4) opening the doors for American commodity and capital exports to Europe; and (5) dividing the two major spheres of influence more deeply and clearly.

At the time Marshall addressed the students and faculty of Harvard University, American families were enjoying a new happiness, brought by opportunity, by the first batch of baby boomers, by the cars and other goods being produced for peacetime consumers. In contrast, the European economy was still in chaos; Europeans saw their homes in ruins and struggled to secure food for their families. The Americans were sending parcels of food and clothing to kinfolk and strangers in the old country. Against this backdrop, Britain—as the major Western Power—reacted first to Marshall's message of all-round American aid, and its reaction lived up to Marshall's expectations. Just one day before the Harvard speech, the State Department had briefed the President that Bevin was deeply concerned about the food situation in Western Europe and potential Soviet exploitation of this situation. He was now considering a plan for dealing with the situation in Western Europe in a unified manner, rather than on an ad hoc and piecemeal basis.[29]

Bevin reported to the British Cabinet on 17 June that he was going to Paris to confer with the French on the Marshall offer. He also explained to the Soviets that, as far as Britain was concerned, the US offer concerned only economic rehabilitation, not politics. And he hoped that the plan would cover Germany, reducing Britain's financial burden there. To disarm domestic criticism, in the Paris conference the French Ministers were emphatic that every effort must be made to secure the participation of the Soviet Union and countries within its sphere of influence. Bevin replied that, even if the Soviets did not come in, they should proceed with the plan; the French concurred. The British and French foreign ministers then invited Molotov to Paris; once he declined to come, they could say that they had done their best. They decided to keep the US posted.[30]

Molotov went to Paris to attend the initial meeting of the European Recovery Plan. Ambassador Smith reported from Moscow that Molotov hoped to destroy the Plan, since any intelligent and well implemented plan for European recovery would impinge adversely upon Soviet political objectives. Ambassador Caffery reported from Paris that many French were concerned over Molotov's visit, since they felt his purpose was to sabotage the discussions.[31] The conference proceedings, however, would later show Molotov's initial attitude to be sincere. Then, upon receiving a directive from Moscow, he would withdrew from the conference—to the relief of the Western countries.

For five days in Paris, the foreign ministers of the UK, USSR, and France argued about a single item: whether the US would leave receiving countries to use the aid at their own discretion, or require that they first propose how they would set their houses in order. Molotov insisted on the former plan, Bevin and Bidault on the latter. Molotov said that he would present a statement of requirements, but that demanding anything further would constitute political and economic interference in the internal affairs of participating countries. He would not yield—nor would Bevin and Bidault. In the end, Molotov said that if they proceeded in the manner they proposed, they would come to rue the consequences and would cause division of Europe into hostile groups.[32] Bevin, in a personal message to Marshall, reported that the talks "to all intents and purposes" had broken down, and that he was glad "the cards have been laid on the table and that the responsibility will be laid at Moscow's door."[33]

The Marshall Plan also further revealed the conflict of interest between the US and the UK. Before Marshall proposed the plan at Harvard, Truman received reports unfavorable to the British government. In late February, Lt. General Hoyt S. Vandenberg, chief of the Central Intelligence Group, reported to the President that the British were displaying a nominally independent attitude in foreign relations, in contrast to their previous close collaboration with the US on practically all international issues. They were reluctant to join the US in formal representations on East European developments, and occasionally declined to support the US in the United Nations on issues such as atomic control and the Pacific Islands trusteeship. And they were making friendly gestures toward the USSR, such as Montgomery's visit there and the invitation for a Soviet parliamentary delegation to visit England. The immediate purposes of this change in attitude were to regain the public's confidence in a time of domestic difficulties and to quiet left-wing criticism that the Labor Government and Bevin did not seek an understanding with the Soviets and were blindly pro-American. Longer-term factors behind the change included a growing concern over the ultimate effect of close economic ties with the US and a desire to mediate Big Three differences in the interest of global stability—for which Britain felt the most vital need among the Three.

The British government then decided, on both ideological and practical grounds, to attempt to mediate between the US and USSR. The net effect of the British change was not a realignment on fundamental issues within the Big Three.[34] The British gestures toward the Soviets were interpreted by the US as basically tactical moves. As noted earlier, a knowledgeable British official repeatedly indicated that every move toward the USSR must be carefully considered and planned so as to protect Bevin against Labor Party rebels.[35]

The effect of the Truman Doctrine on the relationship between US and USSR was not immediately serious; because the doctrine was mainly a statement of intention and policy, its effects might well surface slowly. The Marshall Plan was different. It was an action directly involving every country in Europe. Ambassador Douglas reported from London that, after the Soviet boycott of the Marshall Plan, sentiments in Britain were "disturbed but grimly glad" that the clash between East and West had come into the open. Douglas observed that the public supported Bevin's stand vis-a-vis the Soviets on European reconstruction and would follow him in any measure necessary to make reconstruction effective.[36] The US also believed that the French Communists were isolated as a result of the Soviet refusal on the ERP.[37]

Having acted as the leading sheep in the ERP flock, Britain believed it had obtained new leverage in its relationship with the US. The agreement between the US and the UK on questions concerning German industry also enhanced Britain's position. Bevin lost no time in informing Marshall, in late July, that the British financial situation was critical, and that the UK could play a leading role in the ERP and in Germany only with a loan of $1 billion from the International Bank, which would be sufficient to carry them "over the hump."[38] In early August, Bevin urged immediate high-level US-UK discussions on the British economic situation and its international implications.[39] In fact, the flock—Britain included—were not necessarily inclined to look upon a benefactor with hearty thanks. According to a State Department presidential briefing in September, the Belgian Minister to Portugal informed Ambassador Wiley that, during a short trip through Europe, he found some degree of cheerfulness and friendliness for the US only in Italy and that the anti-American sentiment in England was "terrifying."[40]

Officials in the Truman administration and members of the Congress were still biased against the Labor Government. Treasury Secretary Snyder remarked that "Britain is trying to 'snipe us', leaving us holding the bag."[41] Francis Wilcox reported that, in the bilateral trade negotiations then underway, the UK had no intention of eliminating preferences; he questioned whether the US should enter into any trade agreement at all with the UK, and suggested that the UK's representative be informed that if he continued to refuse to move toward eliminating preferences, "the prospects of Congressional approval for additional aid, under the Marshall Plan or otherwise, will be seriously impaired."[42]   According to Bevin, on 21 September Clayton and the US Ambassador hinted that, if the British were not willing to make further trade concessions, their prospects of obtaining help under the Marshall offer might be jeopardized.[43] In mid-October, Harold Stassen told the White House staff in his *Four Points on Foreign Policy* that "American aid should be conditional." The only "string" he discussed in any detail was "that the British Government should refrain from further nationalization of basic industries."[44]

The US government instructed that its embassy in London express to Bevin serious concern over British plans to make additional jet planes available to the USSR.[45]   The JCS *Guidance to Commander-in-Chief, Europe* of 13 August 1947 stipulated that, pending instructions from the US government, there should be no offensive action by US troops if British troops alone were attacked by the Soviet Union. Only in January 1949 did Truman replace this guidance with the stipulation in NSC-39 that the US should take offensive action if British or French occupation troops in Europe were attacked.[46]   This not only reveals the cool relationship between the US and UK at the time, but also reveals that war was still seen as far away. The Truman administration could play politics at a relaxed pace.

At a meeting of the Economic Planning Board in late 1947, Sir Oliver Franks made a statement on the negotiation of the Marshall Plan. Franks believed that not all Americans were fully aware of the political difficulties involved if conditions affecting the sovereignty of the sixteen participating countries were attached to the aid; members of the Truman administration were generally aware of difficulties, but they doubted the stability of some of the countries in the absence of outside pressure. Then Franks almost directly answered Stassen: "We need not fear political conditions in the simple-minded sense, such as a ban on nationalization." He was confident that, given good leadership by the UK, the sixteen nations could be kept together in close cooperation during the five years of Marshall aid. Franks maintained that in general it would not be necessary to modify major UK policy to conciliate American opinion.[47]   Franks' statement was duly reported to the US Cabinet by the Treasury. For the US government, Britain was obviously a hard nut to crack—or, as the Chinese say, "a porcupine that dogs can't bite."

Both the US and the USSR tried to set their own houses in order after the Truman Doctrine. On the US side, the Loyalty System was launched, and the National Security Act was passed, establishing a new machinery of national security. On the Soviet side, ideology purity was emphasized. Anti-American, anti-imperialist purges started in the USSR and the Eastern

European countries; the Cominform, the Information Bureau of nine Communist and Workers' Parties, was set up. There was also COMCON, the Council of Economic Cooperation, a counterpart to the Marshall Plan and Common Market. Apart from atomic bombs, however, the strength of the US armed forces at the time was still low; regular army enlistments in early 1947 were running far below requirements, and demobilization of wartime military personnel was not yet completed.[48]

The US-USSR relations became more tense following a satirical description of Truman (e.g., "a small man in short pants") by the Soviet author Boris Gorbatov in *Literatura Gazetta* in September. Ambassador Smith was instructed to protest this "wantonly libelous" personal attack on a US President; Molotov's reply was that the Soviet government was not responsible—and that the Soviet press was portraying other countries truthfully and strengthening friendly relations between nations.[49] C.H. Hummelsine of the State Department observed that "if this bird will write about two more articles the President will be elected without having to worry with a campaign."[50] Reeducation of the public in the direction of anti-Soviet and anti-Communist sentiments had achieved effective results.

At the time Smith was instructed by the State Department to protest Gorbatov's "libel"; he reported that the Soviet people were concerned about the imminent possibility of war. And Marshal Montgomery reportedly told someone in Bruxelles that war with the Soviet Union was now unavoidable. However, the year 1947 ended without a shot fired along the demarcation line between the Soviet group and the West. Because the split had come into the open, both sides were strengthening themselves. The US embassy in Moscow reported in early October that there was all-out Soviet propaganda of a war scare, for the purposes of: (1) sabotaging economic recovery, by making other countries hesitant to accept "US imperialist aid"; (2) causing Congress to withhold credits, in the belief that war was inevitable; and (3) bolstering control and discipline within the USSR.[51] As a matter of fact, under cover of a war scare, lay a more stable Europe than before.

CZECHOSLOVAKIA

In the beginning of 1948, a situation developed in Czechoslovakia that was later to be known as the "Czechoslovakia Crisis of February 1948," the "Czechoslovakia Coup," or the "February Revolution"—depending on one's point of view. Among the Eastern European countries, Czechoslovakia at the time held a unique position. It was not a Fascist satellite, not a former part of Germany, not a Germanic nation. It had a government based on a coalition of Benes' and Massaryk's followers with the Communists. Benes served as President, and his followers held most of the ministries. Communist Klementi Gottwald was Premier, and several other Communists held ministerial posts and controlled the security police. By the end of 1945, all of the American and Soviet troops originally stationed in Czechoslovakia were withdrawn by agreement.

On 17 February 1947, non-Communist ministers complained that the Minister of the Interior, a Communist, failed to carry out a Cabinet decision annulling appointments for certain police positions. Given the importance of the police in peacetime, this was obviously a challenge to the Communist Party—and the Soviet Union. Three days later, with no response to the complaints, Ministers from several pro-Western parties resigned in protest. This was a further challenge, and also a golden opportunity for the Communists to get these people out of political life. The Communist Party set up grass-roots organizations and armed them, arresting some of the Ministers who had resigned. On the 25th, President Benes officially announced his acceptance of their resignations and approved a new government formed by Gottwald. The armed forces, led by National Defense Minister Svoboda, supported Gottwald. Thus the Government fell completely under Communist control.

In order to clarify the nature of the situation in Czechoslovakia, it is important to begin by clarifying which sphere the country was in. At the time, views differed—as they still do today. Some said Czechoslovakia was in the Soviet sphere, some said it was neutral, and a few argued that it was in the Western sphere. As early as April 1945, Kennan had already written Czechoslovakia off, maintaining that the US should not send a diplomatic representative because the Benes Government was not independent.[52]

The US embassy reported in January 1946 that tensions were increasing between radicals and moderates in the Czechoslovak government. The former group was determined to bring the country solidly into the Soviet economic sphere and was making progress in that direction. The embassy recommended that no loans be extended to Czechoslovakia until its commitments with the Soviet Union were known.[53] In February, a small American force crossed the Czech border; three soldiers were arrested, suggesting that the Czechs, for whatever reason, were very protective of their sovereignty vis-a-vis the Americans. US Ambassador Lawrence Steinhardt reported from Prague in June that Communist Party gains in the recent Czech election had been accepted with good grace by the general public and by various party leaders; the Communists seemed sobered by their new responsibilities.[54]

In September, the CIA reported that the Czechoslovak Communists were deliberately trying to "weaken if not destroy" the National Front Government.[55] The following month, an informant in Prague reported to the US embassy that if US-Soviet antagonism deepened, it was very possible that the efforts of the Czech Communists would be "more dangerous," as they "resorted to clearly undemocratic measures;" Communist policy was to remain fluid pending the outcome of a CFM meeting in November.[56] Also in October, Ambassador Steinhardt reported finding "clear evidence" that the Czech Communists were determined to "use police pressure and terror" prior to elections the next spring: "Within a few months the Government will have become the subservient tool of Moscow."[57] Hence, four months before the incident in Czechoslovakia occurred, the American ambassador had predicted its coming. Then, in late November, President Benes told him that the "turning point" had been reached in the struggle against the Communists.[58]

After Czechoslovak officials traveled to Paris in July 1947 to attend the ERP meeting, they were recalled due to a warning from the Soviet Union. This should have demonstrated to Western leaders the naivete of believing that Czechoslovakia was not within the Soviet sphere. But Harold C. Vedeler's analysis of the situation suggests that it did not. Vedeler, of Central European Affairs in the State Department, told Steinhardt that, in the prevailing view in his office, the Soviet warning to Czechoslovakia was being exaggerated by some of the other offices in State.

Vedeler compared the situation in Czechoslovakia to the Hungarian government's earlier shuffle on the matter of the Allied Control Commission. He listed reasons put forth in the State Department for not presenting the Hungarian case to the UN Security Council: the US should concentrate on its Greek policy so as not to prejudice its program there, and if the Hungarian case at the UN were postponed, Hungary might come into the ERP. (This was before Molotov boycotted the ERP.) Last but not least, if the US charged the Soviets with unilateral actions in Hungary, the Soviets might level countercharges concerning MacArthur's actions in Japan. Vedeler believed that, as Steinhardt had suggested, some action might be taken in regard to Czechoslovakia for the purpose of encouraging moderates in all the European countries. Steinhardt had also suggested concluding a cultural agreement with Czechoslovakia; Vedeler agreed, but thought it would be difficult to do so.[59] The Vedeler exchange with Steinhardt clearly shows that the State Department on one hand had illusions that the situation might still be favorable to the West, and on the other considered preempting the upcoming overhaul of Czechoslovakia by means that it obviously did not possess.

Detroit banker Joseph M. Dodge, an advisor to MacArthur and the Truman administration, wrote in July 1947 from Vienna that both Hungary and Czechoslovakia wanted to join the ERP but were blocked by the Soviet Union. Dodge stated:

Both incidents show how earnestly the satellites want to get on the band wagon. But they also show how these countries are controlled and whom they fear....[I]t seems to me that the Soviets are deliberately widening the split and drawing the line clearly by their actions in Paris....The fact is their own eastern bloc is all set and under control. Their structure and controls are established except for East Germany and Austria. Our structure has not even had its foundation laid.

Dodge's remarks make an apt footnote to Truman's considerations when he declared his Doctrine in March.[60]

Ambassador Steinhardt wrote in August 1947 concerning his relationship with Benes' Ministers:

In my relations with all of highest officials of the Government—with two or three noticeable exceptions such as Kopecky and Duris—I never felt any suspicion from the Government....Of course there were differences with the Communists, but then the Communists constituted only one half of the Government and any suspicions that they had attained were more than offset by the friendliness by the highest non-Communist officials.[61]

Francis T. Williamson of the State Department had written to Steinhardt in July reporting that the press in the US was writing off Czechoslovakia as a "Russian dominated area." But State thought that the situation could change via "free election," and that "until there is a coup d'etat" the US should consider Czechoslovakia an important aspect of policy for Europe and susceptible to US values. Williamson noted that State was eager to know what the British would think of prospects for close relations with a Czechoslovak government under Communist leadership. According to Williamson, "this presents a real problem in our foreign policy, and one towards which we should adopt a realistic policy."[62] Here again, the British were causing the Americans anxiety.

The US received reports from French intelligence sources on 6 August to the effect that the Soviets were moving troops in the direction of Czechoslovakia in order to keep pressure on the Czechoslovak government.[63] Four days before the Communist takeover in Prague, the CIA estimated that the Communist Party might well precipitate a political crisis resulting in the breakdown of the government.[64] These further demonstrate that the US had warning of the situation that would develop in February 1948, and that the possibility of such a situation was within the calculations of the US government.

In early 1948, the British government discussed the world situation on the basis of a memorandum from Bevin. The government recognized that Soviet influence in Europe had coalesced into a solid political and economic bloc, and believed that the British would "be hard put to it to stem the further encroachment of the Soviet tide." Physical barriers were not enough to guard Western civilization, and the Labor Government believed that it was they—being European and Social Democratic—and not the Americans who could "give the lead in spiritual, moral and political spheres [to] democratic and anti-Communist elements in Western Europe, who were also genuinely progressive and reformist, believing in freedom, planning and social justice—what one might call the 'Third Force'." With the backing of the Commonwealth and the Americas, "it should be possible to develop our own power and influence" to equal that of the US and the USSR. If this line could be followed, the UK "will show clearly that we are not subservient to [the Americans and the Soviets]." Whereas "American propaganda stressed the strength and aggressiveness of Communism which tended to scare and unbalance the anti-Communists while heartening the fellow-travellers and to encourage the Communists to bluff more extravagantly," British propaganda, by dwelling on "Russia's poverty and backwardness," could be expected to relax rather than aggravate international tensions.[65]

The Truman administration might believe that, with the launching of the Marshall Plan, US influence could be enhanced in Europe. But the British were thinking the other way around. As the leading sheep in the Marshall flock, Britain was ready to play spiritual protector of the West. The Chancellor of the Exchequer, reporting to the Cabinet on Britain's 1948 dollar position, discussed the problem in terms of two assumptions. The first was that the US would not agree to provide Marshall aid or that the terms would not be acceptable; the second was that the Marshall aid would come. The Cabinet then concluded that, even assuming full and acceptable Marshall aid, Britain should overcome, as quickly as possible, dependence upon outside economic support.[66]

On the problem of Eastern Europe in general and Czechoslovakia in particular, Bevin commented in January 1948 that "throughout Eastern Europe, the same pattern of a Soviet and Communist dominated political economic structure is becoming increasingly obvious. Even Czechoslovakia is now threatened."[67] In early March, after the Czechoslovakia episode, Bevin reassessed the situation: "Czechoslovakia is in process of being absorbed into the Soviet Orbit as a result of a coup d'etat on typical Communist lines....This outcome is highly detrimental to our interests, but there is nothing we can do about it in Czechoslovakia itself except to express our disapproval." Bevin added that future relations with

Czechoslovakia should be "frigid and correct," and expressed disapproval of the US administration's intention to recall its ambassador. He suggested publicity showing Britain's strength, so that other countries, such as those of Scandinavia, would not think they must throw in with the Soviets while there was still time. Bevin believed that in the long run friends could only be retained if Britain was strong.[68]

People like Kennan had written Czechoslovakia off long before, recognizing that it belonged to the Soviet sphere. But both the US and British governments refused to accept this fact. Of course, neither said that Czechoslovakia belonged to the "Western bloc"; however, they did not take strong action when Soviet threats caused Czechoslovakia to leave the Marshall aid conference in Paris. When the Benes government was dissolved and the Communist Party took over, the British response was, "There is nothing we can do"—that is, the British adopted an ostrich policy. As a matter of fact, anyone in the position of the Soviets and the Czechoslovak Communists would have taken similar strong actions to remove agents of the opposing bloc.

While the US, UK, and other Western countries did make a fuss over the Czechoslovakia episode, the substance of their reaction boils down to three key points: (1) The British admitted that Czechoslovakia had been in the Soviet sphere even before the episode and that their cardinal error was to trust in the Communists' playing by "Westminster rules." (2) The West was more afraid of the possible domino effect on countries such as France and Italy than of the episode itself. Bevin said it was necessary to play along with the Communists, but that they should not encourage a similar line elsewhere (e.g., in Nenni's Socialist Party in Italy); the US State Department decided to handle this case in a way "resulting in greatest beneficial political effect in other countries where serious Communist threat exists or may develop shortly." (3) The British and Americans were impotent, or at least very reluctant, and did not want to aggravate the situation. Bevin said that "continental electorates are impressed by *power*, and in the East of Europe we have not had power." Despite loud protests from people like Allen Dulles who stated, "the end of liberty in Czechoslovakia confronts the free world with the same issues which Europe faced after Munich,"[69] the State Department ordered its UN delegation to avoid a showdown with the Soviets on the Czechoslovak issue, and to handle the matter in a way that would not damage the UN or create frustration in the US and Western Europe. The delegation was not to become an active proponent of investigation, was not to put forward resolutions, and was not to speak early in the debate.[70]

THE BERLIN BLOCKADE

The Soviets continued to take strong action vis-a-vis the Western challenge, especially after announcement of the Truman Doctrine and the Marshall Plan. In order to punish Yugoslavia for its independent actions, the Soviet Communist Party manipulated the Cominform into expelling Yugoslavia and charged Tito and his colleagues with being renegades and agents of the imperialists. Apart from punishing Yugoslavia, the Soviets were, as the Chinese say, "killing a chicken to scare the monkey." The Soviet actions constituted another step toward sanitizing their camp, but at the same time created a cleavage within it. Yugoslav recalcitrance and the adverse effect of the split on Soviet prestige contributed to the Soviets' radical step in Berlin in June 1948.

At the end of March, US Ambassador Smith reported from Moscow that he'd had a long talk with Andrei Vyshinsky on outstanding bilateral issues. It was clear to him that the Soviet Union had no intention of finding a constructive formula for elimination of petty irritations between the two countries; rather, the present repertoire of complaints and protests would be continued for propaganda purposes.[71] The State Department, meanwhile, briefed Truman that the British Foreign Office believed that war with the Soviet Union was not imminent, since the Soviets had little to gain by war.[72] Ambassador Smith and Molotov then met confidentially on 4 May and again on the 9th. Secretary Marshall advised Truman not to discuss these matters with the press.[73] On 14 June, Truman was told that a Paris source reported the development of a highly flexible "appeasement" line on the part of the Cominform, in an apparent effort to prevent further splits in the Communist camp. The same source believed Moscow might contemplate undertaking another "peace maneuver" by accepting the London recommendation on Germany for the purposes of gaining a voice in control of the Ruhr and promoting the idea of German unity.[74] So far, the US and USSR were announcing quite clearly that they had no intention of precipitating war and that there was some chance of improving the relationship between them.

Then, on 14 June 1948, the State Department briefed Truman that Murphy in Berlin believed recent Soviet efforts to tighten restrictions on travel and transport in Germany were intended to cut Berlin completely off from Western supplies or to provoke the western powers into calling a meeting of the Allied Control Council. If such a meeting were convened, the Soviets would use it for propaganda purposes.[75] Soviet provocations soon intensified. On the 16th, the Soviet delegation quit the Berlin Kammandatura meeting of the Allies. On the 19th, the Soviet army halted all surface traffic into Berlin. Ambassador Smith reported from Moscow that he doubted the Kremlin would sacrifice its present position in Germany for a peace offensive; the USSR was forcing the West to make a clear choice between evacuation and digging in. The ambassador said he would work out, with the UK and France, a plan by which the US could "salvage most" from this difficult situation.[76]

Following the failure of discussions on issuance of a single currency for the whole of Berlin, the Soviet authorities announced on 23 June that the new currency for the Soviet Zone would be introduced throughout the city. The Western authorities countered with an announcement introducing their own currency for Germany's Western Zones into the western sectors of Berlin. On the same day the Soviets halted all rail traffic between Berlin and the Western Zones and all electricity supplies from the eastern sector to the western sectors of Berlin.

President Truman, presiding over a Cabinet meeting on the 25th, acted just as one would expect of the head of state of a major power: he did not regard the Berlin situation as a major event. Truman asked the Defense Department to give a report on the "German currency squabble with Russia." Defense Secretary Forrestal reported that the situation was not as bad as indicated in the press. Army Secretary Royall reported essentially the same thing, but maintained that situation was still a matter for serious concern.[77] US Ambassador Caffery reported from Paris that a source close to "Comintern" circles said the present Soviet moves were in the nature of a "war of nerves" designed to secure for Moscow a voice in the affairs of western Germany and not necessarily designed to drive the western powers out of Berlin.[78]

In Britain, Bevin reported the Berlin situation to the Cabinet. The Foreign Office had issued a statement that the UK intended to maintain its position in Berlin and had asked the US to issue a similar statement. Bevin confirmed there could be no question of yielding to Soviet pressure; if the West were forced out of Berlin, the prospect of a Western Union would be fatally weakened. The western allies then discussed supplying West Berlin via airlifts.[79]

When the US suggested referring the Berlin situation to the Security Council, the British disagreed.[80] Meanwhile, the French government had collapsed, and a new one was being formed. The USSR and the western powers exchanged notes in which all persisted in their own positions. The USSR claimed Berlin as a part of the Soviet Zone in Germany, holding that the West had lost their rights in Berlin by violating the Four-Power Accords and blaming the West for the crisis; the West asked the Soviets to remove all traffic blockades and suggested that the two sides enter technical discussions on such topics as the currency problem.[81]

During this period, the US and UK—as usual—did not see eye to eye. Rather, they pursued divergent national interests. Earlier in March, after the Czechoslovakia incident, the British Cabinet concluded that "We should use United States aid to gain time, but our ultimate aim should be to attain a position in which the countries of western Europe could be independent both of the United States and the Soviet Union."[82] On 17 June, just as the Berlin situation was about to develop, Churchill and a group from the British section of the International Committee of Movements for European Unity met with Attlee and Bevin. Bevin's remarks during this meeting show how the British used American strength for their own purposes. He said that:

> for a long time past he had hoped for the creation of a European Union. After the end of the war, however, the United Kingdom had no power to support the European economy, until the offer of Marshall Aid gave us the opportunity to take the lead in promoting a Union of Western Europe. Even then, fears for their future security prevented some European countries from giving full support to this conception until recently, when the United States Government had given their assurance that they intended to retain Armed Forces in Europe until peace was assured.[83]

At the time, the US and UK were negotiating the terms of an Economic Cooperation Agreement. On 24 June, British Cabinet members reacted bitterly upon learning that the US had offered them terms identical to those offered Italy, a former enemy. They observed that the US attitude, at a time of Soviet threat, would gravely damage Anglo-American relations. Following the Cabinet meeting, Attlee asked the US ambassador to convey these views to the US government. Later that afternoon and evening, the US negotiators became more sympathetic to the British position; when the British Cabinet met again the next day, it was able to agree to a revised form of the Agreement.[84] Obviously, the US government urgently needed British support in a time of emerging crisis.

The diplomatic situation developed apace in late July. At a US Cabinet meeting on the 23rd, Marshall analyzed the Soviets' firm attitude in Berlin. In his view, the present tension could be traced to the Russians' loss of face in Italy, France, and Finland (where the West had succeeded), to Tito's "defection," and to desperation in the face of ERP.[85] When the ambassadors of the US, the UK, and France approached the Soviet Foreign Office a week later with a request to see Stalin, Deputy Foreign Minister Zorin's attitude was uncompromising. He said that Molotov was on vacation and that there were no changes in the position of the West suggesting that discussion with Stalin and Molotov would prove fruitful. The next evening, however, the three ambassadors were summoned separately to see Molotov. Two days later, Stalin himself met with them.

The impression of the US ambassador was that "Stalin and Molotov were undoubtedly anxious for settlement."[86]   The way for subsequent negotiations had been paved.

President Truman was in favor of a settlement. During a Cabinet meeting on 6 August, he read a cautious note to the effect that the administration should avoid, in speech and in action, derailing negotiations with Russia. Marshall added that speculation had now reached the point where it was imperative to guard against upset in a ticklish situation.[87]

The Cabinet meetings of August and September dealt repeatedly with the issue of negotiations with the Soviets. During the meeting of 13 August, Truman asked if there was anything new on the Russian front; Marshall replied that it was still too early to report on negotiations in Moscow. On 3 September, Marshall reported that the meeting, now in Berlin, was making progress with respect to the controversy between Russia and the western powers. The key issue concerned whether the powers had a right to be in Berlin or whether they there on the Soviet's sufferance. The State Department reported to the meeting of 10 September that they were trying to move the discussions from Berlin back to Moscow. Since the French government was in a state of collapse, it was difficult to work out a four-power agreement; furthermore, the British were being strained by attacks on the Labor Government and by a fiscal crisis.   If the negotiations were dropped by the US as suggested in the American press, however, the Truman administration would really be in the fire: "We either negotiate or shoot."[88]

While continuing their negotiations with the Soviet Union on the Berlin issue, the western powers were supplying the western sectors of the city via airlifts. The US contributed most of the aircraft, but Britain also played an important part. Though the Berlin situation was not to be relieved until the following spring, it never approached anywhere near war. Both sides treated the situation cautiously and showed a willingness to negotiate. Settlement of the Berlin situation drew the last demarcation line in Europe, a line to be drawn much more boldly with the Berlin Wall in the early 1960s.

The Berlin crisis naturally figured into the US presidential campaign underway in 1948. During the Cabinet meeting of 25 June, Truman had remarked on the cold reception given Dewey by the Republican convention.[89]   On 22 July, the *New York Times* reported that Dewey, having conferred with Harold Stassen, viewed the crisis in Berlin as a result of the Three-Powers Agreement at Potsdam.   On the 24th, the *Times* reported that General Lucius Clay, Military Governor of the US Zone in Germany, accepted blame for failing to get a written guarantee from the USSR on the matter of transportation after V-E Day.

In the run-up to the election, Truman believed it was time to end the Berlin blockade in a dramatic way, so he decided to send Fred Vinson to see Stalin. This idea was rejected by Marshall, after it had leaked to the press. Truman then decided to talk with Stalin personally by telephone and revealed this decision to Senator Vandenberg at the White House. The call was never made. But on 23 October, Vandenberg heard that "some new crazy scheme was being hatched by Harry T. and Co."—a scheme rumored to have Vandenberg's own approval! Vandenberg, having no idea what this scheme might be, informed one of Truman's secretaries about the rumors. He was assured that nothing would be done without prior consultation with him. Vandenberg believed that the Vinson episode had ended any chance Truman might have had in the election.[90]   Truman, of course, was reelected, despite forecasts—and early reports—to the contrary. Perhaps when the Soviet archives are opened up, scholars will determine why the Soviet Union chose to challenge the West just as a US presidential election shifted into high gear.

Though the Berlin blockade did not end until May 1949, from the outset it was clearly not the beginning of a war but rather a show of will. To the Truman administration and the Democratic Party, what was at stake in Berlin was too big to risk losing. But the Democrats were not ready for a war in Europe—nor was anyone else.

7
War Drums in the Far East

In late 1945, the armed conflict between the Nationalists and Communists in China became increasingly intense.

MARSHALL, LOCKE, AND TRUMAN'S CHINA POLICY

On 27 November 1945, the day he accepted Ambassador Hurley's resignation, President Truman announced the appointment of General George C. Marshall as his special representative in China. Truman had always thought highly of Marshall: after V-E Day, the President told his staff that "Marshall was one of the best men in the country today and some means should be found of utilizing him after the war is all over." Eben Ayers observed that the President seemed tremendously impressed with Marshall's abilities.[1]

When Truman asked Marshall to go to China, the general agreed immediately. Marshall's old boss Henry Stimson, however, was skeptical:

> You should insist to Truman that your mission should be purely military. Otherwise you will get into innumerable tangles. Very few white men ever understood the Chinese political mind. In this I speak from sixteen years experience with the present Chinese Government. They will make every effort and use every argument to push us into doing for them what the American people will not do, namely to send troops to fight to expel the remaining Japanese from China. Bear in mind also that Yalta only returned to Russia what she had actually possessed in 1900. The Bear rarely recedes. I doubt if she intends to recede now and the US people will not fight for Manchuria. The main principle for which you fight (if this political problem is forced on you) is equal commercial rights through the ports and over the Manchurian railways. This would be sufficient to conform to the American principle of the Open Door. Remember your political support in the State Department is very shaky. Remember that

119

the Generalissimo has never honestly backed a thorough union with the Chinese Communists. He could not, for his administration is a mere surface veneer (more or less rotten) over a mass of the Chinese people beneath him. Although my knowledge of the Communists is superficial, I believe that their hold on the people underneath them is sounder than his hold over his people.[2]

As sensible as Stimson's comments on Chiang and the Communists may be, how he could separate the military problem in postwar China from the political one is beyond comprehension. There were essentially two issues: the civil war between the KMT and CCP and the allegedly unarmed Japanese forces. Both issues were intertwined with politics.

The presence of the Soviet army in Manchuria was itself in essence a political problem. During the CFM meeting in Moscow in December, Byrnes raised the question of withdrawal of the Soviet troops. Bevin told the British Cabinet that, at the CFM meeting, the Soviets were clearly reluctant to withdraw until the US withdrew its troops from North China. The root of the problem was "the existence of a Communist government in North China." This problem might be overcome by arranging for CCP representation in Chiang's government; the Soviets proposed that the CCP should be represented at all levels but Bevin objected, so it was eventually agreed that the CCP would be represented only in the central government. Bevin said he was embarrassed that China was not involved in these discussions.[3]

Marshall knew Roosevelt's "China Policy" well, since he was Army Chief of Staff. He was especially familiar with what had happened among Chiang, Stilwell, and Hurley. In addition he'd had a memorable experience of his own in China in the 1920s, at the time of the Northern Expedition and the first KMT-CCP cooperation. As a Lt. Colonel and Executive Officer of the US Army 15th Regiment, he was stationed at Tianjin from 1924 to 1927. In a letter to General Pershing in 1926, he wrote that "how the powers should deal with China, is a question almost impossible to answer." The same comment applied equally well in the late 1940s. Marshall in his letter deplored "that a normal solution can never be found [and] we can only hope that sufficient tact will be displayed by foreigners to avoid violent phases during the trying period that is approaching."[4]

Truman understood the importance of China—and of the entire Pacific region. He once said that "our future, I think, lies in the Pacific from a foreign trade standpoint if we can get place in the Pacific, and I think we will eventually get it."[5] In accordance with the policy of his predecessor, Truman believed that economic reconstruction would eventually lead to solution of the China question. In an October 1945 letter to Edwin A. Locke, Jr., whom he appointed as his personal economic representative to China, he wrote:

> I should like you to discuss with the Generalissimo and key officials of the Chinese government the ways in which the industrial experience of the United States can best be utilized to contribute to the sound peacetime economic reconstruction and development of China. You will give particular attention to the immediate situation confronting the Chinese as a result of China's acquisition of large industries in Manchuria and other liberated provinces. On your return, I shall expect you to submit to me a report and recommendation based on your findings and your experience in Chinese economic problems.[6]

Locke, in a report submitted on 5 November 1945, said that Chiang had "expressed his awareness of the need for peace and unity in China as a basis for American economic cooperation [and] fully realized the importance of China's need for American economic cooperation." Locke correctly observed that Chiang put a political solution ahead of economic reconstruction in summarizing his postwar aims as "the liquidation of the rebels and the construction of the nation." Locke also reported that the economic situation in China was more difficult than anticipated. He believed that the departure of Japanese managers and technicians and the uncertain political situation were putting a great strain on the Chiang government and delaying governmental actions to revive production.[7]

In another report, Locke would conclude that the Chinese people were acutely disturbed by the economic situation and rapidly "losing confidence in the Central Government though retaining faith in Gimo personally. There cannot be much basis for practical American economic cooperation until China herself begins to solve internal economic problems."[8] When Marshall went to China at the end of 1945, the economy was not a conspicuous part of his mission—nor was it an area in which he could have made much progress in any case. It remained on the agenda mainly as a lever for bargaining with the KMT.

President Truman was to make a public statement concerning policy toward China on 15 December 1945. On 30 November, Admiral Leahy asked White House aide George Elsey to collect materials dating from the period November 1943-August 1945 (i.e., from the Cairo meeting through the Berlin meeting) that would show US support for Chiang to be a policy of long standing, one that the US had pursued in international negotiations and one in which the USSR and the UK had concurred in international agreements. Leahy told Elsey that the job of drafting Truman's statement, which should be done by the State Department, had been tossed to him, because the people at State would produce six or eight meaningless pages: "The President is all right, he is behind Chiang. But those 'pinkies' in the State Department can't be trusted....The President told me the other day he now knows why FDR didn't trust the State Department." According to Leahy, Truman found that State did not always do what it was told, and was impossible to pin down: "Take the matter of the statement. It shouldn't be more than ten words, and the President knows it. But he could never get anything sharp and clear-cut out of that gang." Elsey collected the necessary material, and Leahy drafted the statement—by no means limiting himself to ten words.[9]

The result, *US Policy Toward China*, was the Truman administration's first public announcement on postwar China policy. Translating the diplomatic language of the statement into plain English, Truman said that the US had always recognized and supported the KMT government alone, and would continue to do so in the future. The KMT government, however, must take in representatives of the CCP and other parties; with representation in the government, the CCP should turn over its army. A united China was of great importance to the US, and the CCP would be held responsible for all consequences if it did not cooperate.

On the day of his statement, 15 December, Truman sent a letter to General George C. Marshall outlining the latter's mission in China. In fact, this letter was drafted by Marshall himself. Three documents were enclosed with it: the original draft of the statement on China policy; the final text of the statement; and a memorandum on China from the Secretary of State to the War Department. In his letter to Marshall, Truman authorized the general to tell Chiang something tantamount to "no peace, no money," in order to force Chiang into making necessary concessions. The day before, Marshall had told Truman:

> in the event that I was unable to secure necessary action by the Generalissimo, which I thought reasonable and desirable, it would still be necessary for the US government, through me, to continue to back the Nationalist government of the Republic of China—through the Generalissimo—within the terms of the announced policy of the US government.[10]

The President and the general might not have been aware that this stance would underlie the failure of the Marshall Mission and ultimately, the American setback in China.

Secretary of State Byrnes, in his memorandum to the War Department, pointed out that the task of broadening representation in the KMT government was not a easy one.

It will not be solved by the Chinese leaders themselves. To the extent that our influence is a factor, success will depend upon our capacity to exercise that influence in the light of shifting conditions in such a way as to encourage concessions by the Central Government, by the so-called Communists, and by the other factions....[Marshall] will endeavor to influence the Chinese government to call a national conference of representatives of the major political elements to bring about the unification of China and, concurrently, effect a cessation of hostilities, particularly in north China.

Byrnes went on to ask that the War Department direct General Wedemeyer to assist in transporting KMT troops to Manchurian ports and to step up evacuation of Japanese troops from the China Theater—but to do so in a way that would permit Marshall to pressure Chiang by speeding up or slowing down these actions. Since Truman's public statement on China had outlined the boundaries within which Marshall was permitted to maneuver, Byrnes' tactics in dealing with Chiang could hardly work; Chiang understood that the US would not desert him and regarded his government as the only legal government and the proper instrument for achieving unification.

However reluctant, the KMT government had to welcome the Marshall Mission. The mission would restrain Chiang's freedom of action—but perhaps it could be used to force the CCP into making concessions. The CCP, meanwhile, understood very well that the mission would not be unbiased in its efforts to mediate, but also believed that mediation itself would be enlightening to the populace and might postpone the outbreak of a nationwide civil war. In the view of the Communists, time was on their side. Hence, the US Army Observers Group in Yanan reported to General Wedemeyer on 20 December 1945 that the CCP spokesman welcomed the suggestions in Truman's statement.[11] Some smaller political factions also welcomed the mission, believing that US might influence Chiang and the CCP to make concessions. In short, then, virtually all political affiliations in China had some hope that the Marshall Mission might be in their own interests.

American officials in China failed to acknowledge fully the critically important role of what might be called the domestic dynamics in China's situation as of late 1945. They put too much emphasis on external influences—political, military, and economic. Due to their lopsided view of the situation, they were dumbfounded when China was "lost." James R. Shepley, a member of the Marshall Mission, wrote on 9 December that Mao had gone to Chongqing for negotiations in August because he was shocked by Moscow's treaty with the Chiang government.[12] Col. Yeaton, new chief of the Dixie Mission in Yanan, commented that a "slight hint in US policy has quickly brought out a desperate cry to stop the civil war earliest and [to] successfully conclude negotiations. I detect a new low in assurance and believe Communists ready to make greater concessions than ever before."[13]

General Marshall arrived in China on 21 December, as the Political Consultative Conference was preparing to convene, with the Communists attending. Luo Longji, a leading member of the Democratic League and an alumnus of the University of Wisconsin, welcomed Marshall, saying: "We don't want to overthrow the government. We just want to be liberalized, to become democratic and representative....For us,...General Marshall's coming and his directive...is a case of what the Chinese call 'hu ying,' or 'call and answer.' We have called and America has answered."[14] Professor Luo did not know that Truman, Marshall and the State Department had already decided to support Chiang Kai-shek, no matter how intransigent he might be.

Marshall and the decision-makers in Washington understood very well that the crux of a rapprochement between the KMT and the CCP was the attitude of the former. Trying to impose strong pressure on Chiang and to convince the CCP of his sincerity, Marshall put forward a proposal allowing the Communists one-third of the Chinese Army, Navy, and Air Force—even though at the time the Communists had only ground troops. Chiang immediately turned this proposal down.[15]

After Marshall began mediation it was decided to set up a Committee of Three as the machinery of negotiations. Marshall was the chairman. The other two members were the Communist representative Zhou Enlai and the Nationalist representative General Zhang Qun (later succeeded by General Zhang Zizhong.) When the Committee first met on 7 January 1946, a new agreement settling a number of points of conflict seemed quite probable. On the 10th, as the Political Consultative Conference convened, the Committee of Three reached a cease-fire agreement, which was made effective by orders from Chiang and Mao to their troops. The Political Consultative Conference itself passed a resolution on reorganization of the government, establishment of a supreme organ of power in which all parties would participate, and the drafting of a constitution. From 14 February until the 25th, KMT and CCP representatives discussed reorganization of the military forces, with Marshall present as an advisor. This discussion led to a Military Reorganization Agreement, stipulating gradual reduction in troop strength on both sides, and a 5:1 ratio of KMT to CCP troops.

Both sides made concessions. The KMT agreed to reorganize the government, to revise the constitution, to establish a State Council as the supreme organ of power, and to cease fire. The CCP agreed to the shipping of KMT troops to Manchuria by US transport facilities and the KMT takeover in Manchuria, to the unfavorable troop ratio, and to dropping its demand that all KMT representatives in the National Assembly should stand for reelection.

The Committee of Three started an inspection tour in late February 1946, visiting Yanan on 4 March. There they met with Mao, and Marshall was royally welcomed. Recalling his China mission, Marshall would write in 1954 that, from early 1946 "the Communist representation and most of their forces in the field seemed to be more responsive to the dictates of the Committee of Three than the Nationalists...until early in June after the postponement of the Constitutional Convention. The Nationalist commanders all seemed to be determined to pursue a policy of force."[16]

The Committee of Three had decided at its first meeting in early January that, to oversee implementation of the cease-fire, an Executive Headquarters would be set up, with officers from the KMT, the CCP, and the US forces. Teams would be sent into the field, in various regions where conflicts between the KMT and the CCP forces occurred. In a memo to Marshall, Wedemeyer was very critical of the KMT government: "During any lull in hostilities the Central Government may attempt to re-dispose forces and to strengthen their overall position, both military and political, so that should hostilities flare up again they will have overwhelming power against the Communists." In Wedemeyer's view, Chiang's determination to hold a conclave of the National Assembly without prior elections indicated that the Assembly was "overwhelmingly packed with old party line members of the Kuomintang." He said that Dai Li's organization continued to suppress organizations and individuals critical of the KMT government, and that the KMT Youth Corps employed violence against students who discussed "in a critical vein the existing conditions in their country."[17] Wedemeyer expected that this "will cause many Chinese intellectuals, small businessmen and the students to affiliate themselves with the opposition."[18] Here, he must have been referring to the "December First Massacre" of 1945, in which KMT troops attacked striking students in Kunming, killing four and wounding at least ten.

STALIN COURTS CHIANG KAI-SHEK, MARSHALL CULTIVATES THE CCP

As a response to the arrival of Marshall and in accord with its own China policy of having "one foot in each boat," the Soviet government courted the KMT—and Chiang Kai-shek in particular. According to Chiang's personal records, his government informed the Soviet ambassador on 15 November 1945 that the KMT's northeastern headquarters would withdraw from Changchun into North China.[19] Chiang believed that since he could not enforce his dictate in Manchuria in any case, he had better leave it to the Soviets. When the Soviets suddenly changed their attitude, permitting the KMT to proceed with the take-over of Manchuria in accordance with the new Friendship Treaty, Chiang nevertheless insisted upon withdrawal. He concentrated his troops at the southern tip of Manchuria. Throughout the winter of 1945-46, the Soviets repeatedly expressed friendliness toward Chiang, and the KMT government in return treated the Soviets with discretion. For example, in the UN Security Council the Chinese representative proposed, against the wishes of the US, that the Council should not take action on the Iran case, but rather permit bilateral negotiations; he also deplored British actions in Greece.[20]

The Americans, meanwhile, were urging Chiang to expedite the take-over of Manchuria, and offered to put a large number of ships at his disposal to transport his troops. Lt. General Du Yiming, Deputy Commander-in-Chief of the KMT's northeastern headquarters, later recalled that, during a KMT military meeting in 1948, Chiang bitterly complained of Marshall's having insisted upon his taking Manchuria. Chiang claimed to have complied only with reluctance, and attributed his own failure to Marshall's insistence.[21] In a memo to Marshall on 7 January 1946, Wedemeyer had mentioned that, should civil strife start again, the KMT government might attempt to dispose forces for a concentrated attack against Zhangjiakou (Kalgan); notably, he did not mention that Chiang might concentrate his troops in Manchuria.[22]

When Marshall left for China, Truman still saw some chance for US-Soviet collaboration to bring the CCP under control. In January 1946 he wrote in a letter that "Generalissimo Stalin says the so called Chinese Communists are nothing but bandits and he has nothing whatever to do with them."[23] But Stalin also thought that he could speak for the CCP: according to Bevin, he and Stalin agreed in Moscow in December 1945 that, in the future, the Chinese Communists would have representatives only in the central government of the Chiang regime, not on other levels.[24] Here, Stalin made an important decision for the CCP, to Chiang's advantage, even before Marshall's mediation started.

Chiang noted in his memoirs how "Stalin took the unusual step of inviting" his eldest son, Ching-kuo, to visit the Soviet Union. Earlier, Chiang Ching-kuo had returned to China following the outbreak of the Sino-Japanese war, having stayed in the Soviet Union for a decade. He took up several party and government posts, and served as Special Commissioner of Manchuria, Foreign Ministry, after the war. Chiang Ching-kuo was assigned to this post because his father thought that, given his experience, he would be well-equipped to deal with the Soviets and because his presence in Manchuria would demonstrate the importance of the Manchurian question to his father.

Chiang Ching-kuo accepted Stalin's invitation, and visited Moscow as his father's special representative. He left for Moscow on 25 December 1945 almost as Marshall arrived in China, and returned on 16 January. According to Chiang Ching-kuo, "Stalin spoke of his hopes for peaceful coexistence between China and Russia and between the Kuomintang and the Communist Party." Stalin said he favored cooperation among China, the US, and the USSR but opposed the introduction of any third power's influence into Manchuria. And he urged the KMT government to adopt an independent policy, "leaning neither to one side nor to the other."

At the end of Chiang Ching-kuo's visit, Stalin expressed the hope that Chiang Kai-shek would visit him in Moscow or meet with him somewhere on the Sino-Soviet border. Chiang Kai-shek believed this communication revealed the real purpose of Stalin's inviting his son to Moscow. After consulting Marshall, Chiang declined the Soviet invitation. The Soviets, however, were insistent. During the first week of May 1946, they repeated the invitation, urging Chiang to set a date. Chiang turned them down again. Some time later, when an official of the American embassy asked Chiang about the invitation, Chiang was quite clear that the US would be offended had he accepted.[25] Chiang's account of this episode cannot be confirmed, since the invitation was extended verbally on both occasions. Judging from the policies of the Soviet Union and the KMT at the time, Chiang's account is highly plausible; examination of a Soviet account of the episode, should one become available, will be very interesting.

While the Soviets were busily courting the KMT, Marshall missed no opportunity to improve US relations with the CCP. According to Zhang Wenjin, Zhou Enlai's assistant in foreign affairs, Marshall found Zhou's position during negotiations compelling, and expressed willingness to persuade Chiang Kai-shek to make concessions and to refrain from obstructing a major agreement.[26] Zhang believed that this explained how a cease-fire agreement could ultimately be reached on 10 January 1946. Marshall also agreed to Zhou's request that the US not interfere in the internal affairs of China. To be specific, his mediation should facilitate the ending of China's civil war, the termination of the KMT's one-party rule, and the realization of a coalition government and democratic politics. According to Zhang, Marshall pretty much adhered to this line during the initial period of his China Mission. At the time, Zhou and Marshall were on good terms. Zhou found Marshall rather fair and candid; he observed, after meeting Marshall twice, "this man reminded me of Stilwell."[27]

During this period, the CCP considered the Marshall mediation fruitful and unbiased. Upon his return from CCP headquarters on

30 January, Zhou Enlai conveyed to Marshall a verbal message from Mao. Mao believed that Marshall's handling of the cease-fire question was fair, and the CCP would like to cooperate with the US in view of this fairness. Zhou added that, though the CCP's long-term goal was socialism in China, at the moment China was not ready for socialism. Rather, in the current stage, China needed promotion of democracy and science and needed to learn, from the US, agricultural reform and industrial development, so as to build a China of independence, liberty and prosperity.

In answer to rumors that Mao was going to visit Moscow for medical reasons, Zhou told Marshall that, if Mao were ill he would rather go to America. This signal was not lost on Marshall, who thanked Zhou for conveying Mao's message, expressed his own belief that the CCP sincerely desired peace, and promised to persuade Chiang to reach an agreement on the basis of this desire and the policies declared by the CCP. Before the conversation ended, Marshall asked Zhou to put Mao's words into a memo, so that he could report to President Truman. Marshall then repeated Hurley's blunder, signing a check sure to bounce: he extended an invitation for Mao to visit Washington, even offering to present to the CCP a plane in which Mao could make the flight.[28]

THE SOVIET LOOTING OF MANCHURIA

Though it was true that the US and the USSR had set their priorities in Europe, the situation in Asia troubled both. *Time* commented in early 1946 that "the touchiest point in US-Russian relations was the Far East—and well the Russians knew it. Because they did not want a showdown with the US, the Russians had behaved with relative restraint in the delicate negotiations between the Chinese Nationalist Government and the CCP."[29] On the stripping of Manchurian industries as war booty, however, the Soviets were adamant. The Chinese Nationalist government had never agreed to the stripping, and charged that it directly violated the Sino-Soviet Treaty of 1945. On 5 March 1946, Molotov replied to an inquiry from US Charge George Kennan, that all properties serving Japan's war needs constituted war trophies, and that the Soviet Union would be the judge as to which properties fell in this category.[30] According to a report in *Time*, Soviet general Andrei Kovtun-Stankovich, Garrison Commander of Shenyang (Mukden), told nine American and British correspondents that the Big Three agreed to these removals "either at Yalta or Berlin—I am not sure, off hand."[31] The US State Department, however, formally denied any agreement on this, "secret or otherwise," and broadcasts from Moscow said the *Time* report was "wholly fabricated."[32] In mid-April, in a letter to the US embassy in Moscow, Vyshinsky insisted that the Manchurian industries were war trophies and that his position was fully supported by the terms of armistices concluded with Bulgaria and Hungary by the Allied governments.[33] Here, Vyshinsky went so far as to treat the territory of a major Allied nation as that of a Fascist satellite.

In his 1954 memorandum to Truman, Marshall observed that the Soviet delay in withdrawing from Manchuria and the Soviet stripping of industrial facilities "had been a continuing cause of complications" in the region. The situation was made worse by Chiang's refusing Marshall's proposal that the Executive Headquarters send field teams to intervene in fighting between the two sides at Yingkou in Manchuria. Later, Chiang would note that field teams entering Manchuria with limited powers would be unable to stop the fighting. It is often said that the KMT's failure in Manchuria was due to Soviet assistance to the CCP. If this had been the case, Chiang would not have blocked the entry of teams who could serve as witnesses; rather, it would have been the Communists, not Chiang, who would want to keep witnesses out. As Marshall's 1954 memorandum pointed out, the "developing situation in Manchuria became one of the determining factors in breaking down all hope of negotiating a political basis for unity and peace in China."[34]

POINT OF NO RETURN

Marshall left China on 11 March 1946 for consultations in Washington—to, in his own words, "apprise the President of the situation and, particularly, to take up the question of the transfer of surplus property and shipping and the problem of loans to China."[35] Marshall's remark is in conformity with his initial assignment to back Chiang up even when he would not cooperate in mediation. In his 1954 memo, Marshall would say that after 10 January 1946, "I in a sense cut myself off from this conference [the Committee of Three], as it was entirely political and I had been sent to China with instructions to bring the fighting to an end, if that be possible." Transfer of surplus property and loans would not halt the fighting. On the contrary, it further strengthened Chiang's hand and made him more uncooperative. The embassy in Chongqing advised in April that, until Marshall returned to China and evaluated the situation, the US should defer making any loan to the KMT government. The embassy believed that announcement of a loan would seriously weaken Marshall's hand in reversing the present trend and bringing the parties back onto the path he intended for them.[36]

Before Marshall departed on the 11th, Zhou Enlai told him of Mao's hope that he could stay on until the situation in Manchuria was stabilized. But Marshall insisted upon leaving immediately. More than two weeks after Marshall's departure, an agreement was reached to dispatch field teams to oversee the cease-fire in Manchuria. But Chiang maintained that the

Nationalist troops went to Manchuria to take over as stipulated in the Sino-Soviet Treaty of 1945, and the cease-fire efforts of the teams became futile. Zhou Enlai believed that the Communists should have no illusions about the intentions of the KMT, and suggested to the CCP leadership that the only way out was to fight in Manchuria. When Marshall returned to China on 18 April, the fighting was already escalating. On that day, Nationalist troops mounted an all-out offensive on Siping, while Communist troops marched into the streets of Changchun.

During the first stage of mediation, it had always been Marshall who took charge and Zhou Enlai who would ask questions for clarification. But after Marshall returned to China, the situation changed conspicuously. On 22 April, Zhou Enlai had a three- or four-hour conversation with Marshall during which Zhou did almost all of the talking. Zhou said that, as he had explained when they first met, the CCP wanted a peaceful and democratic China. He had learned from Marshall how better to understand the democratic traditions of America. He had read a speech by Benjamin Franklin, given to him by Marshall, and had been moved by Franklin's notion that, though opinions may differ, cooperation was still imperative. Zhou thought that the resolutions of the Political Consultative Conference were not completely compatible with the ideals of the CCP, but should be observed since they had been agreed upon by all concerned. Although the CCP had not requested any revisions over the past three months, the KMT was requesting many—and was violating the resolutions it had agreed upon. Marshall told Luo Longji that Zhou was a diplomatic counterpart, the likes of whom he had never met before, and told Wellington Koo that Zhou was more brilliant than anyone else he had dealt with—including those very sly Britons. He also commented that, though he had been warned the Communists were not reliable, the Nationalists were no more so. Zhou and Marshall maintained a good working relationship until the middle of May 1946.[37]

The fighting in Manchuria intensified. Communist troops could not hold Changchun, and KMT troops took the city on 22 May. Chiang Kai-shek became more intransigent, and by the end of the month, all-out civil war was imminent. Zhou held that the CCP should, as a tactical matter, force the Americans "to press Chiang." He told Marshall that his mission represented the good side of US policy, that Chiang had never wanted Marshall to succeed, and that Chiang, now prepared to greatly enlarge the scale of the fighting, wanted to pull Marshall into the water.[38]

In August, the new British ambassador to China reported to London that Marshall believed Chiang could maintain large-scale military operations for about two months, after which China would fall into economic chaos, providing the most favorable conditions imaginable for the spread of

Communism. He said Chiang had told him that the Communists had no intention of coming to a genuine compromise, so the only option was to defeat them militarily—a lengthy process.[39] The civil war was passing a point of no return.

Chiang, not wanting to rely completely on the Americans, tried to obtain arms from Britain. Attlee told the British Cabinet on 14 October that in September, an informal approach had been made to the British ambassador on Chiang's behalf, asking whether the British government would provide the arms needed to continue fighting the civil war. In Attlee's view, Chiang had abandoned the idea of coming to terms with the Communists and was not cooperating fully with the US in attempting to halt the war. The US, apparently, was reducing supplies of war materials as a means of bringing pressure to bear on Chiang. Bevin had already mentioned this to Byrnes on the 13th, to which Byrnes replied that the relationship with Chiang was increasingly unsatisfactory and that the US was considering withdrawing its forces from China. Bevin told Byrnes that the British would not encourage Chiang's hopes of obtaining arms from them, and would advise their ambassador to reject Chiang's request. Attlee supported Bevin.[40] Supporting Chiang, however, had been US policy for a long time, and the US pressure on Chiang was only a tactical move; before long, the Truman administration would become trapped in a China quagmire.

On 11 October, KMT troops took Zhangjiakou, the Communists' center in North China; by the time the KMT-dominated National Assembly convened in November, mediation between the two parties had become impossible. Marshall's China venture was close to its end. Marshall had one golden opportunity to make his mission work: the US embassy in Chongqing reported in April, while Marshall was still in Washington, that relations between the KMT and CCP had seriously deteriorated, that US meditation was still a powerful factor, and that all groups had expressed a desire for Marshall's early return to China.[41] But by autumn, those days of hope were gone.

Henry Luce went to China in November 1946. He told Stimson soon after his return that Chiang was confident he could end the war by defeating the Communists within a few months. Luce believed that the Chinese Communists were "real Communists," that "the difficulty is to get Marshall out," and that the only road was via the Communists being "conquered by the Nationalists." Marshall himself said that carrying out his original mission was now impossible, and everyone else now seemed to agree.[42]

Marshall asked to be recalled on 28 December, almost a year after arriving in China.[43] Truman appointed him Secretary of State in early January 1947. Marshall, in retrospect, did not blame the CCP for his failure in China; on the contrary, he said that throughout this period Chiang had associated with individuals who "were opposed to any effort along the line indicated by American policy. Partially discredited in 1946, they steadily regained their power, and found the development of the China political battle in the United States greatly to their advantage." Marshall and Stuart planned to provoke this "irreconcilable group" of KMT officials with Marshall's statement upon leaving China. But because the news of his appointment at State had already leaked, the group did not take the bait and attack him publicly.[44]

The failure of the Marshall mediation had far-reaching consequences for US-China relations and for the international situation in general. The US missed a golden opportunity in China, chasing a mirage instead by trying to mediate while also supporting Chiang. Incidentally, near the year's end student strikes and demonstrations broke out across China—ceremonial salvos bidding farewell to the general.

THE UGLY AMERICAN IN CHINA

The student protests were generated by an incident in Beijing on the evening of 24 December. In Dongdan Park, about two hundred yards from what is now the Beijing Hotel, two US Marines raped a Chinese girl; they were apprehended by passers-by when the girl cried out, and taken, with the victim, to a police station. The two Marines, no doubt frustrated by having to stay in China after the war ended, probably did not fully understand the gravity of their offense or the hornet's nest it would overturn. As it happened, the victim was a student at Beijing University, one of the most prestigious institutions of higher education in China, and it was said that her father was a professor. The University had a long tradition of protest movements; its students and professors formed the nucleus of the famous May Fourth Movement of 1919, and Mao Zedong himself was for some time an assistant in the University library.

By this time, sixteen months after WWII ended, GI Joe was no longer a war hero in Chinese eyes, but rather a symbol of occupation and corruption. Many American military personnel had forgotten an important lesson, captured in their own Chinese-language training manual: "Ru guo wen jin, ru jin wen su" [when entering a new country, inquire as to what is not allowed; when going to a new place, inquire as to the native customs.] But more important in the changing perception of the US military was the prolonged stay of the US forces and their role in the civil war. Since the war's end, the KMT government had antagonized the Chinese people, who after so many years of war, looked forward to peaceful lives with some degree of security in such basic needs as food and shelter. Instead, they were plunged again into chaos. Many KMT officials, on the other hand, were enthusiastically acquiring "wu zi deng ke" (the five most desirable possessions: gold, houses, status, women, and automobiles) by seizure from the Japanese and their collaborators. When the simmering conflict between the KMT and CCP exploded, the Chinese people well understood that without American aid the KMT would not have had the strength to start a civil war. The CCP had been successfully popularizing the slogan "Fight hunger, oppose civil war", thereby winning popular support, and launched a propaganda war against the US, criticizing the "support Chiang" policy and painting the Truman administration as a "black hand" behind the KMT's mischief. Against this background, the two Marine culprits were looked upon by the citizens of Beijing as rats running in the street: everyone shouted: "Beat them!"

In the view of the US embassy in Nanjing:

> on the whole the recent anti-American demonstrations in China may be interpreted as a manifestation of general discontent and unrest caused by the overall political and economic situation existing in China. Widespread resentment against the government which cannot be openly expressed is being turned almost entirely against the US.…"[T]here exists in China a potentially explosive political situation and it is possible to foresee serious disturbances within the next few months.…[I]n such a situation, the position of the US is vulnerable so long as the presence of US troops in China offers an immediately available target for propagandists of any coloration and for normally latent Chinese xenophobia.[45]

What a wonderful analysis! If only this had precipitated in the Truman administration a thorough review of its China policy.

Under popular pressure, the local judiciary in Beijing decided that the two Marines should be tried by a Chinese court. But higher authorities yielded to US insistence that the two Marines should be court-martialed by the US Navy. This treatment of the case was obviously extraterritorial, invoking a privilege which the US, together with some other Allied nations, formally renounced during the war. A US Navy court set up in Beijing sentenced one of the two Marines to fifteen years in prison, the other to a shorter term. These sentences were approved by the Commanding General of the First Division (Reinforced), USMC, on 21 February 1947, even though two members of the court had recommended clemency. On 6 June, upon interference from a Congressman Riley, the Judge Advocate General of the US Navy reported to the Secretary of the Navy that the case should be "set aside," and copies of his report were sent to President Truman and Secretary of State Marshall.

On 8 July, R.H. Cruzen, the senior member of the Naval Sentence Review and Clemency Board, submitted the view of the Board to the Acting Secretary of Navy:

(1) After careful review of the record...[the] Board is of the unanimous opinion that the evidence is sufficient beyond a reasonable doubt to support the findings of the court on the charge of rape.

(2) Accordingly it is recommended that the Secretary of the Navy approve of the proceedings, the findings on Charge 1 and the specification there under, the sentence of the court, and the action of the convening authority thereon.[46]

Contrary to the judgment and the recommendation of the Naval Sentence Review and Clemency Board, however, John L. Sullivan, Acting Secretary of Navy, approved the 6 June report of the Judge Advocate General and overturned the conviction of the two culprits. A telegram was sent to the Commanding Officer, Naval Detention Bureau, Terminal Island, San Pedro, California: "It is directed that each named man be released from arrest and restored to duty. Letter of promulgation follows."[47]

This incident in the relationship between the US government and the Chinese people was of great importance, because it occurred just as the situation in China was reaching a critical phase. It touched off a spectacular anti-American demonstration, with half a million students in the Nationalist areas going out on strike and demonstrating against the US and the KMT, from the end of December 1946. The students demanded the withdrawal of US troops from China. The CCP was directing this campaign, as revealed by Zhou Enlai himself.[48] But it was the US military presence in China that stoked popular discontent, and it was the crimes of two members of the US military that gave the CCP its opportunity to attack the Truman administration.

This important episode in the American failure in China has not attracted much attention among non-Chinese scholars.[49] They seem to have underestimated its importance or to have believed that the incident was misrepresented in Communist propaganda. Although the struggles surrounding the Christmas Eve Incident marked "a new high tide" of the Chinese revolution, for one reason or another the file of this incident slept unremarked in the Marine archives for some four decades.[50]

ALL-OUT CIVIL WAR

In early January 1947, the US expressed to the USSR and the KMT government that the situation in regard to the status and control of Dalian (Dairen) was unsatisfactory and should be promptly considered by both. In particular, there should be no further delay in opening the port to international commerce, as contemplated in the Sino-Soviet agreement of 1945. This, evidently, was a sign of US insistence upon the Open Door policy in Manchuria.[51]

A month later, the US embassy in Nanjing reported that "the main danger in China is not one of dramatic economic collapse but of insidious economic and political disintegration, which has already set in." The embassy believed that the outcome of this disintegration would be a revival of regionalism and warlordism, and that Communist activities would increase—but perhaps not in the direction of taking over the country.[52] This assessment was wrong: at the time, the CCP had already resolved "Down with Chiang Kai-shek, liberate the whole of China!"

The KMT and the CCP forces had never stopped fighting after the truce agreement of 10 January 1946, but the fighting had remained small in scale. As noted earlier, in late June the KMT launched an offensive that started all-out civil war. On 1 October, Mao Zedong drafted a directive for the CCP Central Committee, in which he summarized the progress of the war over the past three months. It was simple arithmetic. Chiang used 190 brigades of regular troops to make his offensive; 25 brigades were wiped out, and garrison duty used up nearly half the remainder. When the other half advanced, some—perhaps even most—would also have to switch to garrison duty. Mao believed that if the Communists troops could wipe out another 25 brigades, Chiang's offensive would be halted and part of the territory lost by the Communists could be regained. If a third batch of 25 brigades could later be destroyed, the relative military strengths of the KMT and CCP would be changed dramatically.[53] In fact, by February 1947 more than a quarter of the KMT brigades attacking CCP-controlled areas had been wiped out.[54]

By April 1947, it was obvious that the KMT military venture was a failure. The State Department briefed the President that a clear-cut and enduring solution for China by military action was not within the realm of practical achievement. State opposed encouraging Chiang to continue seeking a military solution, but did favor supplying him with more ammunition.[55] At about this time, the US embassy in Nanjing reported that there was no dependable Soviet assistance of a military character to the CCP, and the US Consulate-General in Shenyang reported that the CCP might be getting supplies in return for gold and agricultural products, rather than military aid in the strict sense of the term.[56]

At this point, the State Department not only opposed a military solution, but also came out in favor of suspending US lending to the Chiang government. This was just after announcement of the Marshall Plan to aid Europe. On 24 June, a memo from senior officials to Secretary Marshall discussed an announcement on loans to China, which Marshall was to make the next day. The memo noted that "the wording and tone of the announcement will, however, have important psychological effects in China and in this country; and in these respects it must be satisfactory to the Department as well as to the Bank."[57] The Bank should stress that expiration of the $500 million credit earmarked for China would not prejudice Chinese applications pertaining to individual projects. On June 25, when asked whether he was going to lend to the Chiang government, Marshall replied: "No, I am not. We have been carefully going into that. Everyday, as a matter of fact." On the 26th, Lincoln White of the State Department sent White House Secretary Charles Ross two memos for Truman. One was the State Department memo of the 24th; the other was the transcript of Marshall's press conference of the 25th.[58]

When Communist troops were about to take over large parts of Manchuria in mid-1947, the Truman administration decided to maintain its consulates-general in Changchun and Shenyang. The State Department believed that even if the two cities were taken by the Communists, the long-term value of first-hand observation of the CCP justified this decision.[59] On 2 July, the US Consulate-General in Shenyang reported, "evidence is growing daily that the people of Manchuria are not only prepared for, but are keenly desirous of a change in government."[60]

In September, Chiang Kai-shek submitted to the US embassy a request that he be allowed to buy on credit a six-month supply of weapons, ammunition, motor vehicles, and aviation equipment, since the KMT was "desperately short of ammunition."[61] When the US military attache in Nanjing expressed his suspicion that the KMT did not even know whether or not they were short, the government was aghast. Foreign Minister Wang Shih-chieh and Ambassador Wellington Koo asked the State Department for an appointment with the President. Deputy Secretary Robert Lovett reported to Truman that Wang and Koo feared US preoccupation with western Europe would result in neglect of the KMT's urgent request for aid. The two felt the US had a moral obligation to assist them—partly because of the American role in Yalta, which led to the Sino-Soviet Treaty of 1945 granting rights in Manchuria to the USSR, and partly because they regarded their situation as similar to that of Greece and Turkey. Lovett said they minimized the KMT's own inability to make reforms that would strengthen their hand against the CCP and that were essential to the continued existence of the KMT government. Lovett suggested that when Wang visited Truman, he should be informed that the US "does have a definite traditional interest in China and that it is not being overlooked by the US in its consideration of the problems of economic recovery and rehabilitation throughout the world."[62]   Obviously, the Chiang government was no longer on the priority list for US aid.

Leighton Stuart, however, urged more assistance to Chiang, reporting that the KMT regime "looks like an extremely sick man whose will to live begins to show signs of weakening." He said that absence of substantial military and financial assistance and renewed Communist activity were intensifying the Chinese tendency to panic in times of crisis.[63]   General Wedemeyer was sent back to China to take stock of the situation; the US embassy reported that the Chinese financial situation had sharply deteriorated since Wedemeyer's earlier departure and that run-away inflation could easily lead to complete economic collapse.[64]

Chiang Kai-shek personally complained to visiting US Congressmen that the predicament in Manchuria was due to the Yalta agreement; if the KMT were finally defeated it would not be because of the USSR and the CCP, but because the US failed to give promised assistance at this time of desperate need.[65]   He also tried to impress the US, by showing that he was working toward peace.   Stuart reported in mid-December that Chiang was asking the US to help organize four training centers, and recommended that the US comply.   A week later, General Zhang Zizhong informed Stuart that Chiang had authorized him to resume negotiations with the CCP.   Zhang approached the Soviet embassy urging that they advise the CCP that China "could never be won over to Russia against America."[66]

As to the matter of a peace treaty with Japan, the KMT government had been slow to express its view.   The British Foreign Office favored an early conference on the treaty, believing the KMT was stalling until the US clarified its China policy.[67]   The Soviet government tried to offer a helping hand to Chiang, proposing in December 1947 that a special session of the CFM convene in China to prepare the peace settlement with Japan.   The British considered this proposal inconsistent with the decision of the conference of British Dominions in Canberra, which held that the treaty should be drafted by the principal belligerents.   This would include countries not represented in the CFM; hence, the Soviet proposal was unacceptable.[68]

The situation was now becoming hopeless.   Near year's end, the US embassy advised that the situation was deteriorating in the North, and that all missionary organizations and nonessential personnel should withdraw from inland areas to the big cities.   Stuart had been informed that the KMT was running dangerously low on ammunition.[69]   Just before Christmas 1947, a new channel for explorations by the Truman administration unexpectedly opened.   Feng Yuxiang, a prominent political and military figure in China, wrote to Truman that he had come to Washington and, though hesitant to call on the president, wished President and Mrs. Truman a Merry Christmas. Feng said he was expressing "the sentiments of my people in thanking you for the many kindnesses which you have shown to China."[70]   His letter was obviously a political message.   Given his anti-Chiang and pro-Communist background, he might have been able to serve as an intermediary between the US and the CCP (and other anti-Chiang groups). Truman seems not to have responded.

8
The "Loss" of China

Faced with the inevitable failure of Chiang's military venture and the CCP's rise to national power, the Truman administration urgently needed to review its China policy in 1948. But deliberations on this policy dragged on through 1948, then 1949, and into 1950. Correct assessment of the relationship between the Soviet Union and the CCP was a decisive factor in the crafting of a sound China policy, and making this relationship less harmful to the national interest of the US was a major policy objective. The leaders in Washington owed it to the American people to forge a sound policy. Unfortunately, it was beyond their ability to do so. The only influential figures sophisticated enough to advocate a more or less workable policy were Dean Acheson—and, to a lesser extent, George F. Kennan. The President himself was at times conscious of the urgent need, but for the most part his bias and his preoccupation with domestic politics prevented him from acting.

THE RELATIONSHIP BETWEEN THE CCP AND THE USSR

Before its dissolution in 1943, the Third Communist International was the center of world Communism. Communist parties throughout the world carried out its orders, accepted its supervision, and implemented its policies. The Soviet Union, as the only country in the world that had proclaimed Communism as its aim, had become a sanctuary and Mecca to Communists around the world. Indeed, a department in the Central Committee of the Soviet party was in reality the office of the Third International. Stalin himself was not only head of the Soviet Party, but also the only living teacher of Communism (the others being Marx, Engels and Lenin)—and, naturally, considered himself the leader of world Communism.

Beginning in the 1920s, however, Mao Zedong developed his own interpretation of Marxism, which challenged Stalin's. In a 1926 article, Mao pointed out that the petty-bourgeoisie was among the Communists' closest friends, whereas within the "vacillating middle bourgeoisie..., the right wing may become our enemy and its left wing may become our friend. "[1] This assertion was contrary to Stalin's view that the middle class was most dangerous. During the first period of KMT-CCP cooperation during 1924-1927, the representative sent to China by Stalin and the International supported Communist Party General Secretary Chen Duxiu, who was yielding to the KMT leadership. Chen's course of action eventually brought the CCP to the brink of destruction.

When Mao and his supporters started building the Red Army and the base areas, the CCP had its headquarters in Shanghai. When the headquarters was compelled to move from Shanghai to the central base area created by Mao, Moscow protege Wang Ming began to interfere with Mao's command of his forces; Mao was removed from the leading post in 1933. The following year, when the Red Army could no longer hold the base area, it set off on what would become the Long March. Along the way, the Red Army continued to suffer terrible losses until the extended Politburo meeting in Chunyi, Guizhou, in January 1935. Wang Ming and his followers, as well as their Soviet military advisor, were removed, and Mao was installed as leader of the armed forces and the party—though he did not then hold the title of General Secretary. From this point on, Moscow no longer had strong influence over the CCP.[2]

Chiang Kai-shek sent his eldest son, Ching-kuo, to the Soviet Union to study at the heyday of his relationship with the Soviets. When the elder Chiang reversed his stand in 1927, the son remained in the USSR and married a Russian woman (today his widow in Taiwan). Ching-kuo's presence in Russia could be claimed as a political asset by both his father and the Soviets. (In the ancient days of the Chinese nation, monarchs of smaller states often sent their sons to live in powerful states as tokens of good will.) This asset may have paid off for Chiang Kai-shek. Before the outbreak of the Sino-Japanese war, when Chiang was detained by Generals Zhang Xueliang and Yang Hucheng in Xian, the Soviets interfered; according to Hurley, Molotov told him in 1944 that Chiang was released upon the insistence of the Soviets. And, during the war, the Soviet Union supplied China with loans, equipment, and air support in exchange for Chinese commodities. This aid, however, was channeled to the KMT government, whereas the Communists received only several planeloads of such items as blankets and medicines. The only Soviets in Yanan during the war were journalists and liaison officers.

Recent research reveals that, in the early period of China's War of Resistance (roughly 1937 to early 1941), the CCP's relationship with the Soviet Communist Party and the International was relatively stable. After the Soviet-German non-aggression treaty in 1939, the International instructed all Communist Parties to modify their policies for an anti-fascist united front and to transform the imperialist war into civil wars. Though the CCP was not bound by this instruction to abandon its anti-Japanese united front with the KMT, it considered that, when KMT forces launched an offensive against the Communists in summer 1940, the KMT might seek surrender to Japan. Mao Zedong wrote to the International urging the Soviet Union to impose the heaviest possible pressure on the KMT, to delay the possible surrender and the attacks upon the Communists.[3]

Soviet-German relations soon soured again, particularly after formation of the military alliance of three Axis countries in September 1940. The Soviets needed to stabilize their eastern border, so Chiang Kai-shek became important to them. Stalin cabled Chiang, encouraging him to fight the Japanese, sent him military material, and dispatched General Chuikov as military advisor to the KMT troops. The International instructed Mao Zedong to cultivate relations with Chiang, an instruction against which the CCP argued—to no avail. The Central Committee of the CCP, reluctantly following the instruction, informed the party that Chiang's inclination to surrender had been overcome. Then, suddenly, the headquarters of the Communist New Fourth Army was attacked and destroyed by KMT troops in January 1941, in what became known as the "Southern Anhui Incident." Mao and his colleagues were infuriated, and decided to take strong countermeasures, even though Dmitrov repeatedly cabled them to exercise restraint, and Soviet Ambassador Panushkin and General Chuikov similarly advised Zhou Enlai in Chongqing. The Soviets refused the CCP's demand that they stop supplying the KMT government with weapons.

For the first time, the CCP directly challenged the authority of Stalin and the International. Mao advised Zhou on 14 February 1941 to inform Chuikov that they should not fall into Chiang's trap, and that Chiang's attacks must be reciprocated.

After the outbreak of the Soviet-German war in June 1941, the Soviet Union was very much concerned about a possible Japanese attack. The International instructed the CCP to contain the Japanese troops concentrating on the Sino-Soviet border. Mao ordered his troops to prepare for action, pending further instructions. When the Soviets repeatedly asked the CCP to attack the Japanese concentration, Mao replied that his forces were not strong enough to do so. Georg Dmitrov cabled the CCP with fifteen sharp questions, inquiring as to what actions the Chinese Communists were taking when the Soviet Union was in peril. Later, in May 1942, the Soviet Union would again ask the CCP to commit troops to southern Manchuria, in order to contain Japanese action against the Soviet Union. A *Tass* correspondent named Vladimirov was sent to Yanan as Liaison Officer of the International, to press for action. Mao remarked that once the Soviets went to war with Japan, CCP forces would collaborate, but that their collaboration must be well planned. It was obvious at the time that the Soviets considered their own interests paramount. Their dislike for the CCP and their belief that it was not strong enough to challenge the KMT formed the basis of the USSR's China policy in the ensuing years.

Having proven his judgement correct, Mao believed that the time was ripe for developing a Chinese version of —MarxismMao Zedong Thought. In 1942 the CCP started a Rectification Movement, directly related to the changes in the CCP's relationship with the International. One major purpose of the movement was to relieve the CCP of interventions by the International and the Soviet party.[4]

THE SOVIETS IN MANCHURIA

When V-J Day came, Stalin immediately concluded a friendship treaty with the Chiang government and demanded that the CCP redouble its efforts to reach peace and unity with Chiang's KMT. Stalin said he was opposed to civil war of any form in China.[5] A Soviet representative flew to Yanan on 14 September 1945 and reached a special agreement with the CCP, whereby the Chinese Communists could recruit troops in the name of Manchurian local forces. The Soviets turned over Inner Mongolia and Chahar Province, and suggested that the CCP send 300,000 troops to Manchuria.[6] Stalin believed, on the one hand, that Chiang Kai-shek and his party were the only solid ground that could sustain national rule over China. The USSR had just concluded an agreement with the KMT government—part of the larger deal concluded with the US at Yalta, which Stalin could not afford to reverse. Stalin believed, on the other hand, that although at Yalta the Soviets were given "preeminent" status in Manchuria, they would still need the Chinese Communists as a counterweight to the Nationalists after withdrawal of Soviet troops from the region.

The Chinese Communists, particularly those in the field, held a different perspective: the CCP, once it gained control of the cities and stocks of military material in the region, naturally would not turn these over to the KMT. Frictions occurred between the Soviet Army and the CCP officials and troops. Peng Chen, a member of the Politburo and chief of the CCP Northeastern (Manchurian) Bureau, arrived in Shenyang on 18 September 1945. In their second or third meeting with the Soviet Army Commander, Peng and his colleagues were informed of a warehouse near Shenyang, which stored more than a hundred thousand Japanese rifles. The Soviets said that they would turn these over to the CCP. Upon learning of this, the Central Committee immediately ordered troops under General Huang Kecheng (3rd Division of the New Fourth Army) and troops in Shandong to rush to the Northeast to receive the Japanese weapons, leaving their weapons south of the Great Wall. When the troops finally reached Manchuria, the Soviets notified them that, "owing to various reasons of an international nature, these Japanese weapons will be disposed of in other ways, and will not be given to the CCP as planned." Wu Xiuquan, a senior member of the Northeastern Bureau, later observed that the Soviets feared giving weapons to the CCP would precipitate war with the Americans.[7] A CIA report of March 1948 admitted that Soviet support to the CCP was no more than a possibility.[8] A British Cabinet paper of September 1948 found that "there is no evidence of the CCP being in receipt of financial help or supplies of military arms or equipment from the USSR, nor of there being any Russian advisors, military leaders, or instructors in their midst."[9]

In December 1945, the Soviet Army formally notified the CCP Northeastern Bureau that, according to their agreement with the KMT government, KMT troops were to be stationed in Shenyang and vicinity. The Soviets demanded that the CCP Northeastern Bureau and the Communist troops withdraw from Shenyang before a specified date. CCP Bureau Chief Peng Chen met with the Soviet garrison commander of Shenyang to state his reasons for not withdrawing. The Soviet commander said there was no room for bargaining, and threatened that, "if you are not going, tanks will drive you away." When the issue was referred to the CCP Central Committee, their reply was: "It was decided by current Soviet policy and is not the business of the local commanders. They are carrying out instructions from Moscow." The CCP Northeastern Headquarters and the Communist troops evacuated Shenyang at the end of December 1945.[10]

The Chinese Communists were unhappy about what the Soviets had done to railway transportation in Manchuria. The Russian-built Chinese Eastern Railway had become Soviet property after the Bolsheviks came to power, and, during the Japanese occupation of Manchuria, the Soviets had sold it to the Japanese. After V-J Day, the railroad was supposed to be returned to the Chinese; however, when Soviet troops came into Manchuria, they took possession of the railroad. On the grounds that the route from the Soviet West to Vladivostok along the Chinese Eastern Railway was shorter than that along the Soviets' own Far Eastern Railway, the Soviets demanded that they share in the ownership and proceeds of the Chinese Eastern. Thus, the Soviet government took unjustified advantage of the Chinese.[11]

The CCP was even more unhappy with the Soviet looting of Manchurian industries, which according to US estimates amounted to $858 million.[12] After V-J Day, the Soviet Army took almost all the machinery and equipment that could be moved from factories and mines across Manchuria, for shipment—along with equipment and materials from other places—to the Soviet Union. At the Anshan Steel Works, the Shenyang Arsenal and the Fengman Hydro-Power Plant, the Soviets transferred to

China "free of charge" little more than empty shells. They also carried off all the pianos and luxurious furniture from the homes of Japanese officials and military officers.[13]

In the Sino-Soviet Treaty of 1945, the USSR "reaffirmed" respect "for China's full sovereignty" and "territorial and administrative integrity." But what the Soviets did in postwar Manchuria demonstrated nothing of the kind. China had fought Japan for fourteen years since 1931, first in Manchuria, then in other parts of the country. The Soviet Army had only fought Japan for a week on the eve of its collapse; before this the Soviet-Japanese relationship had been one of non-aggression. According to the Soviets' logic, they were entitled to take Manchurian machinery and equipment to compensate loss of lives and property, while the country Manchuria belonged to, the country that suffered most from the atrocities of the Japanese Imperial Army, had no right to do so. As a leading Soviet historian has pointed out: "One of the reasons that Japanese imperialism did not dare to attack the Soviet Far East during the Second World War, was the heroic struggle of the Chinese people and their Liberation Army....They had tied the Japanese Army's hands in China. Thereby the Chinese people had given the Soviet people great help and had made it easier for the Soviet people to conduct their great struggle in the just Great Patriotic War against the German fascist invaders."[14] Another Soviet historical work says: "Although Japan had occupied a large part of Chinese territory, the war produced severe tension in the Japanese economy....and pinned down considerable Japanese forces."[15] According to one veteran Chinese Communist, Soviet conduct in Manchuria "exposed the tendency toward national egoism, quite the opposite from their pronouncements."[16]

CCP POLICY AND AMERICAN PERCEPTIONS

Compared with pre-war days, the CCP's situation was much improved at war's end. According to official CCP data, regular forces numbered 57,000 when the war started in 1937; regular and guerilla forces numbered 1,300,000 when the war ended. In addition, the CCP had several million men in militia and self-defense forces in the villages.[17] And the CCP had no war liabilities; it had received no military aid from either the Soviets or the Americans. The KMT government had given the Communist forces only 120 light machine guns and six anti-tank guns when the war started. From 1940 on, the CCP forces received no funds, ammunition, clothing, food, medicine, or other supplies.[18] American military intelligence reports tend to confirm the CCP's figures: the Americans estimated Communist forces at 475,000 by the fall of 1944—close to the official count of 570,000 regular troops at that time.[19] Whatever the precise figures may be, there is no doubt that the Communists grew much stronger over the course of the war.

Since Mao Zedong and his colleagues had not followed the instructions of the International and Stalin when they were weak, it would be foolish to expect them to do so now that they were strong. The CCP was obviously not pleased with the deal on China that the US and USSR had made in Yalta nor with its consequences. In his report to a cadre meeting in Yanan in October 1945 upon his return from Chongqing, Mao said that "the capitalist countries and the socialist countries will yet reach compromises on a number of international matters."[20] In an April 1946 document circulated only among CCP leaders, Mao elaborated: "The question in relations among the United States, Britain, France and the Soviet Union is not a question of compromise or break, but a question of compromising earlier or later." Mao's principle for dealing with the situation was essentially the "tit for tat" of his report on the Chongqing negotiations. The April 1946 document, repeatedly endorsed by the CCP Central Committee in 1947 and 1948, stipulated a line that the CCP was to follow for years to come: the CCP would act upon its own judgement, regardless of whatever deal the Soviets had made with the Americans.[21]

The fatal flaw in American judgment of the Soviet-CCP relationship was its one-sidedness. American decision makers had always considered what influence the Soviets could exert on the CCP, but they rarely thought about how the CCP would react to the Soviets. Rather, they took for granted that the CCP would follow, however reluctantly, whatever the Soviets outlined for them. The Truman administration would have done much better if it had heeded Carlos Romulo, the Philippines statesman, who said that "the challenge of Asia, to President Truman and Mr. Bevin, is the challenge of poverty."[22] The mistaken judgment that the Chinese revolution was not indigenous and that the CCP was not an independent entity played a very important role in the failure of Truman's China policy.[23]

As discussed in Chapter 7, at this time the British Labor government believed that Britain, not the US, was the ethical and spiritual leader of Western Europe. After a review of the world situation and of Soviet policies in January 1948, Labor decided that Britain would pursue a policy independent of the US—a position bound to conflict with the US government's expectation that the British government would follow the US lead. The British Cabinet's interpretation of the CCP-Soviet relationship remained a sort of ancient cliche: the success of the CCP was in the interest of the Soviets, and the Soviets were helping the CCP overthrow the KMT.[24]

Some Foreign Service officers and China experts in the U.S. State Department understood the importance of having a China policy that did not rely upon the Soviets. On 23 April 1945, George Kennan, the US Charge in Moscow, sent a memo to Ambassador Harriman, who was then in Washington. Kennan said that, in the months and years to come as in the recent past, the Soviets would have a fluid and resilient China policy, aimed at the achievement of maximum power, with minimum responsibility, on portions of the Asiatic mainland lying beyond the Soviet border. Kennan observed that "It would be tragic if our natural anxiety for Russian support at this stage, coupled with Stalin's cautious affability and his use of words means an undue reliance on Russian aid or even Russian acquiescence in the achievement of our long-term objective in Asia."[25] Kennan came quite close to the key point in his analysis of the Soviets' China policy and the motives behind this policy. But his judgement stemmed from a traditional anti-Soviet and anti-Yalta outlook, and he did not suggest a sound solution to the China question. John Carter Vincent, chief of Chinese Affairs in the State Department, quoted in a letter to Hurley on 2 April a sentence from Owen Lattimore. Lattimore wrote in his *Solution in Asia* that, "the question is not what the Russians are going to do, but what we are going to do." But Vincent, unable to escape the confines of a familiar formulation, said that "it is useless to bring Chiang around to 'coalition' if you can't count on the Communists, and you can't count on the Communists unless you can count on Russia." Vincent "still believe[d], in spite of the reports on Rumania and Poland, that we can reach an understanding with Russia in regard to China on which we can rely."[26]

In reality, the US could not pin the success of its China policy on the Soviet Union; successful policy could only come from a sound attitude toward the Chinese parties and the wishes of the Chinese people. John Paton Davies came closer to this reality. In a memo prepared for Ambassador Harriman on 15 April, Davies reasoned that "though CCP will not admit any disappointment over failure of Kremlin to aid them while acting as a lightning rod to the Soviet Union, they would scarcely be human if they did not feel some resentment on that score." Davies went on that shabby treatment at the hands of the Kremlin over the past nine years and the prospect of the Red Army invading Manchuria and North China and imposing Russian suzerainty on them might lead at least some CCP elements to welcome foreign aid permitting continued independence. Then he put forward a perceptive assertion: "Mao Tse-tung [Mao Zedong] is not necessarily a Tito because he is a Communist." (At the time, Tito was thought to be very pro-Soviet.) As a loyal American, Davies advised that "if any communism is susceptible to political 'capture' by the United States, it is Yenan."[27] His view had no chance of being accepted by decision makers, since Davies was a junior FS officer and Truman had been critical of the State Department since becoming President. Moreover, unless the overall Yalta framework disintegrated, collaboration and vying with the Soviets and support to Chiang Kai-shek would continue to underpin the China policy of the United States.

In a nutshell, as already discussed in previous chapters, Truman's attitudes toward Chiang and toward the Communists were: (1) "We are 'hooked' with the 90 divisions;" (2) "I told them that my policy was to support Chiang, K.S.;" (3) "Chiang's Government fought side by side with us against our common enemy, we have reason to believe that the so-called Commies in China not only did not help us but on occasion helped the Japs." Nevertheless, it is hardly possible that a strong Communist party—and one showing extraordinary independence from the International and from Stalin himself—would have yielded to pressure imposed by Truman, however eager it might be to shape a workable relationship with the US.

THE US FACES FACTS

By early 1948, Ambassador Stuart believed the time had come to make a decision with regard to military assistance for China. Chiang personally informed Stuart that because he was out of ammunition he could not hold the cities of Shenyang, Changchun and Jilin, and that supplies in the Marianas could not arrive in time to be of use.[28] The commander of KMT troops in Manchuria believed the situation was not entirely hopeless—if he could receive reinforcements and additional ammunition. Without these, all of Manchuria would be lost within the next two to three months.[29] In March, Stuart expressed the fear that a complete collapse of the military in the north had become increasingly possible.[30] Truman himself began to talk about the KMT government in noncommittal terms; in March he observed in a press conference that Marshall had gone to China earlier "in an endeavor to assist the CKS government to meet the situation with which it was confronted."[31] On 1 April, the State Department told the president of Stuart's report that the situation was deteriorating at an accelerating pace. There were mounting feelings of helplessness in the KMT government and other circles, and there was a fervent search for means to end the civil war and the resulting economic and political uncertainties.[32]

Faced with a desperate situation, Chiang indicated to Stuart in June 1948 his willingness to accept US military advice "to the fullest extent." Stuart in turn reported this to Washington, and observed that if the elements opposing Chiang succeeded in removing him and in negotiating peace with the Communists, China would revert to regional autonomies. Stuart believed that unless the US was prepared to accept the consequent extension of Communist power, it must "provide Chiang with the character of support which he requires."[33]

This suggestion, however, was not acceptable, even to the Republicans. One important reason that policy on China did not become a major issue during the 1948 election was that the Republicans were pretty sure of winning the White House. As Vandenberg said, military aid to Chiang would be "primarily a problem for Dewey instead of Truman and for the Republicans rather than the Democrats....The vital importance of 'saving China' cannot be exaggerated. But there are limits to our resources and boundaries to our miracles. The new Administration will have to face the bare bones of all of these world-wide realities and make some pretty tough decisions for keeps."[34] After leaving office, Truman and Marshall viewed this question in much the same way. Truman said in 1953 that "if we had transportation and troops available, we would have prevented them from doing what was done in Korea and Manchuria, but had no transportation. Chiang didn't have anything to back him up. His troops were in South China, only can get there by water. Didn't have the means."[35] Marshall wrote in 1954 that "one of the most difficult political reactions arose out of the fact that the Nationalist Government of China was not able to procure quickly the military supplies it desired. The delays were charged to our Government." Marshall said reserves had been reduced so far that they could not be further diminished, there were no appropriations to buy more, and manufacture of the items would be delayed.[36] As it turned out, the KMT forces were not short of arms and ammunition; their captured weapons armed the People's Liberation Army. Vandenberg, more accurately, was appalled at the impotence of Chiang's troops. Replying to a letter in January 1949, he wrote: "I clearly share your basic attitude toward equipped Chinese divisions surrendering without firing a shot—where do we go from here?"[37]

During late fall 1948, the NSC frequently discussed the situation in Qingdao, where the greater part of the US Navy in China was stationed. On 8 October, the discussion expanded to China policy in general. Defense Secretary Forrestal said that it would be impossible to have a realistic policy until after the election; Army Secretary Royall said he never understood why the Americans were in Qingdao, and reiterated his previous opposition to putting money into China; Deputy Secretary of State Lovett said that full involvement of the US in China would dwarf the European Recovery Plan—and even then it wouldn't work. Truman then sent a memo to Forrestal saying he intended that the US should stay in Qingdao. It was decided at a meeting on 3 November to make preparations for evacuation and to strengthen defenses in Qingdao. Earlier, Vice-Admiral Oscar C.

Badger, Commander-in-Chief, US Navy, Western Pacific, had written to Admiral Halsey from Qingdao that he wished the US had the mobility of the Old Asiatic Fleet, so it could "show the flag": "It would do much to solve our immediate problems." Admiral Badger then said that he would "hesitate to consider the situation hopeless as some do. Given proper support, there are capable leaders on the scene who, I am sure, could secure North China to satisfy our policies."[38] Army General David Barr, chief of the American Military Advisory Group to the KMT government, held a different view. In April 1949, he gave secret testimony before a House committee that the Communists would soon win the civil war unless the US invaded the mainland or armed a million more KMT troops.

The CIA held a more objective view—perhaps because they knew more of the truth, from clandestine sources. In a memorandum of 15 December 1948 for the NSC, the CIA strongly opposed continued US support for Chiang, pointing out that "intensive US effort to continue support of a discredited regime and prolong the civil war would increase antagonism toward the US in China, would make more difficult the US position vis-a-vis a successor Communist controlled government, and would probably damage US prestige in other Asiatic countries in which there is still opportunity for successful anti-Communism."[39]

In the summer of 1948, the Truman administration began discussing possible alternatives to Chiang. On 16 July, Marshall asked the other NSC members to consider whether the US embassy should make contact with a Chinese leader who was then planning a separatist movement; Stuart had reported being asked to send an observer. Marshall remarked that it did not look as if US could do this, but he believed that the separatist was far more competent than many of the present leaders. Royall wondered whether the US would not be better off if a condition of banditry resumed in China.[40] On 31 August, Rusk told the daily meeting in the State Department that there was some possibility of sending former general Frank Meril to see General Sun Li-jen, who was in command in Taiwan, in the hope of working out a plan to "save Formosa."[41]

Truman and his close associates knew very well that Chiang's government was hopeless and that it would be futile to aid him. Marshall told the cabinet members on 3 September 1948 that "30 percent of the Chinese budget is collected in taxes. 70 percent of the budget is spent in military operations. That is the situation."[42] He again reluctantly told his colleagues on 26 November that "the Nationalist Government of China is on its way out and there is nothing we can do to save it. We are faced with the question of clarifying this to the American people and by doing so deliver the knockout blow to the Nationalist Government in China—or we can play along with the existing government and keep facts from the

American people and thereby not be accused later of playing into the hands of the Communists."[43] When Congressman John McCormack suggested that a fact-finding commission be sent to China, Truman drafted a reply saying that, "if the facts were told that is exactly what would happen [the rug would be pulled from under Chiang]—there would be no Government of China." But in the final text of the reply the President did not speak so candidly.[44]

There was still aid for Chiang, but on a much smaller scale than in the early postwar months. Wedemeyer, as the Director of Plans and Operations of the Army, reported to the White House on 20 October 1948 that some small arms and ammunition could be made available for early shipment from General MacArthur's stocks.[45] Answering Truman's inquiry concerning such shipment, Royall reported on the 29th that there were seven or eight hundred tons available in Japan, and he had ordered them sent to China.[46] In December, the NSC sent a memo to Truman saying that aid to Chiang was in danger; the NSC also decided that US forces would withdraw from Shanghai.[47]

With the decay of the Nationalist regime on the mainland, the Truman administration turned its attention to Taiwan. During the NSC meeting of 17 December, Acting Secretary of State Lovett announced that the "Formosan Chinese" had approached the State Department and the CIA about setting up "a separate state in Formosa." Discussions were continuing. Lovett said the value of Formosa lay not in the possibility of Chiang's return, but in securing the future of the island by integrating it with Japan or by setting up a government free from Communist influence. In view of the awkward situation at the time, efforts toward such ends had to be clandestine.[48] On 6 January 1949, the NSC showed the first official sign of a two-China scheme in *The Strategic Importance of Formosa* (NSC-37).[49]

THE SOVIET UNION AND BRITAIN

Strangely, the one country that tried to rescue the KMT government and to relieve the embarrassing US position in China, was none other than the Soviet Union. As early as January 1948, Stuart reported several incidents suggesting that the Soviets had offered mediation between the KMT and the CCP, and that certain influential elements in the KMT government were prepared to accept. The Political Science Group was strongly in favor of a rapprochement with the USSR. On 26 February 1948, the US embassy in Nanjing received confirmation from Chiang's secretary that the Soviet military attache did offer to mediate. Chiang's secretary said that the USSR had changed its policy in China, so as to bring about an understanding between the KMT and the CCP. But pursuit of this mediation offer did not have Chiang's approval.[50]

Stalin always maintained that sending US troops to fight in China would threaten destruction of the Chinese nation. He sent Anastas Mikoyan, a Politburo member, to see Mao. Mikoyan arrived at Mao's headquarters in Hebei Province in mid-January 1949. According to Zhou Enlai, "the situation was pretty good then, both militarily and politically. We were preparing to go south, ferry across the Yangtze and liberate the whole of China. The Soviet Union held a different view and asked us 'to stop the civil war.' This was virtually the making of the 'South and North Dynasties,' the two Chinas."[51] Mao himself mentioned, in a conversation on 11 April 1957, that Stalin had said not to cross the Yangtze, or US troops would come.[52] The same story has also been told by other veteran Communists.[53]

It seems, however, that Stalin's offer to mediate either was not known to Truman, or was ignored by him. The NSC paper of 11 January 1949 said that "the immediate aim of the US therefore should be to prevent China from becoming an adjunct of Soviet power. [The US should prepare] to exploit opportunities in China while maintaining flexibility and avoiding irrevocable commitments to any one course of action or to any one nation."[54] The NSC hinted that the US should use any avenue, including recognition, to prevent New China from aligning with the Soviet Union. Almost simultaneously, Truman declared in a Cabinet meeting on the 19th that "we can't be in a position of making any deal with a Communist regime." Cabinet members Forrestal, Snyder, Clark, Krug, Sawyer, Fleming, Barkley, Steelman, and Tobin all expressed agreement.[55] It is curious how one could have flexibility and at same time be unprepared to make any deal at all. And wasn't the Soviet government a Communist regime? Hadn't the US made a number of deals with the Soviets? Clearly, there was an internal contradiction in America's China policy.

The British government was very attentive to the China situation. When the Cabinet discussed recent developments in China on 18 December 1948, Bevin said that the Nationalist government had virtually lost control north of the Yangtze, and that in the course of time the Communists would secure control over the rest of the country. Bevin sought authority to discuss, with the other governments immediately concerned (i.e., France, Holland, and the US), means of containing the Communist threat in the Far East. In the Cabinet discussion, it became clear that no firm conclusion could yet be reached on the ultimate nature of Chinese Communism or on the relationship between the CCP and the Soviet Union. Far Eastern Communism might develop along distinctive Chinese lines. Although at the moment Chinese Communism was an agrarian movement, it might be forced to modify its principles in order to secure the support of industrial and mercantile interests. It would be unwise to pursue a policy that might drive the CCP into the arms of the Soviets, and the interested powers should reach agreement as soon as possible on their attitude towards a CCP government. The British authorities in Hong Kong, in dealing with KMT refugees, should not appear to depart from strict neutrality between the two sides of the civil war.

The sophistication of the Cabinet's analysis is admirable. The Cabinet in the end decided to consult first with the US government on containing the Communist threat to Anglo-American interests in Asia, then to consult with the Commonwealth countries, discussing steps to strengthen their position in the British Asian colonies. In February, Bevin reported to the Cabinet that there were signs the CCP would be willing to make barter deals with the British. He advised British merchants in China to trade with the Communists, though the attitude of the CCP toward foreign-trade interests was not predictable. The Cabinet members agreed that every endeavor should be made to maintain trade, on condition that the government would not compensate for any losses.[56] Bevin also proposed establishment of adequate liaison between the various police and intelligence organizations in China.

Ambassador Stuart reported from Nanjing on 10 January 1949 that the KMT government had handed notes to the ambassadors of the US, the UK, the USSR and France, suggesting that the Four Powers mediate between the KMT and the CCP to end the civil war. Stuart agreed with his British and French colleagues that this was an effort to gain time and to avoid loss of face, and that there was little chance of successful mediation—especially since it seemed that the USSR would not act in concert with the other three. Washington instructed Stuart to refuse mediation.[57] British Foreign Secretary Bevin had suggested that the US inquire of the Soviet and French governments before refusing, but the US was unwilling to do so. The Colonial Secretary felt that British relations with Asiatic peoples and with the Commonwealth might well be prejudiced if the UK intervened in the Chinese dispute, and Bevin said he much preferred not to intervene, since the Soviet Union was likely to accept and to exploit the chance to extend its influence throughout China. The Cabinet authorized Bevin to inform Chiang that the British, too, refused to intervene.[58]

It was revealed by a CCP source that, around this time, the Soviets received a letter from the KMT government asking the Soviets to mediate between the KMT and the CCP. The letter cited an ancient Chinese proverb that when brothers fight against each other, enemies outside prevail. The Soviet government made no comment, but simply turned a copy of the letter over to the CCP. In Zhou Enlai's view, KMT Foreign Minister Wang Shijie must have had a hand in drafting the letter.[59]

On 21 January, Chiang Kai-shek was forced to announce his "withdrawal," and turned the government over to then Vice-President Li Tsung-jen, who became Acting President. (Chiang retained control of the party and the troops.) On the 24th, the State Department briefed Truman that Li Tsung-jen had reached agreement with the Soviet ambassador on three points, as conditions for mediation: (1) strict Chinese neutrality in any future international conflict; (2) elimination of as much American influence from China as possible; and (3) establishment of a real basis for cooperation between the USSR and China. Two days later, the State Department reported that Li had attempted to secure Soviet intervention, to prevent the Communists from crossing the Yangtze; Li had argued that the US would intervene in the civil war if the crossing took place. On 24 March, State reported to the President that Li was contemplating a journey to Moscow, and had said he might also visit Washington and London. Li wanted to know the position of the US. The State Department instructed the embassy in Nanjing to inform Li that the Chinese must take responsibility for the decision, and that a visit to Washington would not result in increased US aid. Indeed, the Senate Foreign Relations Committee had shown no enthusiasm even for extending the authority to use unexpended ECA funds for China.[60] The embassy in Nanjing reported on the 29th that Li might provide formidable opposition to the Communists or to Chiang, and that Li could be counted on to keep part of China under his control.[61] This optimism proved unfounded.

By this time, the People's Liberation Army was about to cross the Yangtze. Since they did not have modern vessels, they had to cross before the end of April; otherwise, spring floodwaters would make the crossing too difficult. Also by this time, Dean Acheson had succeeded Marshall as Secretary of State. (During the Korean War, Marshall returned as Secretary of Defense once Louis Johnson had been ousted from that post.) Truman praised Marshall immensely: "The more I see and talk to him, the more certain I am he's the great one of the age. I am surely lucky to have his friendship and support."[62] Marshall returned the favor: toasting Truman, he said that he'd never in all his career been backed up as he had been as special envoy to China and as Secretary of State. He also said, "the United States has a President and Commander-in-Chief who is loyal to those who work for him."[63]

THE US AND THE CCP

Under Acheson, the State Department developed a policy targeted more at estranging the CCP from the Soviet Union. According to a report from the embassy in Nanjing on 31 January 1949, the apparent lack of Soviet enthusiasm for the success of the Chinese Communists suggested (1) high level USSR-CCP discussions on overall policy in the Far East were "running into snags"; (2) the Kremlin feared that the CCP might be able to develop a state too strong and independent for the Soviets' tastes, or (3) the Soviets, remembering previous experiences in China, were distrustful of all Chinese.[64] As proved by later events, this analysis was not entirely unfounded. In its report to the NSC on 28 February 1949, the State Department said that "the germs of friction between a Chinese Communist regime and the Kremlin undoubtedly exist in the Chinese situation....[T]he interest of the US would be served if operations or factors such as those indicated above were to result in successful resistance by a Chinese Communist regime to Kremlin attempts at political and economic exploitation of China."[65] During the State Department's daily meeting of 8 March, "it appeared that Mr. Acheson would like to have this subject looked into in a careful manner and that he had some doubts as to whether we had to continue to shore up the Nationalist Government to the extent that we had in the past."[66] Meanwhile, the US Air Force was publicizing its strength off the China coast. Charles Bohlen of the State Department believed this "very damaging to this country in its effect on European nations. Especially so in connection with negotiation of the [North Atlantic] Pact." Acheson agreed. Deputy Secretary of State James Webb talked with Secretary of the Airforce Symington who promised to discontinue the show of force at once.[67]

The Truman administration also sought to prevent Taiwan from falling under CCP control and to separate it from China. Members of the NSC agreed upon a document—NSC 37/2 of 3 February 1949—saying that "the US should seek to develop and support a local non-Communist Chinese regime which will provide át least a modicum of decent government for the islands,...[would use] influence wherever possible to discourage the further influx of mainland Chinese, [and] seek discreetly to maintain contact with potential native Formosan leaders...to make use of a Formosan autonomous movement."[68] The State Department briefed the President on 18 April that it had instructed US representatives in Taiwan to inform T.V. Soong "there was no question of US employing armed forces to affect the destiny of Formosa. Failure to make this point clear to Soong would inevitably result in eventual failure of US efforts to prevent Chinese Communists domination of the island."[69] Here, the State Department was forcing the Chiang regime to seek means for its survival by collaborating with the native population of the island.

Since Truman had won the 1948 election and would be in the White House for another four years, the Republicans now had a freer hand to stress the necessity of aiding the Chiang government. In February 1949, contrary to the NSC's suggestion, Congressional leaders unanimously advised sending munitions to the Nationalists; accordingly, the NSC decided to do so.[70] But when the McCarran Committee, the Senate watchdog committee on China, introduced a bill for $105 million in aid to the KMT government, Truman disagreed.[71]

The People's Liberation Army crossed the Lower Yangtze in late April 1949. Shortly before this, Li Tsung-jen informed the ambassadors of the US, the UK, France, and Australia that the CCP's peace terms amounted to unconditional surrender, and that the terms were unacceptable. The British ambassador, the spokesman for the four, replied that nothing could be done to help Li.[72] This was Li's last diplomatic effort before leaving Nanjing. Immediately afterwards, the PLA took the Nationalist capital and other cities along the river, including Shanghai. At this point, the US and the USSR each showed its expertise in international politics. As Zhou Enlai later observed: "On the eve of the liberation of Nanjing, the Soviet Union still maintained a diplomatic relationship with the KMT government. Chiang Kai-shek could not stay in Nanjing anymore and moved his capital to Guangzhou. Roschin, the Soviet Ambassador, followed the Chiang government and moved the embassy to Guangzhou, while US Ambassador Stuart did not go but stayed in Nanjing and watched how the situation would develop."[73] Indeed, Stuart refused to leave Nanjing even at the personal request of Li Tsung-jen. Bevin had reported to the British Cabinet on 26 April that "it had been decided that the British Embassy should remain in Nanjing and should not follow the Nationalist Government if it retired to Formosa or some other parts of China. Other countries, except the Soviet Government and the Governments associated with it, had decided to pursue a similar policy." The British government had also resolved on 13 December 1948 that the British communities in China should not be urged to leave.[74] The different lines taken by the western powers and the Soviet Union reflect the facts that the Western governments were not afraid of offending the KMT and the Soviets were not afraid of offending the CCP.

The Soviets—as the Chinese would say—had always "kept one foot in each boat" in China. In April 1945, Kennan had already commented that the different attitudes of the Soviet Union and the CCP toward Chiang might "represent a delicate warning (to the CCP) that the Kremlin has more than one string to its Chinese bow."[75] Why shouldn't the Soviets let Ambassador Roschin follow the KMT government south? Once the CCP took national power, he could reverse direction swiftly and serve as ambassador to the new government in Beijing. Roschin's move also could be construed as a warning that Mao should not replicate Tito's recalcitrance.

On the other hand, the US was so gentlemanly that it would not desert even a lost cause. As Truman would later say:

> The Far Eastern situation has been a peculiar one, as is often the case in a horse race--we picked a bad horse. That was the development of the situation in China. It turned out that the Nationalist Chinese Government was one of the most corrupt and inefficient that ever made an attempt to govern a country and when I found that out, we stopped furnishing them with material. Most of the Communist material was material which was surrendered by the Chinese Nationalist Government for a consideration. If Chiang Kai-shek had been willing to listen to General Marshall, General Wedemeyer and General Deane, he never would have found himself in the condition he is in now. After the surrender of Peiping [Beijing] where ammunition, trucks, and artillery material we had furnished was turned over to the Communists I cut off everything to the Chinese Government. It had to be done gradually, however, because Nationalists were still holding the line of the Yangtze River and I didn't want to pull the rug from under Chiang Kai-shek at that time.[76]

Though Truman did not follow the Soviet example of riding two boats at one time, he did let the State Department instruct Stuart on 25 April 1949 that the ambassador should remain in Nanjing during the Communist takeover to render all necessary assistance to the American community and that, once the Communist regime was firmly established and he had done everything possible for the Americans in Nanjing, he should proceed to the US for consultation.[77] This instruction could hardly be taken at face value, since there was not a big American community in Nanjing and looking after it did not require an ambassador. Stuart's stay in Nanjing seems to have had been intended to take stock of the situation and to wait for opportunities—as Mao Zedong commented.[78]

The State Department briefed the President on 27 April that Stuart had filed a report that the CCP was in thorough accord with the Kremlin.[79] This report completed contradicted the embassy's report of 31 January, discussed earlier in this chapter. The January report was much closer to reality; Stuart, as the chief observer on the spot was apparently doing a poor job appraising the China situation as of April. It was around this time, however, that Stuart made contact with the CCP and the "Zhou demarche" allegedly occurred.

According to American records, the offices of the US foreign services in Communist-controlled areas had, apart from various minor informants, at least four major avenues for communicating with the CCP leadership during the late spring and early summer of 1949. These avenues ran through (1) Philip Fugh, personal secretary to Stuart; (2) Chen Mingshu, of the Revolutionary Committee of the KMT; (3) Zhang Dongsun, his son Zhang Zhongbing, and other members of the Democratic League; and (4) Michael Keon of the United Press, Assistant Military Attache David Barrett, and other players in the "Zhou Enlai demarche."

Philip Fugh had been Stuart's confidant since their days in Yenching University. Fugh phoned the foreign office of the PLA's Nanjing Military Control Commission on 13 May 1949, and left his name for Huang Hua, director of the office and Fugh's Yenching classmate. The next day Huang returned the call and invited Fugh to visit him. This developed into a direct contact between Stuart and Huang. Stuart reported to Washington that he and Fugh brought up with Huang an incident where PLA soldiers had intruded into Stuart's bedroom, and were told that Zhou Enlai and Liu Bocheng, Commander of the 2nd Field Army and head of the Nanjing Military Control Commission, were distressed over the incident. Their more important discussions concerned the relationship between New China and the US. Stuart had two definite impressions: first, the CCP was anxious that foreign governments, particularly that of the US, abandon the KMT; second, Huang Hua was deeply sensitive to China's right to make her own decisions in the international field. In early June, Fugh asked Huang on his own initiative whether Stuart could travel to Beijing for his birthday and for commencement at Yenching; Huang called Stuart on the 28th, to say that he had received word from Mao and Zhou that they would welcome Stuart should he wish to visit. Stuart reported the message to Washington. Kennan, the State Department's policy planning chief, believed the message extremely significant and was in favor of the trip. The US Consul-General in Shanghai was also in favor of it. But on 1 July, Acheson cabled Stuart that, following instruction from the highest levels, he was under no circumstances to visit Beijing. The reasons were as listed in Stuart's own telegram: a visit would start rumors and embarrass the Department; it would be misunderstood by the diplomatic corps and viewed as breaking the united front policy, which would start a trek of mission chiefs to Beijing; visiting either of China's two capitals (Guangzhou and Beijing) would constitute interference in Chinese internal affairs; and the Beijing trip would enhance the prestige of the CCP and of Mao himself.[80]

Chen Mingshu, a general known for his stand against both the Japanese and Chiang, was a senior member of the KMT Revolutionary Committee. Chen visited Stuart in Nanjing on 10 June 1949; later he would give Stuart a memorandum dated 19 July in which he explained the success of the Chinese revolution, enclosing memos on his own conversations with Mao, Zhou, and Beijing Mayor Ye Jianying. The essence of these conversations was that the CCP hoped the US would not aid Chiang again and would act in the manner of FDR, Stilwell, and Wallace. If the US behaved in this manner, New China would treat the US with similar friendship. Chen quoted Zhou as saying, "I do not depend on you, you do not depend on me. If you should seek to come in a private capacity, it is possible that you would be able to meet a person in a responsible position." But Stuart did not respond with action. He took the message with him to Washington and submitted it to the State Department.[81]

Zhang Dongsun and his eldest son Zhang Zhongbing (Joseph Zhang) were, like Luo Longji, Democratic League personalities.[82] In May 1949, Stuart asked O. Edmund Clubb, U.S. Consul-General in Beijing, to ask Zhang Dongsun to come to Nanjing, as Stuart was confident that Zhang had information useful to Washington.[83] Clubb reported on the 28th that, when Zhang had seen Zhou Enlai the day before, "latter indicated receptive attitude *re* particular question trade with foreign nations." Zhang said Mao, Zhou, and Liu Shaoqi "were aware of the need *re* foreign trade and foreign relations," but needed to educate the lower strata of the party. He believed that there was a tendency toward adjustment of their position vis-a-vis the Americans but that the CCP acted very slowly. Clubb reported on 2 June that in three different conversations, Zhang Zhongbing "unsolicitedly indicated belief Communists would eventually 'be prepared to accept American aid.'"[84] Clubb passed along on the 8th and 9th Zhang Dongsun's information on the formation of a coalition government and on the possibility that the Soviets might yield at the CFM meeting in Paris. Zhang Zhongbing also reported that, in a recent speech, Zhou Enlai had said the CCP would not take Tito's line. Zhang Dongsun observed that Zhou's claim might indicate that in fact the CCP was considering emulating Tito. Clubb reported on 19 July that both Zhangs, Luo Longji, and another member of the Democratic League urged that the US sever relations with Chiang and recognize the Communist government. Clubb believed that Mao might have had prior knowledge of this meeting. According to one member of the Democratic League group, quoting Mao, the statement that China would side with the USSR in the event of war between the US and USSR was not official, and the CCP did not have such a commitment. Clubb told them that if China "desired to get on the road to construction it could best do so by making use of help from all quarters possible [and] the Communist side should note our own present attitude was one of noninterference in Chinese affairs."

The US government believed that Zhang Dongsun could exert influence on critical matters. Acheson cabled Clubb on 4 November 1949, in the name of Stuart, transmitting a personal message for Zhang. This message asked Zhang to act on the case of Angus Ward, US

Consul-General in Shenyang, who was being detained by the Chinese authorities. The message said: "Friendly relations our two countries now seriously damaged by unprecedented harsh treatment." Zhang later told Clubb that he had written a letter to Zhou Enlai, and that Zhou admitted receiving the letter—but had not replied. Earlier, when the US Consulate-General in Shanghai had some trouble with PLA troops in July, Stuart instructed Clubb to contact Zhang Zhongbing, asking his father to intervene.[85] The American records on Zhang Dongsun's activities have not been confirmed by the Chinese authorities, either verbally or in documentary sources. Zhang might have had the acquiescence of CCP leaders when he contacted the Americans, but it seems unlikely that he acted as an officially assigned intermediary.

Of all the alleged US-CCP contacts during this period, the most enigmatic and controversial is the so-called "Zhou Enlai demarche". Clubb reported to Acheson in late spring 1949 that Colonel David D. Barrett, Assistant Military Attache in Beijing, had received a message from a "reliable intermediary"—who turned out to be one Michael Keon, an Australian journalist working for the United Press. The message Keon delivered was reputed to have originated with Zhou Enlai, who had desired that it be transmitted to the "highest American authorities on a top-secret level, without his name being mentioned." Otherwise, he would disavow the message. Zhou also desired that the message be conveyed to the British, through the US State Department.

Zhou's message said that the CCP was now divided into liberal and radical wings. Zhou belonged to the liberal wing; his group suggested coalition with KMT. But they had failed to prevail in a dispute involving all the top Communist leaders except Mao. As the coalition had been rejected, the CCP must now obtain outside aid—from the US and the UK, since the USSR was unable to help. Zhou mentioned advantages the US would gain by aiding China. In Clubb's view, the Zhou demarche had two alternative explanations. One was that Zhou's wing had in fact been seriously at odds with the radicals and might be inclined towards Titoism; the other was that Zhou had taken his action with the full knowledge of the CCP and even of the USSR. Clubb tended to favor the second explanation, as "it would be premature accept development Titoism at this juncture," and China was in grave economic trouble, evidenced by Zhou's request that the US provide aid. Clubb suggested that the US respond to the effect that the US and China had long been friends and the US desired to develop social, economic, and political relations if China were to reciprocate with like intentions.[86] Stuart said that the State Department might want him to reply to the message in a "somewhat personal tone," and that he had other suggestions as to how the message might be followed up. Stuart assumed that Clubb would develop channels of communication superior to Keon's.[87] When Clubb's report arrived in the State Department, Acheson was not in Washington. Webb reported the demarche to Truman on 16 June, and read part of a reply to Zhou. The President approved, and directed that State not indicate any softening toward the Communists, but judge their intentions by their actions.[88] The reply was said to be in line with Clubb's original suggestion, but it referred to the cases of Angus Ward and Smith/Bende as causing serious concern to the US.[89] The reply was reportedly sent on 22 June to Zhou's secretary, origin unspecified.[90] The next day, however, the demarche ended.[91]

The U.S. State Department did not transmit Zhou's alleged message to the British government, and did not contemplate doing so unless the names of the intermediary and the source were revealed.[92] The British Foreign Office officially learned of the incident in a telegram from Hong Kong on 10 August, which coincided with a *London Times* report dated 8 August. The *Times* said that reports from Beijing had spoken of a divergence of opinion at the top of the CCP, with one school—headed by Zhou—advocating a period of moderate cooperation with the West on purely economic grounds and the other favoring alignment with the USSR. The first British Foreign Office official to handle this information commented that:

> the tale was too like the one that so many travellers have told in Hong Kong to merit serious attention....The fairly extensive diffusion of this top secret information by Chou [Zhou] and his choice of journalistic channels makes the thought of a plant very obvious indeed, [this being a trick] much used by the Japanese as well as the Nazis to get concessions even when a hostile policy had in fact been decided on....The Communists now use this technique deliberately before policy is finally adopted.

The official believed that, whether the demarche was fact or not, it did not much affect British policy, since its aim was economic cooperation. He added that the "possibilities of there being difficulties" confirmed that Britain's keeping a foot in the door in China would be the best way of weakening Soviet influence.

One subsequent commentator agreed that "the possibility of this message being a plant cannot be dismissed," but argued that it should be treated as a genuine, if partial, statement of Zhou's views. Another commentator said that if "we can assume" Zhou did ask to convey this message to the British government, then "we must ask ourselves" whether the cleavage in the CCP existed, and what might be Zhou's motive in informing an "imperialist" government of it? The commentator's answer to the first question was yes; as for the second, he believed the CCP moderates hoped the British would not adopt a policy contributing to ascendance of extremists within the party. British Foreign Office officials differed as to whether the message was a plant or should be assumed to be genuine.[93]

As it happened the Foreign Office official who first handled information on Zhou's demarche was none other than Guy Burgess.[94] He might have suggested that the message was a plant for his own special purposes. And, since the information passed through the hands of Burgess, it is probable that the entire substance of the demarche was known to the Soviet government in August 1949, if not earlier.

The "Zhou demarche" has never been confirmed by the Chinese authorities. Questions about it were raised during a conference on China-US relations in Beijing in the fall of 1986—a conference attended by Chinese and American scholars and diplomats. Former senior diplomats denied having any knowledge of the incident. The demarche remains an enigma that will only be illuminated when the relevant Chinese archives are opened to the public. It seems almost incomprehensible that Zhou Enlai should have sent messages of similar language and content to the US and the UK—as Colonel Barrett has observed. The demarche might be entirely fictitious, but it is also possible that someone in the CCP used Zhou's name without his knowledge.

If there really was a demarche, the following points warrant consideration. First, it must have been a party decision. Second, Barrett was chosen because of his relationship with the CCP since Dixie Mission. Third, the CCP was exploring possibilities for influencing the US to abandon the KMT—or perhaps the CCP was exploring possibilities for economic aid. Finally, the demarche might have been aimed at neutralizing US forces that could have intervened when the PLA advanced southward. After having crossed the Yangtze, the PLA deployed two field armies, the 2nd and the 3rd, in the coastal provinces; this deployment was aimed at possible US military intervention.

"LEANING TO ONE SIDE" AND THE US "LOSS" OF CHINA

A CIA report of 16 June 1949, *Probable Developments in China*, incisively examined possible developments in the CCP-USSR relationship. The report identified "points of potential conflict between the USSR and the CCP...such as possible inability to assist in China's industrialization, Soviet designs in China's border regions, the CCP's intention toward Communist movements in Asia, and the general issue of subservience to Moscow." Another significant feature of the report is that it used the name "Taiwan" throughout instead of "Formosa," which had often been used in US official documents. The CIA approved of recognizing the Communist government, but advised that the action should be taken some months, or a year, later. The intelligence organization of the State Department dissented, however, "on the grounds that it [the CIA report] does not give adequate treatment to the implications of the anticipated desire of a Communist China for international recognition," and criticized the CIA as having "accorded this highly complex and technical subject" a treatment best characterized as "oversimplification."[95]

On 30 June, the official news agency *Xinhua* broadcast Mao Zedong's *On People's Democratic Dictatorship*, commemorating the 28th anniversary of the CCP. Mao declared that the foreign policy of New China would "lean to one side"—the side of Soviet Union. General Wu Xiuquan, the PRC's delegate to the UN in 1950, wrote in his memoirs that Stalin was particularly sensitive to the possibility that China might go the "Yugoslavian way." Wu said that Mao put forward the policy of "leaning to one side," to address this sensitivity.[96] The northern department of the British Foreign Office did not consider Mao's language particularly serious, commenting that "after what happened to Tito, Rajk & Co., it would seem reasonable to interpret Mao's orthodoxy as a very sensible form of reassurance rather than a necessary proof of Soviet dictation."[97] Earlier, the British Consul-General in Tianjin had reported that "Mao and his lieutenants are moderates who have at heart the interests of their own country and its people rather than those of international Communism."[98]

Shortly after Mao's *Xinhua* broadcast, Acheson met with Wellington Koo, the Nationalist ambassador, and Kan Chieh-hou, the representative of acting Nationalist President Li Tsung-jen; the two had come to the US to seek support. Acheson was contemptuous of them and commented that retaining 300,000 inactive troops on Taiwan did not appear the most effective way of resisting Communism in China. The US stood ready to assist China, but first China would have to give concrete evidence of a desire to help itself.[99] President Truman also received Koo and Kan—and was even more impolite than Acheson.[100]

For quite some time, the State Department had been preparing a *China White Paper*, which Truman believed would be one of his administration's "most important actions for some time to come."[101] The paper was supposed to tell the American people and the world how China was "lost." The JCS and Defense Secretary Johnson doubted the wisdom of publishing the paper, but Truman and Acheson wanted to go ahead with it—although the timing would have to be considered in connection with Stuart's exit permit, to be issued by the Chinese Communist authorities.[102]

State issued the *China White Paper* on 5 August 1949, at the president's direction.

Whether it was wise to publish the *China White Paper* is still debatable. The British government believed that the paper "failed to stifle the critics and indeed provided them with further ammunition" (and, in particular, abundant material showing the corruption that led to defeat of the KMT and ascendance of the CCP) and that the Soviets would use it to unseat the KMT at the UN.[103] In fact, as of March 1949, the State Department was already considering that it should have "a careful study made of the question of US public opinion on China versus the feeling that full airing of the question would have an adverse affect on the Chiang regime."[104] People in State apparently felt that they should let the American people know what had really happened, regardless of whether or not they might want to desert Chiang once they knew the truth. Then too, when the American people knew the truth, they would support the administration in forsaking the KMT. This would mitigate the claim that it was the Democrats who "lost" China.

The *China White Paper* certainly did give the CCP more ammunition for propaganda batteries pointed squarely at the Truman administration. Mao himself wrote several comments on the paper for *Xinhua*, further heightening the anti-American mood in China.

9

Adapting to the Communist Accession in China

The People's Republic of China was established on 1 October 1949 with the accession of the CCP. Whether the Truman administration could adapt its policy to this new reality remained to be seen.

Drew Pearson wrote, in his *Washington Post* column of 14 July 1949 that Acheson had placed an anti-Chiang proposal before the NSC. It was defeated, 5 to 1, by Louis Johnson, the Treasury Secretary, and the heads of the services. Pearson noted two reasons for this defeat: Mao's inclining toward Moscow, and the shoddy treatment of US officials in China (Vice-Consul William Olive, in particular). Declassified NSC records do not confirm Pearson's report, but the two reasons he suggested are worthy of discussion.

Anyone in Mao's position would have felt himself in a difficult situation. Neither of the two world powers really supported the Chinese revolution. The US had been supporting the KMT regime all along, and was openly hostile to New China. The USSR, on the one hand, admitted its past misjudgment of the Chinese revolution—Stalin apologized to Liu Shaoqi in July 1949 and to Mao Zedong in December—and, on the other hand, strongly suspected that New China was in fact another Yugoslavia.[1] The US attitude, though unwise, was understandable to Chinese leaders; the Soviet attitude embittered them. But they were unable to challenge it, since at the time the Soviet Communist Party was at the center of a strong international Communist movement and Stalin was the teacher of world revolution. When Soviet pressure became intolerable, the CCP proved its sincerity and allayed Soviet suspicion by proclaiming publicly the policy of "leaning to one side" (as already discussed).[2]

The Soviet government recognized New China on 4 October. Upon learning of this, Dean Rusk suggested that the policy planning staff consider making a general review of the US situation and denouncing the Far East portion of the Yalta Agreement.[3] Webb met with Truman the same day on the problem of recognition, stating a position similar to Rusk's. Truman said the US should be in no hurry whatever to recognize New China, remarking that the US had waited twelve years to recognize the Soviet regime.[4] Truman could not have imagined then that the US would not recognize the People's Republic until twenty-two years later!

Because it upset the balance of power in China as designed by the Big Three at Yalta, the birth of New China doubtless ran counter to the wishes of the US government. But it was also against the wishes of the Soviet government: "The Soviet Union worried that the Chinese civil war would disrupt the spheres of influence divided by the Yalta Agreement, and would invite U.S. involvement and jeopardize the Soviet Union."[5] The "Soviet Government is not at all interested in any revolutionary movement it cannot control and subordinate."[6]

As to Pearson's second reason for the defeat of Acheson's proposal, it was true that Vice-Consul Olive had not enjoyed diplomatic privilege after he interfered in a mass demonstration in Shanghai. The new government's way of treating diplomats of the US, the UK, and some other western countries was certainly abnormal, in the eyes of the countries concerned. The Consulate-General was now called the "ex-Consulate-General," or simply the "office of the person in charge." These persons in charge did not register as diplomats at the Foreign Ministry and the local foreign affairs offices, but rather at the Alien Affairs Offices of the local public security authorities.

ANGUS WARD AND THE SHENYANG SPIES

The case of Angus Ward actually overshadows that of Olive. On 24 October 1949, Ward, the US Consul-General in Shenyang (Mukden), was detained by the municipal public security bureau. It was said that a Chinese employee of the consulate had been assaulted by the American staff, and Ward was held responsible. Truman remarked on the 31st that he was prepared to take the strongest possible measures, including force, if he was sure such measures would be effective.[7] On 14 November, Truman indicated to Webb, Acheson's deputy, that State should thoroughly explore the possibility of blockading coal shipments from North China ports to Shanghai, so the CCP would understand he meant business and would release Ward. Truman believed that, by so doing, the US would gain prestige internationally and make independent British action on such matters as recognition more difficult. In Truman's view, if the US meant to go into this, it should be prepared to sink any vessel that refused to observe the blockade.[8] Webb reported to Truman on the 18th that the "next move would be to secure assistance from the British and the French in making representations, but at the same time Secretary Johnson was making a study of possible means of applying force."[9] Acheson went to see Truman on the 21st, advising against the blockade. He and Truman agreed to wait for reactions to a note sent to countries having official representatives in China.[10] On the same day, Angus Ward was sentenced to six months detention; on the 27th the verdict and sentence were reported in the Chinese media. He left Shenyang on 7 December, and was deported.[11]

Kennan believed "the Angus Ward Case [to be] a retaliatory measure for US actions in the Amtorg and Gubitchev cases."[12] Whether Kennan's belief is well-founded has not been verified; the Ward case seems more a purely Chinese reaction than a Soviet scheme. At least two aspects of the case warrant attention. First, while Ward was in detention, the US Consulate-General in Beijing reported to the State Department that the Ward case was more complicated than it appeared because it was connected to a spy case. The Chinese news media reported on 2 December that, during the summer, the Chinese security service had cracked a spy ring directed from the second floor of the Consulate-General; several Chinese and Japanese were arrested. This case not only made the Chinese government more suspicious of the Americans, but also gave them evidence supporting their public claims that the US had long been scheming to sabotage New China. Second, the Chinese government might have used the Ward case to retaliate against the US for failing to recognize the new government and for influencing other countries to follow suit. The Chinese government probably wished to show that its slogan "The Chinese people have stood up!" and its anti-US pronouncements were not mere rhetoric. Maury Maverick, a veteran Democratic politician and an old friend of Truman, wrote that "I have an idea that Chou En-lai [Zhou Enlai] is treating Angus Ward as he is because Ward has no *exequatur*. I think, however, that the President should have this explanation. Thus, our pride is causing us to slip rapidly in the Orient."[13] Maverick added that Angus Ward's tribulations could be traced to E.V. "Ever Victorious" Ward of the Taiping period, since Angus had the same family name as did E.V.[14] Of course, this was intended as a joke—but there may be a grain of truth in it.

From the fact that Truman wanted to rescue Ward (setting a precedent for the Delta Force venture decades later) and to use the Navy to blockade Chinese coal transport, one could well conclude that he lacked means of handling this awkward situation. Although the Ward episode came to an end when Ward was released, its implications were far-reaching. Later, Truman frequently cited it as evidence showing the hostile attitude of the PRC. In fact, Truman was genuinely hurt. How dare the Chinese Communists detain and sentence a senior American diplomat! The Chinese leadership, on the other hand, had no doubt that the Shenyang spy case was not the only such clandestine venture of the US. Whether they had hard evidence of other incidents at the time is yet to be disclosed. The Chinese media did not report anything more about the US intelligence network in China until the Korean War broke out; from these later reports, the Shenyang case appears to be one part of a larger scheme.

By the end of the war, the OSS in China had started to build up a network covering Manchuria, North China and East China. When the OSS was dissolved, its clandestine functions, personnel, and contacts were turned over to the War Department under the name of the Strategic Service Unit. In 1947 this unit joined the new CIA as its Office of Secret Operations. Regardless of these changes in affiliation, the outfit in China was active all through the late 1940s. In the immediate postwar period, it was known as the ALG (American Liaison Group); it was later known as SSU (Strategic Service Unit); and finally as ESD-44 (External Survey Detachment). We can assume that these names correspond to its affiliations with the OSS, the War Department, and the CIA. The headquarters of this espionage network was to be found in a big compound on Hengshan Road, Shanghai (once Rue Petain, in the French concession). Although one of its chiefs was a Navy captain, it was not a military intelligence network, but rather operated both overtly and covertly with regular CIA functions.

US MOVES TOWARD A NEW CHINA POLICY

At the end of October 1949, Truman decided to evacuate American women and children from Taiwan. He indicated "that the Communists could take Formosa almost on their own timetable, and that he did not wish to face another situation where Americans had remained behind with all the problems involved."[15] As instructed by the President, Secretary Acheson then organized a meeting to discuss the Far Eastern problem. This meeting took place on 17 November in the Cabinet room. Apart from Truman and Acheson, it was attended by Jessup, Butterworth, and three consultants on the Far East, and some other people from the State Department. Acheson recorded his comments at the meeting as follows:

> Broadly speaking, there were two objectives of the policy: one might be to oppose the Communist regime, harass it, needle it, and if the opportunity appeared, to attempt to overthrow it. Another objective of policy would be to attempt to detach it from subservience to Moscow and over a period of time encourage those vigorous influences which might modify it....This second alternative did not mean a policy of appeasement any more than it had in the case of Tito....The consultants were unanimous in their judgement that the second course was preferable. The President thought that in the broad sense in which I was speaking

this was the correct analysis and that he wished to have a thorough understanding of all the facts in deciding the question.[16]

Truman observed after the meeting that it was tremendously helpful to him and that "he had gotten a new insight into the reasons for the Communist success in China, a better understanding of the whole situation, and found himself thinking about it in a quite new way."

On November 15, Maury Maverick had sent a memo to members of the State Department's China Committee—namely, Jessup, Case and Forsdick. In the memo, Maverick said:

> The position of the State Department does not gain the friendship of the new government of China, nor the Chinese people. Rather, our lecturing and smug attitude solidifies hostility to us with the Chinese people, whatever may be the future government of China. [US accusations] fall flat on unsympathetic ground, do no good whatever. In making the charge we ignore our own continuous backing of the corrupt nationalist administration long after we knew it was morally wrong. We also ignore Chinese history of European and American intervention beginning with the Opium War in 1840. Above all, we ignore human emotions which the Chinese must have, like we have....According to International Law, nations should be recognized who are entitled to it. This is true even if friendly to Russia.

On the 19th, shortly after the Truman-Acheson meeting, Maverick wrote to Truman, attaching a copy of his memo to the China Committee. Maverick said in his letter:

> [I am] inclined to believe that a way should be found to recognize the new government, or at least to negotiate. I understand the arrest of our consul and know it is bad. However, it is my opinion that this improper conduct by the Chinese should not be permitted to get us out on the limb. In my opinion, the new government is anxious for recognition. Also, we can make a friend out of China.

Truman replied to Maverick's letter on the 22nd, saying:

> [yours is] the most sensible letter I've seen on the China situation. I can't tell you how much I appreciate it. There are so many crackpots who know all about what to do and who really know nothing about what to do, it is pleasure to hear from somebody who has a little common sense in the matter.[17]

Subsequent actions suggest that at this point the Truman administration decided to put the policy of driving a wedge between the USSR and the PRC above its principle of not appeasing a Communist country. The case of Yugoslavia had not only warned the Soviet Union to beware of recalcitrants within the Communist ranks, but also shown the US that the socialist group was not monolithic. The US ambassador to Yugoslavia reminded the State Department in February 1950 that "the Yugoslavs are most anxious to establish contact with the [Chinese] Communists in order to hasten their break with Moscow which they confidently expect."[18]

But not everybody held the view decided upon at the State Department meeting in November. Prior to this meeting, the NSC circulated to its staff the draft of a paper, *The Position of the United States with Respect to Asia*. The draft said:

> In the light of the present situation and of all intelligence reports it would be folly, however, to base United States policy on the faint hope or distant prospect of 'Titoism' in China, and thus to deny to the United States the moral strength of opposing communism because of its basic evil....[If the US were forced for tactical reasons to enter relations with the PRC] every effort should be made to avoid recognizing the communist regime as the sole government of China. The possibility of recognizing a Communist regime in part of China and continuing to recognize another government in non-communist China should be explored.[19]

NSC paper 48/2, *The Position of the U.S. with Respect to Asia* (30 December 1949), moved closer to the policy decision made during the State Department meeting:

> The US should exploit, through appropriate political, psychological and economic means, the rifts between the Chinese Communists and the USSR and between the Stalinists and other elements in China, while scrupulously avoiding the appearance of intervention. Where appropriate, covert as well as overt means should be utilized to achieve these objectives....While Formosa is strategically important to the US, the strategic importance of Formosa does not justify overt military action....The US should make every effort to strengthen the overall US position with respect to the Philippines, the Ryukyus and Japan.[20]

A few days later, President Truman said, in a statement on China policy:

> The US has no predatory designs on Formosa or on any other Chinese territory. The US has no desire to obtain special rights or privileges to establish military bases on Formosa. Nor does it have any intention of utilizing its armed forces to interfere in the present situation. The US Government will not pursue a course which will lead to involvement in the civil conflict in China. Similarly, the US Government will not provide military aid or advice to Chinese forces on Formosa.[21]

Although the US had already been proven insincere in its early postwar statements opposing fratricidal conflict in China, the President's announcement at this late moment, which came close to saying "US to keep its hands off Taiwan," could not be neglected. Within the Truman administration there still was no coherent view as to the future of Taiwan. A draft of Truman's statement, prepared by the State Department, was opposed by White House and NSC aides Clifford, Murphy, Souers and Layn, and by Defense Secretary Louis Johnson. NSC Secretary Souers called Acheson, saying that JCS Chairman Bradley suggested deleting a phrase about the US having no desire "to detach Formosa from China," because the JCS might want to do so at some point in the future. Acheson agreed to the deletion, although he would have preferred to retain the phrase in question.[22] Acheson then personally persuaded Truman that the statement should be released.[23]

There were also divergent views within the military. Several days after the statement, Rusk said during a meeting in the State Department that the JCS might reverse its position on Formosa. The Pentagon was debating whether or not Formosa was important enough to warrant military action; Rusk was sure the JCS would raise this question.

Truman himself had reservations about the statement. He added three words to it: "at this time." Acheson was not happy that Truman inserted three words of great significance without consulting him. The Press Secretary was not happy, because the text had to be retyped at the last moment.[24] Johnson was not happy that the statement was released at all.

Truman's statement, as released, was tantamount to inviting PRC troops into Taiwan—clear evidence that the policy decided upon at the State Department meeting was being followed. One Vietnamese official informed the US embassy in Saigon that Truman's speech was generally approved by Vietnamese public opinion, as US occupation of Taiwan would appear to be an expression of Western imperialism. The US embassy in New Dehli reported that Truman's statement was doubtless received by the Indian government with relief.[25] One week after the statement, Secretary Acheson discussed the China question in a speech at the National Press Club. His comments echoed Truman's.

There were further signs showing this trend of moderation toward the PRC. On 6 January, the State Department reported to Truman that it had instructed the US mission to the UN to vote against any motion in the Security Council intended to unseat the KMT or seat the PRC—but to explain that the vote was not a veto. If it were considered a veto, the mission should request a re-vote, and then abstain.[26] UN Secretary-General Trygive Lie met with Acheson and other US officials on the 21st. During this meeting, Rusk said that the US would not veto China's being seated. Rusk went on:

> Probably in a matter of several weeks seven members of the Security Council will have recognized the Communist regime and when that happens a Communist representative will be seated on a procedure vote....We regard it as a procedural matter and we would neither ourselves exercise the veto nor acquiesce in a veto by anyone else."[27]

Ambassador Kirk reported from Moscow that:

> Our long-range interests would best be served by early recognition of the Chinese Communist regime. We cannot exploit the situation in China to our advantage unless we have official representation on the ground there....It would be highly dangerous for the free world to split over the issue of the recognition of the Peiping regime, serious repercussions would be felt in the UN and elsewhere.

Kirk opposed any action to strengthen the KMT regime in Taiwan, as he believed such action could not succeed, would be costly, and would evoke strong adverse reactions in Southeast Asia.[28] The US Consulate-General in Shanghai reported that the great majority of Americans in that city believed US recognition should and must come in time.[29] Truman himself, in a meeting with Philippine President Quirino in February, said he "did not regard Formosa in the hands of the Communists as a threat to the Philippines."[30]

For the Chinese, this was not the time to nod approval to mercurial statements of Truman or Acheson. They were reaching a critical juncture. In November 1949, the CIA sent Truman three reports concerning the situation in China. (1) CIA Director Hillenkoeter reported to Truman on 18 November that the CIA had received a message that morning from a reliable source, concerning the whereabouts of Angus Ward and some of his staff members. The message said Ward had been interrogated by two public security officials on 2 November, and it quoted questions and answers from the interrogation. Hillenkoeter advised that he was reporting this information only to the president, and that once it was more widely disseminated, it would jeopardize the source.[31] This means that the CIA probably had an informant within the Chinese public security establishment. (2) Hillenkoeter reported on the 21st that Chennault had recently met MacArthur and given him personal messages from Chiang and General Bai Congxi (considered to be one of the ablest generals under Chiang). MacArthur regretted that US policy prevented him from helping Chiang, and asked Chennault to tell Chiang and Bai that he wanted them to fight to the end. MacArthur's chief-of-staff leaked that Japanese volunteers, mainly in aviation, were being allowed to slip out of Japan to Taiwan.[32] (3) Hillenkoeter reported to Truman and Acheson on the 19th and the 21st concerning Zhou Enlai's remarks in late October on the subject of Chinese foreign policy. The CIA's source quoted Zhou as remarking that:

> [Since] Chiang and other reactionaries are allied with the US, the Communist Party (China) must ally with the USSR. It would be a dream on the part of the American Government to expect the CCP to split with the USSR, but they can expect that the CCP will not always be anti-American. The CCP cannot afford two enemies at one time, but there is nothing to keep them from having more than two friends.[33]

This seems to dovetail with the strategy Mao always maintained and which became a line the Party followed.

Later developments proved the significance of three key points Hillenkoeter reported: that American espionage had penetrated the apparatus of the PRC, that MacArthur took a hard line in the Far East, and that the PRC's attitude toward the US was not intransigent.

MAO'S VISIT TO MOSCOW

Mao Zedong led a large delegation to the Soviet Union in late 1949, arriving in Moscow on 16 December. The celebrities of the international Communist movement were all present, to attend a celebration of Stalin's 70th birthday. This was Mao's first visit to the Soviet Union.

Mao had planned a visit as early as April 1948. At that time, with final victory over the KMT fast approaching, he had many problems to discuss with Stalin. But when he asked Stalin about the visit, Stalin replied that, at the decisive moment of China's revolutionary war, the supreme commander should not leave his post; if there were questions requiring consultation, Stalin would send a Politburo member to hear Mao's views.

Mao accepted this suggestion. Owing to the military situation, however, the Soviet representative—Anastas Mikoyan, one of Stalin's close associates—did not arrive in China until January 1949. Mikoyan reached Xibaipo, the headquarters of the CCP Central Committee, just as the PLA entered Beijing. Accompanying him were I. Kovalev (Vice-Minister of Railways), E. Kovalev (a China specialist), and two bodyguards. Mikoyan met with CCP Secretariat members Mao Zedong, Liu Shaoqi, Zhou Enlai, Zhu De and Ren Bishi, with Mao himself serving as speaker for the CCP group (This visit was discussed in Chapter 8.) In early May, the CCP decided to send a delegation to visit the Soviet Union in secret. This delegation, headed by Liu Shaoqi and also including Gao Gang and Wang Jiaxiang, was supposed to discuss various important issues with Stalin and make preparations for a future visit by Mao himself.

Liu and his colleagues met with Stalin five times. At the second meeting, Stalin admitted his mistakes in regard to the Chinese revolution. Stalin asked, "Have we handicapped you?" When Liu replied "no," Stalin said, "We did, we did, we don't understand China very well." At the fourth meeting, in Stalin's dacha, Stalin made the following toast: "The center of the world revolution has moved to the Soviet Union, later it will move to China. May the little brother overtake the elder one." Liu could not accept this toast. Whether Stalin was sincere in his toast and his earlier apology can best be judged from what happened during Mao's visit in December.

During his third meeting with the Chinese delegation, Stalin asked when the new central government would be formed. Liu Shaoqi replied that the CCP's major concern was international recognition, and that the capitalist countries would not extend recognition quickly. If the socialist countries could promptly recognize the PRC, China would not feel isolated—but the CCP was not sure they would do so. Stalin did not clearly answer these concerns. Rather, he advised that the period without a new central government should not be long, or it would invite foreign intervention, and expressed his view that a new world war would require at least twenty years' preparation on the part of the imperialists. Stalin noted, however, that nobody could guarantee that a madman would not emerge, citing the suicide of James Forrestal in support of this caveat.[34]

When Mao Zedong stayed on in the Soviet Union after Stalin's birthday celebration, all sorts of rumors started to circulate. US Ambassador Kirk reported in early January that Mao's delayed departure from Moscow was due to failure to reach an amicable agreement with the USSR.[35] This was basically correct. According to authoritative Chinese sources, Mao was then waiting for the conclusion of a friendship treaty with the Soviet Union. When Mao went to Moscow, Stalin was skeptical of the situation in China, bitter about the CCP's independent action vis-a-vis the International, and suspicious that China would go the "Yugoslavian way." He was also suspicious that, with the participation of some non-Communists in the government, the CCP might take a pro-British and pro-American line. The Soviets therefore discussed signing the treaty only in the later stage of Mao's visit, and only because Mao insisted that it be signed; otherwise, he would not leave. Stalin, although fearful of violating the Yalta Agreement, finally agreed, and the treaty was signed on 14 February 1950.

The initial text of the friendship treaty was drafted by the Soviets. One passage said that should one of the signatories be invaded by a third country, the second "will be able" to come to aid of the first. Zhou Enlai did not think this was definite enough. After long deliberation, the wording was changed to "immediately and with all-out effort." During the treaty deliberations, the Soviets impudently invited the Chinese delegation to see the ballet *Red Poppy*, which is offensive to the Chinese people; the delegation boycotted the performance, sending one member to see it and voice criticism.[36]

Other episodes warrant discussion in connection with Mao's visit to Moscow. First, almost all of the various avenues of communication between the CCP and the US (discussed above) were blocked in late June, by either the CCP or the US. Most importantly, Acheson instructed Stuart that he should not go to Beijing, and Mao wrote his article commemorating the 28th anniversary of the CCP. Second, in his letter transmitting the *China White Paper*, Acheson encouraged the development of "democratic individualism" in China, which meant that the US was in favor of greater participation of non-Communists in the political arena. Mao took pains to repudiate this view, in his comments in *Xinhua*. Lou Longji, one so-called "democratic individualist" of prominence, suggested to the US that "it would be helpful if Americans refrained from open announcement of support for Chinese democratic elements." Lo "felt he would have enjoyed a more influential position in the CCP had there not been statements regarding democratic individualism in the Acheson letter."[37] He added that "there was to have been set up a foreign relations committee headed by Chou En-Lai [Zhou Enlai] with Lo and Chang Tung-Sun [Zhang Dongsun] participating, but that project had been abandoned after issuance of the *White Paper*."[38] Third, the non-Communists were not the only ones plagued by their connections to the US. Gao Gang reported to Stalin in 1949 that Mao and Zhou were pro-American.[39] This further increased Stalin's suspicion of the CCP, leading him to humiliate Mao by letting him "sit on a cold stool."[40]

It was reported that, during his visit, Mao repeatedly expressed his displeasure both at what had previously happened between the Soviets and the CCP and at the treatment he was receiving in Moscow at the time. During their first meeting, Stalin had praised his youth and vigor and his great contributions to the Chinese revolution. Mao replied that he had been pushed aside for a long time, with no one to whom he might appeal. Stalin interrupted, saying that "victors are not to be accused." Then, when the Soviets failed to have the text of a trade agreement ready for the signing ceremony, Soviet staffers falsely accused the Chinese of causing the delay. Stalin asked that this be translated to Mao; Mao commented to his colleagues that "the Chinese are to blame for all the mistakes, after all!"[41]

After the signing ceremony, the Chinese delegation, Soviet Politburo members, and other senior Soviet officials attended a banquet at the Metropol Hotel. Zhou Enlai, speaking for the Chinese, said that Sino-Soviet friendship should last for generations to come and that China should learn from the Soviet Union. Stalin then expressed regret that there was one party absent—Yugoslavia. Stalin claimed that Yugoslavia had cut itself off; this, of course, was not true.[42]

DULLES AND THE EMERGENCE OF A BIPARTISAN US POLICY

During this period, circumstances forced the PRC to mount attacks on the US. Acheson alleged in his press conference on 12 January that the Soviet Union was preparing to incorporate four northern areas of China into the Soviet Union.[43] In March, Acheson made a similar reference to Soviet advances in China. Such references were obviously aimed at estranging Sino-Soviet relations; indeed, the first was made while Mao was in Moscow. China responded by charging publicly that Acheson was slandering Sino-Soviet relations.[44] Soon after the PRC expropriated the US compound in Beijing, the US government announced, on 14 January 1950, that it intended to prepare instructions for withdrawal of all US officials from China—an action that had been long delayed. O.E. Clubb, Consul-General in Beijing, reported on the 20th what an American with access to a "highly-placed source" in the Chinese Foreign Ministry had told him. According to this source, there had been "heavy gloom" in the Foreign Ministry upon discovering that the US was not bluffing and "meant business." There had been "guarded criticism and discontent" with the decision to seize the US compound.[45] The Foreign Ministry's official spokesman put fat in the fire by announcing on 5 February that most US diplomatic personnel had not yet applied for exit and asking whether the US government might regret its announcement. In his view, this instance once again revealed that US imperialism was "strong in looks, weak in essence."[46]

Around this time, a bipartisan Far East policy was shaping up in the US. When John Foster Dulles discussed the Taiwan problem with Acheson on 22 December 1949, he said that the US should take over Taiwan and make it a "showpiece"—but with three conditions: (1) the US must not fight Chiang, (2) the US must not be present in Taiwan as Chiang's guest, and (3) Taiwan could have no strategic importance. Acheson asked how could this be done. Dulles had no ready answer, but said he would give it some thought.[47] Three months later, Truman's staff sent him a memo outlining eight measures for dealing with the situation vis-a-vis the USSR. The last item in the memo was "restoration of a bipartisan approach. In implementing the above program, and particularly in matters relating to such troublesome areas as the Far East, real care and thought should be given to lifting this area of national action out of the realm of hard political infighting."[48]

Republican Congressman Christian A. Herter called on Acheson on 21 March 1950, to discuss in detail the foreign and domestic problems facing the US. In the end—according to Acheson—Herter said that "he hoped that we would be able to work things out, that he wanted to be helpful, that he was sorry I had so much trouble on the Hill recently and that he realized that made my problems more difficult." Herter's visit was definitely a token of good will on the part of the Republicans.[49]

Republican Senator Vandenberg, who had been instrumental in keeping the bipartisan approach alive since the UN inaugural conference in April 1945, was critically ill in the early spring of 1950. The Truman administration urgently wanted to see not only that Vandenberg would have a successor to carry the torch of bipartisanship but also that his successor would help in forming a coherent bipartisan policy toward the Far East, and toward China in particular. On March 26, Truman wrote to Republican Senator Styles Bridges, observing that his joining with the "wolf-hounds" in attacking Acheson indicated that he did not fully understand "all the implications involved in this unwarranted attack on the bipartisan foreign policy." Bridges replied that he would talk with Acheson in person. Truman wrote to Vandenberg on the 27th, expressing his concern over "the situation as it has been developing in the Congress with regard to the whole bipartisan foreign policy." Truman said the bipartisan policy had originated when Hull was Secretary of State. Its first great result was the setting up of the UN, followed by aid to Greece and Turkey and the Marshall Plan, and, still later, the North Atlantic Pact and the military aid program. Truman went on to say that "the breakup of the bipartisan foreign policy at this time would mean but one thing—victory for Russia in Europe, and in all probability a definite approach to a shooting war, which none of us wants....The unfortunate situation in the Far East, which came about as a result of the corrupt Chinese Nationalist Government, has caused us more much difficulty, through no fault of ours that I have been able to discover."

Truman was asking the Republicans to cooperate in the Far East and China policies. Vandenberg replied on the 29th that "certainly we cannot fundamentally 'divide at home' in respect to foreign policy and expect to have much effective authority abroad." Vandenberg expressed his regret that he could not "take full part in these recurrent Senate crises." Truman continued the exchange, expressing his hope that Vandenberg would recover completely—he was on sick leave at the time—and would train the young men in the Senate to carry on with what Vandenberg, Hull, and others visualized with regard to "a continuing foreign policy for this great Government of ours."[50] Vandenberg wrote to Acheson, on the 29th, saying "we disagree at many points but never in respect to the final unity which will be a major source of our national security," and on the 31st, saying that appointing a Republican in the State Department was excellent. Vandenberg also believed that bringing John Foster Dulles back "into active and important cooperation with the State Department [was] an indispensable necessity in recapturing some degree of bipartisan liaison in respect to foreign policy."[51]

In preparing the Japanese peace treaty, the State Department encountered two big hurdles, the Pentagon and the Senate, and two minor hurdles, Britain and Australia. According to State Department official Randolph Burgess, it was Butterworth of FE who suggested bringing Dulles in at this point. At first, Acheson was opposed to this suggestion, since Truman was annoyed with Dulles and had said he would never appoint Dulles to office again. Truman had appointed Dulles to the UN's Paris meeting in 1947, but Dulles failed to call on Truman when he came to Washington.[52] Acheson called Truman on 4 April and mentioned the subject of an appointment for Dulles, saying that he thought Dulles could be appointed as "consultant to the Secretary of State on Bipartisan Foreign Policy." Acheson mentioned the Vandenberg letter recommending Dulles, adding that he was going to see Dulles and would like to have Truman's ideas on the matter. It seems likely that Acheson had discussed the Dulles problem with Truman prior to this telephone call, and that the title, "consultant to the Secretary of State," was Truman's idea. Truman said that such an appointment would do no harm to "Mr. Dulles's dignity" and that, in view of what Dulles had said on domestic matters during the election campaign, Truman could not bring him into the administration on domestic affairs. Acheson agreed. Acheson immediately told Webb and Rusk about his conversation with Truman.[53]

The next day, Acheson phoned Dulles, initiating an interesting sequence of events. Acheson said that, having secured the President's approval, he would like to have Dulles come to Washington to work with him as a consultant. Acheson had already talked with Vandenberg, who would get in touch with Dulles to urge him to accept.[54] Dulles replied that he had called Vandenberg the previous night, and then suggested he should talk with Truman himself so as to feel that there was "reestablishment of personal confidence." Acheson said that Dulles could make an appointment when Truman returned to Washington (from Florida), though he did not feel that this was necessary. Acheson hoped Dulles would come to Washington, to be briefed on all of the major issues and to help deal with Congress and to "get these matters on a basis of unified support." He noted in particular the problems of the Far East—the Japanese peace treaty and the peace in India—and reviewed the question of the US position in the Cold War. Dulles said if he could do interesting work and make himself useful, he would not enter the Senate campaign in New York the following fall—but he did not want to make an immediate commitment; rather, he would like to discuss, that afternoon, the language of the statement appointing him.

When Dulles phoned Acheson that afternoon, Acheson read the statement to him:

> At the request of the President and the Secretary of State, Mr. John Foster Dulles has agreed to serve as Consultant to the Secretary of State. In this capacity Mr. Dulles will advise Secretary Acheson on broad problems in the field of foreign affairs and on specific lines of action which this Government should follow....Mr. Dulles...will take office April ____ after completing a brief vacation.

Dulles wondered if "there might not be inserted some mention of his experience with the United Nations." Acheson complied. Then Dulles inquired about the term "office." Acheson replied that it was not a statutory office requiring confirmation, but rather a regular office in the Department; he suggested the language "will assume his duties" might be used instead. Dulles, commenting that it "wasn't a very distinguished sounding office," said that he would like to let Governor Dewey know of his plans and that he would phone Acheson "if he had any change in plans." It was agreed that Butterworth would go to New York before Dulles left for vacation, to brief him on the Japanese peace treaty.[55]

Acheson called Dulles the next morning and said that Truman was pleased with "the whole thing." When Dulles asked whether Rusk had passed on his message, Acheson said Rusk told him that Dulles had spoken to Dewey and that Dulles would like to have something "corresponding to Ambassador-at-Large." Acheson, however, hesitated to bring this up with Truman, who had said explicitly that he did not want to make such an appointment. Furthermore, John Cooper had just been appointed Consultant, and it would create complications if Dulles' appointment were to differ from Cooper's. Dulles said that Senators Vandenberg and Smith and Governor Dewey all felt that "the Republican Party was selling out awfully cheap," and "if the word 'top' were inserted somewhere, that would take care of it." Acheson hesitated, but in the end said that Dulles could say that he, Jessup, and Cooper were all "top advisors." Dulles appeared to be satisfied: now, "nobody 'was above me'."[56]

Dulles called on Truman around noon, on 28 April. He said that in the past, his political strength had come from Dewey and Vandenberg; with Dewey's defeat in the election and Vandenberg's declining health, it seemed desirable for him to gain some political stature in his own right. Now he wanted to tell the President that his having a desk in State did not in any way ensure bipartisanship in foreign policy or protect State against Republican criticism. But if foreign policies he could whole-heartedly support were developed, he had confidence that they would receive sympathetic consideration by Republicans on the Hill and that few Republicans would attack them on partisan grounds. But he needed to be in a position where he could help work out policies that he could genuinely endorse. Truman expressed agreement. Dulles conveyed his impression that many Americans had lost confidence as a result of what had happened, particularly in the East. This created opportunities for men like McCarthy. "If we could really get going, the American people would fall in behind that leadership and attacks like McCarthy's would be forgotten." Truman again expressed agreement.[57] This finalized the deal between Dulles (and, to a larger extent, the Republican Party) and the Democratic administration on cooperation in foreign policy and especially in Far East policy, which had not enjoyed two-party endorsement.

There were more signs of the gradually maturing bipartisan approach. On 10 April, Dewey called Acheson from Albany to clear portions of a speech he was to deliver at Princeton. He referred in strong terms to "China being given away in Yalta," and said that refusal to heed dissenting opinions on China had been a cause of failure, and claimed that "the only flicker of hope for China and the Far East was in Formosa." Acheson did not object to the first two points, but was very unhappy about "the flicker of hope" statement. He said that the best hope for the Far East was to drive a wedge between Peking and Moscow and to reach agreement on a Japanese treaty, or at least a settlement. Dewey agreed to strike out "flicker of hope." He and Acheson decided that he would not mention the "wedge" either. Rather, Acheson suggested Dewey say something about "heartening bipartisan consultation on the Far East."[58] On the 27th, Truman made a statement concerning the formation of eight subcommittees in the Senate Foreign Relations Committee, to correspond with offices in the State Department; it was hoped that the House would follow suit, in this "true bipartisan approach." On the 28th, Acheson met with Senator Wiley concerning bipartisan foreign policy. UN Secretary-General Lie visited Truman on 20 April, prior to his trip to Moscow, and on 29 May upon his return. At the time of the first meeting, the Soviet representative was boycotting the Security Council over the question of China's seat. Lie urged termination of the Nationalists' membership to solve the problem. Acheson asked whether this would be enough. Would seating the Communists be necessary? Lie replied that the Soviets seemed to have changed their view and were not insisting upon seating the Communists—but he was not sure. Lie believed that Stalin was misinformed about American intentions and policies, and suggested that Truman meet with him. Truman said he had met him and was completely disillusioned with him, but would be willing to invite him to visit Washington. After visiting Moscow, Lie told Truman that Stalin thought "there were so many difficulties now existing between the East and West that a meeting of heads of state would not be profitable." Stalin thought that a meeting might be considered at some point in the future, but couldn't foresee when that might be. Stalin had informed Lie that acceptance of the Chinese Communists was indeed a condition for the Soviets' return to the Security Council. Truman was very unhappy; he told Lie that he did not regard it as necessary at this time to comment on future meetings of the Security Council, and that he "had the gravest difficulty in seeing how the relations of the United States and the Peking Government could be worked out in view of the total disregard by the Peking Government of international obligations and in view of its treatment of the United States Government and its representatives."[59]

THE BRITISH FACTOR

Decision-making in the US government was influenced by the fact that the US could not rely upon its major ally—Britain—to endorse its China Policy. Britain certainly did not want to drive China into Moscow's arms, but did have its own special considerations. Aside from its more sophisticated diplomatic philosophy and its traditional business interests in China, the UK was concerned about the future of Hong Kong. Prime Minister Attlee sent a note to the Cabinet on 5 May 1949 regarding the possible threat to Hong Kong. The Ministers observed that "the British community in Hong Kong felt great uncertainty about the Government's ultimate intentions in regard to the Colony," and felt that, since Hong Kong could not be held against attack from the mainland, the "Government must be careful to avoid drifting into a position in which, after pouring valuable resources into Hong Kong, they had at the end to withdraw with great material loss and loss of prestige."[60] On 26 May, it was said in a Cabinet meeting that:

In the long term, if a strong Communist Government established itself in control over the whole of China, it would be impossible for us to maintain Hong Kong as a trading center unless that Government acquiesced in our continuance there. These considerations seemed to suggest that the aim of our policy should be to find a basis on which a Communist Government of China could acquiesce in our remaining in Hong Kong."[61]

When the US was consulted as to whether it would support a British policy of "defending Hong Kong against aggression," Acheson raised questions covering the whole problem of long-term policy with respect to Hong Kong. Bevin proposed in the Cabinet meeting of 23 June that no reply, not even an interim reply, be sent to Acheson. He said that, from the responses to Britain's approaches made to the Commonwealth and the US, it now appeared that Britain would have to bear the main responsibility for devising effective means of safeguarding Hong Kong and should lose no time in formulating a policy for dealing with the situation. The Cabinet agreed with Bevin's view.[62] On 29 August, Bevin reported to the Cabinet that since the Nationalists were blockading the passage by sea to Shanghai, the British government was prepared to escort merchant vessels into Shanghai. But at the last moment, Foreign Office legal advisors reported that an international court might hold that the blockade was legal, making the British position difficult. Bevin proposed seeking the opinions of the Law Officers.[63] The British eventually did send warships to convoy merchant ships running the blockade. Truman was twice informed of this in October 1949, and was not pleased.[64]

But the most sensitive problem was recognition of the PRC. Truman "thought that the British had not played very squarely with us on this matter."[65] On 27 October 1949, Bevin presented a memorandum to the Cabinet discussing pros and cons of recognition; his conclusion was that, on political and practical grounds, the UK should recognize the new regime. It was clear from his talks with Acheson and Schuman in Washington that the US was not in favor of early recognition. According to Bevin, the attitude of the State Department was being influenced by attacks in Congress upon its China policy; the British should recognize that State would be influenced more by internal American politics than by the realities of the situation in China.[66] After long discussion, the Cabinet authorized Bevin to consult with the Commonwealth, the US, and the other western powers. The Cabinet hoped, in particular, to reach agreement with the US on the matter of recognition.[67] This approach was consistent with the global perspective of the Labor Government, which gave up the idea of forming an independent third force and believed that, "for the present at any rate, the closest association with the United States is essential." Nevertheless, it wanted to apply "a brake to American policy, if necessary."[68]

Bevin reported to the Cabinet on 15 December the results of the consultations and his recommendations. The US "felt strongly that as long as there was any opposition to the Communist regime it would be a stab in the back if recognition were to be accorded. They attached great importance to obtaining an assurance that the Communist Government is prepared to accept China's international obligations." Bevin added that, at a press conference on 7 December, Acheson had said that recognition of the new Chinese government in the immediate future—and even consideration of such recognition—would be premature. He did not exclude the possibility in the more distant future. Acheson subsequently told UK Ambassador Oliver Franks that there would be "a large-ish time gap between a decision on the date and the act of recognition" in order that public opinion in the United States might be properly prepared. He hoped that the UK would not seek concerted action by Commonwealth members, since he feared this would suggest that the US and the UK were going separate ways. The US would favor Commonwealth members' according recognition "at several intervals of time."[69] When the Cabinet meeting started, Bevin said that "the interests of the United Kingdom Government would be best served by according early recognition to the Communist Government of China....Although it was now clear that the United States Government would not follow this lead, he had good reason to believe that a large number of other friendly Governments would be willing to accord recognition in the near future."[70] In accord with the Cabinet's decision, the UK sent a message to the PRC on 6 January 1950, announcing recognition and willingness to set up diplomatic relations. The PRC replied on 9 January.

At this point, the US embassy in London believed that relations between the US and the UK had reached an all-time low. It reported in early January that "while our basic relationship rests on solid grounds, we must not at any time take it for granted....There have been several periods of tension between the US and UK since the war, with the present one being potentially the most serious of all in view of the numerous and complex problems between the two governments and the likelihood that they will remain a source of friction for some time."[71] The embassy reported on the 30th that there was uneasiness in the British Foreign Office "over failure of Chinese Communists to respond more cordially to British note according recognition of Chinese Communist regime," and also over the demarche asking for diplomatic relations going unanswered.[72] In fact, during the spring of 1950, the British did feel that recognition of the PRC had not evoked a satisfactory response from the PRC government. Four months after recognition, the PRC had still not agreed on an exchange of diplomatic representatives.

The PRC's attitude towards the UK remained unfriendly. Prospects for British commercial interests in China seemed to be deteriorating. The British did not, however, conclude that the policy of recognition was wrong. Bevin suggested to the Cabinet that the present policy be continued and that, in forthcoming discussions with Acheson, he seek to secure assurances that the US would not follow courses harmful to the common UK-US aim of preventing permanent alienation of China from the West. He would also try to persuade Acheson to modify the US attitude toward PRC representation in the UN Security Council. He would not, however, press Acheson to an extent that might antagonize the Americans. Bevins also believed that, unless the UK could find some means of putting pressure on the PRC, relations between the two countries were not likely to improve. The UK could say that if the PRC were to extinguish British commercial and financial interests in China, the UK would not support China in the UN and would not persuade the Americans to adopt a more friendly policy toward the PRC. The Cabinet approved Bevin's suggestions.[73]

Bevin reported to the Cabinet on 8 May that, in early discussions among the UK, the US and France in preparation for a meeting of their foreign ministers, there were as yet no indications that the US had been able to formulate any fresh policy toward China. The continuing uncertainty about American policy was undoubtedly embarrassing to a number of Commonwealth countries.[74] During his talks with Acheson on the 9th and 10th, Bevin emphasized the importance of preventing differences over China policy from developing into an open split, prejudicing cooperation elsewhere. He noted that the UK's position was not reversible.[75] Bevin reported to the Cabinet that "it became apparent from my talks with Mr. Acheson that the United States Administration, owing in part to pressure and attacks from the Republicans, have no positive—or indeed any—policy towards China at all."

THE SOONG EPISODE

There was one person who would not yield to fate at this juncture—Chiang Kai-shek. After his "withdrawal" in January 1949, he had remained in actual control of the KMT political and military apparatus. Sensing that the US was about to desert him, he once again appeared from behind the curtain, to resume the "presidency" on 1 March 1949. Li Tsung-jen was in the United States at the time, and was coolly received by Truman. On 8 March, the State Department reported to Truman that Chiang had arrested thirty-six generals who supported Li.[76] The US embassy's office in Taiwan reported that, after his resumption of the presidency, Chiang would continue to "divide and rule"—with the usual fatal results.[77] (In July, the State Department would discuss personal assets held in the US by Chiang and his close associates, placing those of the Soongs at $200 million and the total for all important Nationalists at $1.5 billion.[78])

On 16 March, Defense Secretary Louis Johnson told Sidney Souers, former NSC Secretary and now a special consultant to the President, that Congressman Boykin had some startling information. Johnson thought he himself had better stay out of this matter, so he arranged for Boykin to give the information to Souers. When Souers called Boykin the next day, the latter said that the informants were T.V. Soong and T.L. Soong, Chiang Kai-shek's brothers-in-law. The Soongs claimed to know what the Russians were doing at the time and were planning to do; Boykin wanted Souers to hear them tell their story in person. Souers agreed to meet them, not as special consultant, but in line with his previous work in intelligence and as a "friend at court."

Souers met with Boykin and the Soong brothers at the Washington Hotel on 21 March. The Soongs had no inside intelligence regarding the Russians; T.V. Soong said that he knew from reading the papers that Russia's purpose was to dominate all of Asia. But T.V. said he could gather information on the intention of the CCP, and felt that the only way to prevent the CCP from moving southward and westward would be through holding Taiwan and Hainan Islands. These islands could be held if the US gave modest economic and military assistance. He wanted $15 million a month, plus surplus planes, fuel, artillery, and wheat. In due time, the Nationalists would be able to land 250,000 troops on the mainland. When they did, warlords would join in—and much of China could be taken. Souers said he was in no position to help them. Boykin asked Souers privately if he could think of an attorney who could assist the Soongs, and the Nationalists, in saving Taiwan and Hainan. Souers replied that they had fired many lawyers in the past and he did not believe they needed any more—and that hiring additional lawyers would have no effect on the administration's policy.

Boykin called Souers on 28 March, attempting to make an appointment for the Soongs to confer with Souers and Webb. Souers himself refused, pointing out that Truman had already announced his China Policy, and said that Webb was busy and that Boykin might contact him at a later date.[79] This ended the Soongs' effort to change Truman's policy (i.e., "hands off Taiwan"). The Soong episode further confirmed that Truman's announcement on 5 January concerning China was not mere rhetoric.

Shortly after the Soong episode, Bevin analyzed the American situation in a paper for the Cabinet; this paper was discussed in preparation for his meetings with Acheson, starting on 24 April. Just before the UK announced recognition of the PRC, Republican elements in the US Congress had pressed for active assistance to Taiwan. At a most opportune moment, Acheson and Truman issued statements that helped greatly in minimizing any adverse effects the UK recognition might have had on American public opinion. Meanwhile, the Republicans had picked China as the weak link in the Truman administration's policy. In a mid-term election year, the Truman administration had to act with extreme caution, the net result being that there was in fact no US China policy beyond "waiting for the dust to settle." This passive line was itself subject to attack. Bevin listed indications of a hostile attitude on the part of the US government toward the PRC for political and emotional reasons, commenting on the statement, in the *China White Paper,* that the Communist regime served the interests not of the Chinese people but of the Soviet Union. Bevin then noted that the Sino-Soviet agreements of February 1950, "at any rate in their published texts, demonstrated complete equality between USSR and PRC.[80]

From Truman's statement and Acheson's speech, both in January 1950, until June of 1950, the NSC did not discuss anything of significance in regard to China. The question of Chinese representation in the Security Council was at a stalemate. The Soviet representative continued to boycott Council meetings. Then a war broke out in Korea.

10

The Blood-Tainted Peninsula

Before being occupied by the Japanese at the end of the 19th century, Korea had a long history as an independent state. When China and Korea were defeated in the Sino-Japanese War of 1894-95, Japan colonized Korea, forcing the Koreans to adopt Japanese names and to consider themselves subjects of the Japanese Emperor. The Koreans, however, never submitted to Japanese rule: there were successive revolts aimed at national liberation.

During WWII, Roosevelt and Stalin believed, for no apparent reason, that it would take decades after the war for the Koreans to be ready for independence. The Cairo Conference of 1943 declared that Korea would become independent "in due course," with no mention as to how long this would take. At Yalta in February 1945, the US, the USSR and the UK decided that Korea would be put under international trusteeship—in other words, that Korea could not have independence after the war. Right after Japan surrendered, Dean Rusk (then a major in the US Army), and another officer devised a plan to draw a demarcation line at the 38th parallel, separating the US and Soviet troops in Korea. This nearly duplicated the line separating the spheres of influence of Czarist Russia and Imperial Japan in the 19th century. The new line might have been designed as a temporary expedient, but it came to perpetuate the spheres of influence, now of the USSR and US. The Soviet Union began to support a government in the north and to help it build up its armed forces; the US did the same in the south—and went even further. A UN commission was set up in the south, to oversee elections in both parts of Korea. With a Soviet ban on the commission's work in the north, however, its activities were in fact limited to the south alone.

On 25 June 1950, armed conflict erupted between the northern and southern parts of Korea. This conflict evolved into the Korean War, which directly involved all major nations except the Soviet Union—the first war with extensive international participation since WWII. Who started it? This question remains unanswered, because many official documents relating to

187

the start of the conflict are still classified. The crux of the issue, though, is really not who "started" the Korean conflict, but rather who divided Korea and thus made the conflict possible. The ongoing debate on the start of the conflict, then, has not been to the point at all.

US ACTIONS IN THE INITIAL STAGE OF THE CONFLICT

On 27 June 1950, two days after the outbreak of the Korean conflict, President Truman ordered that American troops be sent to Korea. At the same time, he announced that the US 7th Fleet would patrol, and neutralize, the Taiwan Straits. Thus, the United States would not only directly fight in the civil war in Korea, but also interfere in the civil war in China. Truman's two decisions of 27 June have been subject to much debate. His decision to fight in Korea, however, seems a natural response. Regardless of who started the war, the US was bound to fight in defense of South Korea, and the prestige of the US was at stake. In fact, during the US Cabinet meeting of 8 July, it was reported that Europe had never had a greater lift than when it learned of the US decision to fight in Korea. Truman mentioned that, on the 7th the Lutheran Bishop of Berlin had told him 70 percent of the Russian attitude was bluff.[1]

Truman took the conflict in Korea very seriously. In the Cabinet meeting of 21 July, attended by all the members plus Harriman and Symington, Truman announced that those present would constitute a War Cabinet. When Vice-President Barkley pointed out that there might be a demand for Republican representation, Truman said this demand would be handled by having Republican advisors for Cabinet members.[2] Several days later, Truman said there would be no exemptions from service, except for key personnel whose removal would injure the operations of their departments; it was decided that a list of those so exempted would be sent to the Defense Department.[3] At the time, Truman also considered enlisting Germans to serve in the US Army or in British and French forces in Korea.[4]

The Truman administration was not entirely sure that the US forces could hold on. On 27 July, Paul Nitze reported that the Planning Staff had prepared a paper on US policy in the event UN forces were unable to remain on the Korean Peninsula. The staff agreed that this paper should be kept confidential, since word of it would have a negative effect throughout the world. It was agreed that Ambassador Muccio in South Korea would be advised to keep members of the South Korean government together if their evacuation became necessary. Kennan suggested that, rather than cabling this instruction, someone should be sent to Korea to brief Muccio on the thinking in Washington.[5]

At the time, the US government was very sensitive to the attitude of the Soviet Union. According to CIA Chief Hillenkoeter's report of 29 June, there was no evidence that the USSR was prepared to support the North Koreans and there appeared to be little Soviet military activity anywhere in the Far East.[6] Acheson mentioned in a Cabinet meeting on 14 July that troop movements by the US would not impress Russia; Russia would have been more impressed by a speed-up in US industrial production.[7] The State Department instructed the embassy in Moscow to use all possible sources for obtaining indications of Soviet reactions and intentions, and to report immediately the slightest change of tone or emphasis, pointing out that in 1939, the embassy had obtained an initial tip about the Soviet march into Poland from a propagandist speaking in Moscow's Park of Culture and Rest.[8] On 14 July, the embassy reported that the Soviet press did not give the impression that any threat to the USSR was imminent or suggest that the Soviet army would take offensive actions.[9] Ambassador Kirk reported from Moscow that neither the press nor official statements indicated Soviet reaction when the tide turned against the North Koreans, and that the USSR had been very careful to avoid investing its own prestige in the conflict. Kirk believed that when the critical phase came for the North Korean regime, the USSR would not commit its own forces—or any other forces at its disposal. Kirk advised, though, that the US should not take on any obligation to use troops north of the 38th parallel.[10] In an analysis of Soviet policies in August, Kirk observed that, although the Soviet Union was prepared to assume risks in pursuit of its objectives, it did not wish to engage in a global conflict in the near future.[11]

The intentions of the People's Republic of China caused the US even more concern than did those of the Soviets. On 13 July, the US ambassador in London reported the British Foreign Office's belief, on the little evidence available to them, that the PRC leadership was focusing its attention on Korea and the land approaches to it, and would delay an attack on Taiwan indefinitely. As early as 17 July, the British were looking for signs of an international brigade from the PRC, but found none.[12]

Bevin and Acheson exchanged several messages about the Korean situation during this period. The Commonwealth Relations Office briefed the British High Commissioners in Commonwealth countries on 19 July concerning the Bevin/Acheson exchange, saying that Taiwan was the focus. Bevin reportedly suggested to Acheson that, if the West were to seek reestablishment of the *status quo ante* in Korea, the questions of Taiwan and Chinese representation in the UN would almost certainly arise. Acheson replied that, in regard to Taiwan, there was a short-range military problem and a long-range political problem. Because the US could not allow forces cooperating with Moscow to seize Taiwan for use as an air and naval base against the US, the US had taken military measures to neutralize the Taiwan Straits. Acheson believed that the ultimate fate of Taiwan should be decided in the Japanese settlement or by the UN. He remarked that the US could not submit to Russian blackmail, on either Taiwan or on the Chinese seat in the UN, and that the US did not have a closed mind regarding the Chinese seat. Bevin replied that the PRC had communicated its intention of "liberating Taiwan" to the Security Council and that this might lead to hostilities with the US, leading the Soviet Union to accuse the US of aggression. Bevin hoped Truman would say something to remove whatever misapprehensions the Russians were encouraging and to make it clear that the matter would be settled on its own merits. Bevin said that, since neither the UK nor the US wanted to see China irrevocably alienated, the present situation must be handled carefully so as to avoid pushing China further in the direction of the Soviet Union.[13]

Harriman suggested on 4 August that the time had come to publicly link the PRC with the Korean conflict, but this suggestion was not received very enthusiastically in the State Department's daily meeting. Kennan had apprehensions about this link and warned that the US should proceed with care. Matthews said he would pursue the matter with Rusk.[14] On 17 August, the US threatened the PRC: the State Department instructed the ambassador to India to inform the Indian government that the US was anxious to avoid any extension of the conflict, but that the decision as to whether hostilities in Korea were to be localized or to spread southward rested with the Chinese Communists, who were presumably under pressure from Moscow. Should the Chinese enlarge the scope of hostilities, the US would have no alternative but to retaliate. Should the Chinese act as a "cat's paw" for extending military aggression, this would bring destruction to China's transportation system and industrial facilities, setting back the country's progress toward modernization. The State Department felt there was a strong possibility the Chinese Communists might attack Taiwan during August, regardless of the progress of the Korean campaign.[15]

MacArthur went to Taiwan in August 1950. After his visit, Chiang Kai-shek made a statement concerning US-Nationalist "military cooperation" and "the joint defense of Formosa." Canadian Foreign Minister Pearson noted to Acheson that MacArthur was a UN—as well as US—Commander. Pearson sent Bevin a copy of his letter to Acheson and expressed his concern that the US had decided to assume responsibility for defending Taiwan. He was afraid that the UN might be asked to sanction an act for which there was no general support, and that the Korea and China questions might become confused.[16]

MacArthur's views and actions conformed to what he had expressed to British officials Joseph Gascoigne and Alexander Grantham in October 1949. He said then that the PRC could be "choked out of existence" by an Anglo-American economic blockade. Since China would not get much material supply from the USSR, it would have to trade with the US and the UK. In his opinion, the Pacific was an "Anglo-Saxon lake" where the two countries could do as they liked. As for Taiwan, MacArthur believed that the island was under trusteeship pending decisions to be made at the Japanese treaty conference, and that the West should never give Taiwan to the Communists. He still felt the US government had been wrong from the word "go" in handling the Chinese situation—the Communists would have been defeated long ago if the US had dealt with them with a firm hand from the start. MacArthur told the British officials that his suggestion would not come to fruition.[17]

The British government clearly did not want to link the Korean War with Taiwan. The Labor Government's position was that, as of 1950, Taiwan was still *de jure* a part of the Japanese Empire as it had been at the time of Cairo Conference in 1943, and not a part of China. But Labor was afraid that a confrontation in Taiwan between the US and China might lead to war and jeopardize British interests in Asia.[18] At its meeting of 4 July, the British Cabinet maintained that recent US actions in the Pacific had increased the potential threat to Hong Kong, and that this was not the time for the UK to make a gesture, like imposing control of strategic exports, alienating the PRC.[19] In reply to a Labor M.P., Attlee said in August that "we are well aware of the dangerous possibilities [and] have made it quite clear that our action in Korea is in accordance with the Security Council resolution and is not concerned with Formosa."[20]

Why Truman wanted to get involved in the Taiwan issue is a perplexing question. After the outbreak of civil war in Korea, the US government, contrary to its own announcement several months earlier, considered the fighting between Nationalists and Communists in China not a civil war but a "military aggression" on the part of the Communists. To this day, no convincing explanation based on international law has been given to support this position. It is also strange that, at one moment the US was waiting for the PRC to take over Taiwan, and at the next it was denouncing the PRC's right to do so simply because a civil war had broken out in Korea. As to the mission of the 7th Fleet, the US said it had neutralized the Straits, thus making it impossible for either the Nationalists or the Communists to launch an attack. Acheson stated during the NSC meeting of 27 July 1950 that "if it were not for the 7th Fleet, no amount of military assistance and supplies could possibly result in the holding of [Taiwan]."[21] This statement shows that the Truman administration had changed its strategy, from withdrawing from Taiwan and South Korea to continuing to hold them. Clearly, the progress of the Korean War had by then greatly changed US estimates of the international situation. The US now believed that the Communists were working concertedly against it in Asia and, therefore, retreated from its strategy of driving a wedge between China and the Soviet Union to its previous strategy of treating both of them as enemies. Alienating the Chinese would prove to be one of the great mistakes of American Cold War foreign policy.

Was the Chinese government preparing to attack Taiwan? The answer is no. China realized in 1949 that, without naval and air support, it was not possible to take Taiwan, and decided to postpone liberating Taiwan until preparation of a Navy and Air Force was completed. Then, after the outbreak of the Korean War, China decided to shift the focus of its military deployments to the north. A resolution was passed on 11 August 1950 that Chinese forces would not attack Taiwan during 1951. US intelligence reports at the time indicated that Chinese troops were in fact moved northward rather than southward.[22] These reports, however, might have not attracted the attention of US decision-makers.

The Truman administration not only judged Chinese intentions incorrectly, it also failed to understand the mentality of the Chinese leaders. During the civil war, CCP leaders were always alert for possible American military intervention. That is why there were two field armies deployed along the coast when the PLA crossed the Yangtze. Then, as in 1950, any military move aimed at China would provoke Chinese antagonism without gaining China's submission.

It seems, however, that the measures China was taking were not widely known to the outside world. The General Secretary of the Indian Foreign Ministry informed the US ambassador on 24 August that India's ambassador in Beijing believed the PRC had no immediate intention of attacking Taiwan. According to the same source, the Chinese were convinced that the US was supporting Chiang in order to provide a "legal cover for future aggression against the mainland." The ambassador said the PRC might be persuaded not to press the Taiwan issue if assurances could be obtained that the US would withdraw protection for the Nationalists after the Korean situation had eased; or the UN would accept the PRC government as the sole representative of China; or the UK, India, and the other powers that recognized the PRC would use their influence to prevent the Americans from using Chiang as a cover for aggression against the mainland, and from keeping the Nationalists permanently under their protection. The ambassador believed that the USSR was trying to persuade the CCP to attack Taiwan, but the Chinese were holding back. The Indian government suggested that the US give assurance that it would withdraw protection from Chiang after the Korean situation eased.[23]

The State Department conveyed to the President on 30 August information obtained from the British Foreign Office. Nehru had reportedly directed his ambassador to impress upon the Chinese that India, while not unsympathetic to the PRC's claim to Taiwan, would strongly deprecate any effort by the PRC to use force in achieving its ends. The Indian ambassador then told the Chinese that such action would further aggravate the international situation and would prejudice the PRC's position before the UN, and that the PRC's attitude toward Taiwan would be regarded by India as a test case.[24] Though the PRC would never recognize any foreign interference concerning the Taiwan question, it could be expected that Chinese leaders would act very discreetly in the face of hard realities. It might be possible for the US to keep the PRC from direct involvement in Korea if the two countries could reach a compromise on Taiwan.

The State Department told the President on 5 September that the US ambassador in New Delhi had told the Indian Foreign Minister the US was not irrevocably committed to supporting or opposing any particular political group in China. The primary concern of the US was that other nations act in accord with the UN Charter, and the attitude of the US toward the PRC resulted not from any prejudice but rather from the CCP's hostility toward the US and from the support they were rendering to "forces of aggression in Korea."[25] Unfortunately, at the time the US was preparing for the landing at Inchon, and nothing concrete was being done on the Taiwan question; therefore, the seemingly conciliatory attitude of the Truman administration could only be interpreted as a tactical move.

In mid-August, the State Department informed the US ambassadors in London and Paris of growing public and Congressional concern that the allies were allowing the US to bear the brunt of the fighting in Korea.[26] America's allies in Western Europe were greatly concerned about the increasing tension between the US and China, which might expand the conflict into a general war. Boon, Secretary-General of the Dutch Foreign Office, informed the US ambassador of this concern, and said that "political thinking" in Western Europe held that no time should be lost in admitting the PRC to the UN. Boon also believed that though the US said it would not oppose a majority vote in the UN, there might be "pressure behind the scenes" to block admission of the PRC.[27]

In early September 1950, the State Department advised Warren Austin, US representative to the UN, that it was in the American interest to air charges in the Security Council in the case of Taiwan. The PRC was to be given a hearing before the Council took action on the question.[28] Eventually, the Security Council did decide to invite the PRC to speak during its debates, and a Chinese delegation headed by General Wu Xiuquan, then a senior official in the Foreign Ministry, participated in the debate at Lake Success in November 1950. The PRC delegation condemned the US for aggression in Taiwan and the Straits, and for other acts of aggression against the PRC. General Wu believed that the US did not manipulate the UN vote so as to foreclose Chinese participation in the debate, because it wanted an opportunity for dialogue with the PRC. In his memoirs, Wu said "the US wanted very much to have some kind of diplomatic contact, in order to know what was in our minds and at the same time try to prevent us from standing completely on the Soviet side vis-a-vis the US."[29]

The foreign ministers of the US, the UK and France met in September 1950. At this meeting, Acheson outlined the US position on the question of Chinese representation in the UN. Bevin then suggested that support for Chiang risked alienating the Asian peoples and provided China with no alternative but "domination by the Soviets." The State Department reported to the president on the 15th that Bevin did not make a commitment to oppose seating the PRC and that the three ministers agreed that, if the proposal to seat the PRC proved unsuccessful, they would support an examination of the criteria for seating rival claimants on the understanding that the PRC's claim would be considered on its merits. The ministers also agreed to support the US proposal that a commission be established to investigate charges of aggression against Taiwan, and that the western powers would oppose appearance of the PRC before the Security Council.[30]

Pretty much as the Chinese had forecast, US troops under General MacArthur landed at Inchon on 15 September. The US government subsequently requested that India express to the PRC that it was of the utmost importance that the PRC avoid any intervention in the Korean hostilities. The US wished India to present this as its own view or as one it supported. India fully agreed to this approach and instructed its ambassador in Beijing to present the view as that of the Indian government.[31]

Long before the Inchon landing the Truman administration had discussed the possibility of crossing the 38th parallel. In the NSC meeting of 8 September 1950, it was noted that "the north across the 38th parallel plan" was based upon an assumption of noninterference by major forces from the Soviet Union and China.[32] The State Department reported to the President on the 21st that, in conversations with Zhou Enlai, Panniker was told repeatedly of the peaceful intentions of the PRC government, and that "even in respect of Formosa they have preferred to follow a peaceful line." Pannikar believed that the PRC's interest in Korea had slackened and that their direct participation in the fighting seemed beyond the range of possibility—unless a world war started after UN forces went beyond the 38th parallel and the Soviets decided to intervene. He added that the PRC was not taking even "elementary precautions against air raids in the major cities." He believed that the turn of events in Korea had helped to bring home to the Chinese the weakness of Soviet policy and that they would likely follow their own line even while publicly "leaning toward the Soviets." He emphasized the considerable influence exercised by the non-Communist leaders in China who were by no means figureheads, saying that their positions had been strengthened "by the nature of the Korean invasion," and concluding that China was not a Soviet satellite.[33]

The British ambassador in Moscow reported that the USSR might regard the occupation of North Korea by UN forces as cause for war. He believed the Soviet leaders were anticipating that UN forces would occupy North Korea and considering ways to forestall such an occupation or, failing this, neutralize the danger posed by occupation. He felt the Soviets would be hesitant to put forward detailed proposals on either count, that the main Soviet effort would be in the propaganda field, and that they might distract attention by staging a diversion elsewhere (in, e.g., Berlin or Indochina). He concluded that the USSR would not fight a total war to restore its prestige and eliminate a threat to its security. The ambassador's report was made known to Truman on 26 September.[34]

This was days before US troops crossed the 38th parallel and the PRC decided to send troops to Korea. The US assessed Chinese intentions incorrectly, while correctly assessing Soviet attitudes. Both of the US assessments made the US more optimistic in the heady days after the victory at Inchon. As the military situation rapidly turned favorable to the US, Truman reversed his position opposing crossing of the 38th parallel. Bevin remarked on 11 September that events of the past few days had jeopardized Britain's objective of localizing the Korean War. Attlee believed "it is possible that the Chinese Government may consider the crossing of the parallel as provocative or even as a challenge to Chinese security."[35]

As early as 21 August 1950, Kennan had advised Acheson that the US should have as a policy objective terminating involvement on the Asian mainland as rapidly as possible and on the best terms possible; in Kennan's words, "it was not essential to us to see an anti-Soviet Korean regime extend to all of Korea for all time [and] it is beyond our capabilities to keep Korea permanently out of the Soviet orbit."[36] Apparently the Truman administration did not take Kennan's advice—particularly after the Inchon landing.

The State Department's brief to the President on 29 September was cast in an unusually relaxed tone.[37] The Truman administration seems to have convinced itself that the war in Korea would end soon after the UN enforced its police action throughout the North. But then on 3 October, State conveyed to the President information obtained from the British. Zhou Enlai had reportedly told Pannikar that China would send troops to defend Korea if UN forces crossed the 38th parallel, but that China would not take such action if South Korean forces alone crossed the parallel. At the same time, according to Dutch Foreign Minister Stikker's report to the American embassy, an "absolutely authentic source" reported that the PRC was preparing a major military move. Stikker indicated that he had information about increased quinine stockpiling, which "means war in the Far East."[38]

Outwardly, the Truman administration regarded Zhou Enlai's warning with disdain. The next day, the State Department instructed the US ambassador to India to point out to the Indian government that "such a Communist demarche lacks legal and moral justification and threatens overt defiance to the will of the United Nations." The Dutch Foreign Office informed the US embassy of the view of the Dutch Charge in Beijing—that the PRC did not want war but might take precipitate action "in a moment of panic" if US forces crossed the 38th and penetrated deeply into North Korea. The Dutch Charge believed that there was "some bluff" in the PRC's attitude, although they did have very bitter feelings toward the US. He said that when Zhou was told that China's industrial potential would be completely destroyed in a war against the US, he replied that China would have no choice but to defend itself against "further aggression."[39]

Roger Makins of the British Foreign Office reported to Attlee on 3 October that MacArthur, who discounted the Chinese position as bluff, planned to move troops into North Korea as far as a line through Pyongyang about 10 October. Makins observed that the Chinese had 400,000 troops in Manchuria, and at least 100,000 of these could move into North Korea at fairly short notice, "if indeed they have not done so."[40]

High up in the US military establishment, preparations for possible Chinese intervention were underway. Deputy Defense Secretary Lovett forwarded a draft directive to MacArthur for Presidential approval on 7 October; Lovett said previous documents did not specify what action MacArthur should take if the Chinese intervened in Korea without prior announcement. The JCS believed such intervention possible, in light of current conditions in Korea, and therefore had recommended, with the concurrence of the Secretaries of State and Defense, that the directive be approved and sent to MacArthur. The directive stated:

> Hereafter in the event of the open or covert employment anywhere in Korea of major Chinese Communist units, without

prior announcement, you should continue the action as long as, in your judgement, action by forces under your control offers a reasonable chance of success. In any case you will obtain authorization from Washington prior to taking any military action against objectives in Chinese territory.

Truman approved this directive on the 8th, the day that Mao Zedong ordered Chinese troops into Korea.[41]

The State Department, meanwhile, had instructed the ambassador to India to inform the Indian government that the question was not whether the PRC intended to intervene in the Korean conflict, but rather the degree of that intervention. The State Department believed that the PRC statement of intent was an attempt to dissuade India and other UN members from taking firm action at this critical point, and that giving the North Koreans a chance to regroup north of the 38th parallel would result in increased defiance of the UN and make the unification of Korea more difficult.[42]

The Truman administration decided to cross the parallel despite China's warnings, still hoping to block Chinese military intervention at the last moment through a direct approach to the PRC. The State Department instructed Ambassador Henderson in India to try to meet the PRC's ambassador and to make clear that: (1) the US desired no hostilities between the UN and PRC, as this would be a tragedy for the world and especially for the Chinese; (2) the UN operation constituted no threat to Korea's neighbors; (3) the US had no desire for establishment of bases or for any other special position in Korea; and (4) the US was prepared to accept a neutral investigation and assessment of damages (in response to Communist charges of bombing incidents).[43] China, of course, would not buy the American gesture at this late stage.

CHINA ENTERS THE WAR

China fully realized the critical situation facing her. On 7 July 1950, the day the UN Security Council resolved to set up a UN Force Headquarters in Korea, China decided to establish a Northeastern (Manchurian) Border Force. On 13 July, the 13th Army Corps became the basis of the Border Force, with Deng Hua as commanding general and political commissar. The Force had four armies and three artillery divisions under its command, with a total strength of 255,000 troops.[44] The Northeastern Border Force received instructions on 5 August that it should be ready to fight by the first week of September.

On 15 August, China's General Staff and Foreign Ministry began to meet to discuss the Korean situation, in the belief that the US would soon wage a counter-offensive. The operations room of the General Staff staged a model manoeuvre, the results of which showed US troops landing in one of the six ports to the rear of the North Korean troops. The most probable site was Inchon. The General Staff briefed Mao and Zhou on 23 August; on the same day, General MacArthur selected Inchon as his landing site.[45] On the 31st, the Chinese Border Forces forecast that after the US troops landed, they would either advance northward or turn toward the south to sandwich the North Korean troops in South Korea.[46]

After MacArthur's troops had landed successfully in Inchon, Kim Il-sung was very much concerned about the future course of the war. He sent the North Korean internal minister to Andong (Dandong) to see the commanders of the Chinese Border Forces. On behalf of the North Korean government, his internal minister requested that China send troops to fight in Korea.[47] On 1 October, the North Korean foreign minister brought Mao a letter from Kim and requested Chinese troops. During the small hours of that night in Pyongyang, Kim summoned Chinese Ambassador Ni Ziliang and Political Counsellor Chai Chenwen, requesting that China send troops as soon as possible.[48]

The top leaders of the CCP immediately began to discuss extending assistance to North Korea. The scale of these discussions expanded as members of Politburo and other senior officials were brought in. Mao stressed during the 2 October session that sending troops to Korea was necessary "because if the whole of Korea were occupied by the US, the Korean revolutionary forces would suffer fundamental failure, the American aggressors would be more reckless than ever, and it would be to the disadvantage of the entire Orient."[49] Other views aired at the meeting have never been officially disclosed. According to Peng Dehuai, though, on the 4th Mao asked the participants to list reasons for not sending troops. Mao then concluded that "your points are all reasonable. But now their country is in a critical moment. Whatever reasons we may have, if we only stand by and watch, we will feel sorrow in our hearts." Peng spoke the next day in full support of Mao's view.[50] Zhou Enlai said later that "there are over 1,000 *li* to defend along the Yalu.[51] How many troops will be needed! And who knows when they will attack us!"[52] The leadership ultimately resolved to organize a Chinese People's Volunteer Army (CPVA), with Lin Piao as commander-in-chief. Lin was familiar with the Manchurian area, and most of the troops were from the Fourth Field Army, which he commanded. But Lin said he was sick, so Peng Dehuai, commander of the First Field Army, was commissioned as commander-in-chief instead.

In an attempt to avoid armed conflict between China and the United States, Zhou Enlai summoned Indian Ambassador Pannikar; the two met at 1:00 a.m. on 3 October. Zhou told Pannikar that China had maintained that the Korean issue should be localized, and still believed this to be so. The US government was not trustworthy: though the meeting of foreign ministers had agreed that, without consent of the UN, the 38th parallel was not to be crossed, the US government had reneged on this commitment. Zhou asked Pannikar to forward to the governments of the US and the UK, through Prime Minister Nehru, a message expressing China's desire that the Korean question be settled by peaceful means. Zhou also emphasized that if troops other than South Koreans crossed the 38th parallel, China would not sit idly by. The Chinese preference for peaceful means was not reciprocated by the US.

The US wanted to prevent China from intervening when its troops advanced northward. The Indian ambassador told Chinese Vice Foreign Minister Zhang Hanfu that a message had reached Nehru from Bevin. Bevin reportedly said he had been informed by Acheson that the US regretted the intrusion of American planes into northeastern China, and the damage they had caused. The US had repeatedly indicated that it would like to have neutral countries investigate and evaluate this damage. Zhang noted that American planes had intruded repeatedly, and that the PRC had already presented the case to the Security Council and demanded that representatives of the PRC participate in the Council's discussions.

On October 7, the UN General Assembly passed a resolution calling for unification of Korea. The next day, Mao Zedong ordered the CPVA "to proceed rapidly to Korean territory."[53] On the 10th, Peng Dehuai told the generals of the CPVA that at the moment there were still two different views. Adherents of the first view held that troops should not be sent to Korea—at least not at the moment. The trauma of China's own civil war was yet to be healed, land reform had yet to be completed, remnant bandits and secret agents had to be thoroughly liquidated, the equipment and training of the troops were insufficient, and a part of the population was tired of war. Adherents of the second view believed that, although the Chinese troops might not be well prepared, neither were those of the enemies—particularly those of the United States.[54]

What role did the Soviet Union play in China's decision to send troops into Korea? First, there is no evidence that the Soviet Union pushed China into the war. Stalin's blind optimism of the early days of the war dissolved; he had not expected that the US would send combat troops. He later told Zhou Enlai that, "if China had not gotten involved, Comrade Kim Il Sung would have come to Northeast China to set up an exile government."[55]

Before China decided to send troops into Korea, Stalin promised that the Soviet Air Force would control the Korean skies so the Chinese would only have to worry about the fighting on the ground. After having learned of China's decision, the Soviets informed China that their Air Force was not yet prepared to fight in Korea and, therefore, would not be able to assist Chinese ground troops. Mao believed the real reason behind the Soviets' message to be Stalin's desire to avoid any risk and his preference that China fight the United States alone, and that the advance of the Chinese troops should now be postponed. The Chinese Politburo decided to send Zhou Enlai to Moscow to negotiate. Stalin was astonished when Zhou told him that movement of the Chinese troops had been delayed, but remained firm in not sending Soviet planes. Zhou reported by telegram, and on 13 October the Chinese Politburo reviewed the Korean situation. Despite the fact that Soviet planes would not enter combat, the Politburo agreed unanimously that troops should still be sent, since they believed that the CPVA could easily handle the South Koreans and that, if several divisions of South Koreans could be annihilated, the situation for China and North Korea would be greatly improved. On the other hand, if the CPVA did not fight in Korea, the enemy might come right up to the bank of Yalu, leaving domestic and foreign reactionaries in a position of great advantage. Northeastern China would bear the brunt of the incursion and the entire Border Forces would be pinioned; in addition, the supply of electricity to southern Manchuria would be under enemy control.[56]

Mao sent Zhou, still in Moscow, a telegram informing him of the Politburo's decision to send troops into Korea. Zhou then informed Stalin. He saw tears come to Stalin's eyes as the old man murmured: "Chinese comrades are good,...Chinese comrades are good."[57]

While the troops of the US and its allies were advancing northward from the 38th parallel, the Soviets did not react and even sent signals to the US indicating that they would not do so. On 20 October, the State Department briefed the President that, in the view of the embassy in Moscow, the failure of the USSR to intervene openly in Korea, the mild tone of the Soviet note about the strafing of an airfield in the USSR, and Soviet attempts to seem "cooperative" in the UN were not indications of a basic change of Soviet policy, but might be the early fruit of the American policy of containment.[58]

TURNING THE TIDE: INITIAL ENCOUNTERS

At this point, General MacArthur was still confident that the North Koreans would soon capitulate. He stated on 9 October that if the Korean People's Army (KPA) did not cease resistance, the UN troops would immediately launch an offensive and take measures to forcibly carry out the UN resolution. Readers in the West are no doubt familiar with the US version of events after MacArthur's statement. But what were China's decisions concerning the prosecution of the war, and how were they made?

Commander Peng Dehuai of the CPVA reported to Mao on 10 October his intentions to send in two armies and two artillery divisions. For fear that the bridge on the Yalu would be destroyed, CPVA troops would concentrate south of the river. Mao gave Peng his approval to carry out this plan.[59] MacArthur's headquarters stated on the 14th that recent CCP announcements that the Chinese would come into North Korea were nothing but diplomatic bluffing. On the 19th, Peng Dehuai crossed the Yalu with a small staff to meet Kim Il-sung, who was retreating northward from Pyongyang. At twilight on the same day, the bulk of the CPVA troops walked across the frozen river. Mao instructed that the advance should proceed in extreme secrecy and that reconnaissance teams should wear the uniforms of North Korean forces.

Peng Dehuai met with Kim Il-Sung again on the morning of the 20th. Peng told Kim that the PRC had decided to send a total of 39 divisions, the first group to include 12 infantry divisions and 3 artillery divisions, or approximately 260,000 men. The second and the third groups were just being massed at that time. The CPVA would first build defenses, and would not attack until the enemy launched its own offensive. Peng explained that it was not easy for China to decide to enter the war, since China itself had just been liberated and the new regime still had serious difficulties of its own. Peng described three possible outcomes of China's entry into the war. First, the CPVA might annihilate the enemy and secure peace for Korea. Second, they might stand firm against the enemy, but remain locked in stalemate. Third, they might never gain a foothold and be forced to return home. Kim admitted that, at the moment, the North Korean Command had no more than three divisions on hand—two infantry divisions and one tank division—plus one workers' regiment and a tank regiment. Troops trapped in the South were in the process of pulling out.[60]

China decided in late October to send another army (of three divisions) to Korea, bringing the total to 18 divisions. Stalin had expected China to send only 6 divisions; Peng later remarked that if China had sent the number of troops Stalin expected, the Chinese could not have won their first battle.[61]

Before China's entry into Korea, Mao had thought it possible to first train and equip the troops and then start offensive actions six months later. But no sooner had the Volunteers arrived than the situation changed dramatically. On their second day in Korea, the CPVA found that UN troops were moving at a very rapid pace, and that they could not overtake them. Mao instructed on 21 October that "the question now is to grasp the opportunity to fight, completing the campaign deployment in a few days so as to start fighting after that. It is not a question of first having a period for arranging defenses, then discussing attack."[62] Peng Dehuai felt that it would be difficult for the KPA to keep up with the UN troops and that the latter would continue to march northward until they encountered the Chinese. Peng said it was highly probable that the CPVA could wipe out the UN troops by a warfare of movement.[63]

On the 25th, the CPVA fought its first battle. Troops of the South Korean Sixth Division met the CPVA's 40th Army 118th Division (40A 118D). One battalion and one battery of the South Korean troops were routed.[64]

The lack of information on the part of the US in the days leading up to the first battle is astonishing. On 15 October, President Truman and General MacArthur met on Wake Island. MacArthur assured Truman that China would come to fight in Korea—one week after Mao had ordered that the CPVA be sent in. (Marshall and Acheson were not informed prior to the President's deciding to make this trip.[65] Truman would later tell Acheson that, before the meeting, he knew there was a possibility that things could go wrong.[66]) After this meeting, Syngman Rhee made several demands to US Ambassador Muccio concerning assumption of power north of the 38th parallel. He suggested that China's warnings had meant nothing at all.[67] On the 23rd, the State Department reported to Truman that the Indian government was embarrassed because its recent warnings about Chinese intentions in Korea had proven groundless. In conversations with the British ambassador, the Indian Foreign Ministry's General Secretary expressed great indignation that the PRC should have completely misled the Indian government concerning their intentions in the matter of the 38th parallel, and that India was placed in the position of a cat's paw for the Soviet-Chinese maneuver.[68]

The CPVA posted more victories. On 1 November, the CPVA 39A wiped out most of the US First Cavalry Eighth Regiment (8R) and the South Korean 15R. CPVA Headquarters formulated an ambitious plan to ensnare the US 24D, but did not achieve this result because part of the CPVA 66A arrived too late.[69] Peng reported on 4 November that "if the enemy moves forward again, we plan to let them come in deeper and annihilate them later on," and Mao approved.[70] To lure in the UN troops, the Volunteers released 100 US POWs, having told them that, because of a food shortage, the CPVA was retreating to China.[71] On 15 November, Kim Il-Sung and Soviet Ambassador Stikov came to the headquarters of the CPVA to meet with Peng Dehuai. Gao Gang, Chief of the CCP's Northeastern Bureau, was also present. The four discussed the problems of fighting to the enemy's rear, unifying command of the KPA and the CPVA, and policy toward POWs.[72]

As of 6 November, the Truman administration still could not ascertain the extent of the Chinese military intervention. The President was informed that, while there was not sufficient information to permit a satisfactory assessment of the situation, there was no doubt that the Chinese military intervention was substantial and there was no reason to suppose that it would not increase. The US wanted a special meeting of the Security Council, not to extend the fighting into China by proving aggression, but rather to localize the conflict.[73] It was suggested that the Yalu River bridge in Antung should be bombed. The State Department was against this, but Truman said he "would approve the action if it was necessary because of a serious and immediate threat to the security of our troops."[74]

As of the 14th, the situation still remained in doubt. The State Department instructed Austin, Ambassador to the UN, that the US must play its hand in the UN with some care, since there was no reliable and accurate picture of the PRC's ultimate objectives and the military situation in Korea was not clear. The US objectives at the UN were: to localize the Korean conflict, so as to bring about the withdrawal of Chinese forces and prevent a world war or a war between the PRC and the UN forces; to obtain maximum international support for action, as the situation worsened; and to bring about a final settlement of the Korean question along the lines of the UN's resolution of 7 October. State believed that the overall national interest of the US did not permit branding the PRC as the aggressor. State instructed certain US ambassadors to discuss with the countries where they were stationed, the problem confronting US forces in Korea as a result of Manchuria's being used as an enemy sanctuary, and the fact that it might be necessary to permit UN aircraft to pursue enemy aircraft for two or three minutes flying time into Manchuria. The US ambassador to Holland reported that Foreign Minister Stikker expressed great concern over the possible consequences of US aircraft operating near the Manchurian border and inquired whether the decision to do so was made by the US or the UN. A high French Foreign Office official seemed to regard it as a decision made by the Commander-in-Chief—that is, by MacArthur.[75]

THE BRITISH, THE BOMB, AND THE KMT

By late 1950, Britain was very apprehensive. Bevin expressed his "personal view" to US Ambassador Douglas, saying that the Chinese were so deeply involved that they would not now settle for less than a considerable voice in the solving the Korean situation. He also expressed concern that Korea might tie up resources of the western powers and thereby undermine the defense program in Europe. On 23 November, Indian Ambassador Pannikar told Chinese Vice Foreign Minister Zhang Hanfu that Bevin's attitude had changed. Bevin had remarked that the UK recognized China's interest in Korea, and suggested that, after the Chinese delegation arrived at Lake Success, the British delegate should discuss the Korean question with them. Pannikar said the Indian Government believed that these two remarks were the beginnings of consultation. When Zhang asked exactly what the view of the Indian Government was, Pannikar replied that the Security Council could not discuss the Korean question without PRC participation.[76] Meanwhile, Yugoslavia's UN delegate, Bebler, stated to an American diplomat that the PRC action was an "infantile disease." Bebler was convinced the Chinese felt that the UN forces constituted a genuine threat to Manchuria and, in particular, to hydroelectric works along the Manchurian border. He believed that the Soviet Union was cultivating this feeling.[77]

The State Department informed Truman on 22 November of its instructions to the US Charge in London. Bevin was to be told in the strongest terms that it would be most harmful for the UK's representative to the UN, Gladwyn Jebb, to propose a demilitarized zone in northern Korea in the immediate future; with an offensive about to start, it would be most confusing to MacArthur and his forces. Furthermore, the proposal, if presented before the Chinese delegation arrived, would constitute a commitment that the Chinese could regard simply as a starting point in bargaining for something more. And, until the results of the forthcoming offensive in Korea were known, it was impossible to ascertain what course could and should be safely adopted.[78] At the time, the Truman administration was betting on MacArthur's offensive and would not allow a demilitarized zone to hamper his operations. This stance would cost the US a bargaining opportunity.

The British government did agree not to present its proposal before the PRC delegation arrived at the UN, and it was also understood that the six-power resolution would not be voted upon before that time.[79] Bevin explained that there had been some misunderstanding regarding his attitude, and he had "no desire to upset the applecart." He sent a strictly confidential message through the UK's ambassador in Washington to the effect that Commons was concerned over the possibility of MacArthur's committing the UN forces in Korea (of which UK troops were a part) to large-scale hostilities with the PRC. It was important to assure Commons that MacArthur's objectives were no more and no less than those of the UN, that proper consultation was taking place on MacArthur's instructions, and that MacArthur was in fact an agent of the UN. Bevin demanded that those member states of the Security Council who were providing forces in Korea be consulted confidentially on any contemplated action beyond the troops' mandate and that the US should not issue instructions to MacArthur to proceed with such action unless those states expressed agreement.[80]

Meanwhile, on 24 November, MacArthur ordered his troops to launch an all-out offensive to end the Korean War, which he believed could be completed before Christmas. The general, victimized by his own miscalculation and blind confidence, left a gap between his two northward forces. Prior to MacArthur's offensive, Peng Dehuai found that this gap (between the western and the eastern groups of UN troops) had widened, leaving the western group more isolated. Peng also found that the weak points in the enemy's western group were the South Korean 7th and 8th Divisions. On 22 November, he ordered the CPVA 38A and 42A to wipe out these two divisions. MacArthur was completely unaware of the Chinese plan.[81] The Volunteers, under the direction of General Han Xiancu, Deputy Commander of the CPVA, wedged into the gap and encircled the two divisions. When the battle ended on 8 December, the CPVA and the KPA had annihilated approximately 36,000 UN troops. The entire US and South Korean front collapsed, and their forces retreated southward.

On the 28th, MacArthur reported to the UN that Chinese forces with an aggregate strength of over 200,000 men were arrayed against the UN forces in Korea. MacArthur, dumbfounded, said that this situation posed issues beyond his command and called for a political solution.[82] This was perhaps the only moment in the general's life other than Coregidor when he felt unable to handle a situation militarily.

On 30 November 1950, Truman made a statement concerning the Korean War—a statement interpreted in some quarters as hinting at the possibility of using atomic bombs. The State Department's original draft made no such implication. The White House staff, however, revised it. On an outline of the redraft, George Elsey wrote the three letters "A.E.C.," which stood for "Atomic Energy Commission." These three letters figured into the development of the final text of Truman's statement.[83] Attlee was so concerned that he rushed to Washington to confer with Truman. Oliver Franks, British Ambassador to the US, and someone in the State Department devised a final communique which was satisfactory to both Truman and Attlee.[84] The *Washington Post* reported, based on an Associated Press news item from London on 13 December, that Attlee returned from his talks with Truman "with a firm arrangement binding the US not to act alone in using the atomic bomb." When Acheson appeared before a joint meeting of the Foreign Relations Committees of both houses, he was questioned about the language in the Truman-Attlee communique. Acheson said the language was clear and refused to comment further—and he asked Truman to do the same.[85]

In fact, nobody knew how the atomic bomb would fare in combat, as evidenced by the following conversation during the Cabinet meeting of 1 December 1950.

Vice President Barkley: "How effective is the atomic bomb in destroying an army?"

General Marshall: "I simply do not know whether I could answer."

President Truman: "What the Vice President wants to know is how effective in the field."

Marshall: "I cannot answer the question."[86]

In view of the seriousness of deploying atomic weapons, Marshall wrote to Truman on 16 December, proposing to transmit future military requests for issue of atomic weapons to the NSC's special committee on atomic energy. Marshall said he had asked the JCS to advise him prior to decisions that would transfer previously issued atomic weapons from one theater of operations to another. This procedure would enable Marshall to keep Truman and the Secretary of State fully advised of any activities involving atomic weapons that might create political problems between governments.[87] Vandenberg, concerned that the Democratic administration might use atomic weapons in Korea without Congressional consent, cabled Francis Wilcox on 29 January 1951 to inquire whether the President had authority to use such weapons. Wilcox replied that the Atomic Energy Act did not provide for any specific Congressional role in determining when they should be used. The President did have authority to make such a determination.[88]

Study of the draft of Truman's statement of 30 November reveals two additional points of interest. First, the State Department draft mentioned that Russia was the "traditional enemy" of the Chinese people—probably intended to drive a wedge between the two countries. The White House redraft omitted these words. Second, General Bradley deleted from the original draft the word "necessarily," in "the battlefield situation is necessarily uncertain at this time," and the word "temporary," in "we may suffer temporary reverse as we have suffered before." The general was not optimistic about the future course of the war.[89]

In early December, an important paper entitled *Soviet Intentions in the Current Situation* became an approved Inter-Agency Committee report. Acheson took the paper to Truman on 2 December 1950. Its highlights include the following. (1) The PRC understood the risk of a general war between China and the US, and would not have accepted this risk without explicit assurances of effective Soviet support. (2) The Soviet Union would probably continue to support PRC operations with material, technical personnel, and even "volunteer" units, as necessary; or with aircraft and anti-aircraft artillery, and trained personnel to man them; or with open military support—under treaty terms, if there were major US operations against Chinese territory. (3) The Soviets knew the increased risk of global war and were ready to accept it. (US intelligence was inconclusive as to whether the Soviets intended to precipitate a global war at that time.) (4) Even if the Soviets did not intend to precipitate a global war, they must have calculated that a broadening of the Korean War into a general war between the US and China would be advantageous to the them.

In view of the deteriorating US military situation in Korea, in mid-December Truman was ready to proclaim a national emergency (i.e., total mobilization). Acheson said during a Cabinet meeting that Soviet propaganda would call any effort to increase US strength a step toward war; it was the duty of the US government to both offset Soviet propaganda and to get the war economy moving with all possible speed.[90] Acheson also reported that the UN conferences would be looking toward a cease-fire order in Korea. The Chinese said they would agree, if the US pulled out; Truman said that he would not do so.[91]

At this juncture, an interesting episode occurred. Congressman Frank Boykin wrote to Sidney Souers on 12 December 1950, recommending a proposal from General Claire Chennault, the old Flying Tiger. Boykin said he had every confidence in Chennault and knew that Truman would agree; he was willing to have Truman handle Chennault's proposal as he saw fit. Chennault proposed sending an ultimatum to the PRC to the effect that if Chinese troops were not withdrawn within 72 hours the US would act, with or without the concurrence and assistance of other UN members. Specifically, the US would arm and train KMT forces and other anti-Communist Chinese, with the objective of "liberating" China, and would use atomic bombs and other weapons to destroy Chinese troops and material in Korea and Manchuria as well as centers of war production and transport in China. The US would also blockade the entire China coast in cooperation with the KMT and would support and encourage KMT forces to land on the mainland. Chennault suggested the appointment of MacArthur as Supreme Commander, US Forces, FE, and Wedemeyer as assistant to MacArthur and Commander, US Forces, China.[92] This proposal was a complete departure from the existing policy of the Truman administration; it was not accepted.

A week later, Truman was informed in a Cabinet meeting that the Congress had asked State to testify as to reasons the US should not follow an isolationist policy, withdrawing from commitments in Eurasia and the Far East (which would result in complete control of Eurasia by the Soviet Union). Truman said that a non-isolationist policy was approved by the National Security Council and himself. It was important that this be made clear to the US and the rest of the world, especially in view of the isolationist speech made by former President Hoover. He said his position rested upon studies and decisions made since January 1946, and that the present US policy originated in December 1945, when he had reversed the position of Secretary of State James Byrnes and decided upon a firm policy toward the Soviet Union.[93] The Truman administration was obviously under heavy attack for its overseas commitments by the end of 1950.

CHINA, THE "AGGRESSOR"

During the initial period of Chinese military intervention, Mao Zedong's eldest son, Anying, was killed in an American air raid. Mao Anying had joined the CPVA when it was organized, and became the confidential secretary of Peng Dehuai. When American planes bombed CPVA Headquarters in Korea on 25 November 1950, Anying was burned to death at the age of 28. This incident may have had a profound and long-term effect on Mao Zedong. He had five children—three sons born to his first wife, Yang Kaihui, and one daughter each to his second and third wives, He Zizhen and Jiang Qing. His sons roamed the cities of the lower Yangtze when their mother was imprisoned and then executed by the Nationalist government and while Mao Zedong was off in Jiangxi. Eventually, Anying and one of the other sons were found; Anying went to the Soviet Union during the war and returned to China after it ended.

Despite the loss of his son, Mao became quite optimistic after the initial victories of the CPVA. He estimated on 4 December 1950 that the war might well be settled quickly, though he also warned China to be prepared to fight for a year, and noted that armistice negotiations could only begin after the US acknowledged intent to withdraw its troops from Korea and retreated south of the 38th parallel. For the moment, Mao advised the Volunteers to concentrate on destroying South Korean troops, thus expediting the withdrawal of the Americans. Once the US agreed to withdraw, the UN might agree to let the Korean people elect their own government, under UN supervision and with the PRC and the USSR participating in that supervision. But Mao believed that the promises and agreements of the US, like those of Chiang Kai-shek, were not to be trusted, and that the Chinese should not be caught by surprise in the event the US disappointed them.[94]

In the midst of this uncertainty, Peng Dehuai was calm. He reported to Mao on 8 December that, since the two past campaigns, the UN troops had shifted from the offensive to the defensive and had shortened their front line. Politically, it was not advantageous for the US to give up Korea; the UK and France would ask the US not to do so. The CPVA faced a severe winter and needed time to shift from a warfare of movement to one of attacking fixed defenses, so it was not advisable to cross the 38th parallel. Peng therefore suggested postponing any fighting south of the parallel until the following spring.[95] But when Zhou Enlai met with Pannikar of India three days later, he said that since US forces had crossed the 38th parallel, the demarcation line no longer existed. On the 13th, Mao informed Peng that the US, Britain, and other countries were asking the CPVA and KPA forces to stop north of the 38th only to benefit their own forces in future operations. The Volunteers must cross the parallel.[96]

The third campaign of the Volunteers—the New Year's Offensive—began on 30 December and ended on 10 January. In the west were the CPVA 38A, 39A, 40A and 50A, and the KPA 1A. These forces were to attack Seoul. In the east were the CPVA 42A and 66A, and the KPA 2A and 5A. These were to assist in the Seoul offensive, by cutting traffic to the city. On 7 January, when the UN forces retreated to areas near the 37th parallel, Peng ordered his troops to halt their pursuit. He said that mines had to be cleared, roads repaired, and food and ammunition replenished, and that the troops needed to rest. In fact, he believed the retreat of the UN troops was a ploy designed to lead the CPVA into an ambush.

Peng was correct: the retreat was a trap. But Stikov, the Soviet ambassador in North Korea, demanded that the troops continue in pursuit. When Peng refused, Stikov commented that "such a way of fighting a war is something never seen in the world." Peng reported to Mao that, "After two victories...the mood of quick victory and blind optimism have been growing in all aspects. The Soviet ambassador says that the US troops will flee and demands that we go forward quickly." Peng believed that the war would be a protracted one and that the CPVA should now proceed cautiously; "not much will be gained by chasing a modernized enemy on foot." Mao approved of this assessment, and told Peng that Stalin "believed that the command of the Volunteers was correct. He criticized many incorrect comments and understood the difficulties of operating in Korea. He offered to provide 2,000 more trucks to meet your difficulties."[97] Some Chinese shared the view of the Soviet ambassador: at one point, even the *People's Daily* advocated "Driving the US Invaders to the Sea!" To this, Peng Dehuai replied, "How can so many well-equipped enemies be driven to sea by one thrust? It is not possible."[98] In retrospect, some Chinese military historians believe that the CPVC should not have continued to push southward after the Third Campaign. However, it is also debatable whether the Volunteers should have crossed the 38th parallel at all. Perhaps they should have stopped after the second campaign, and turned the 38th parallel into a diplomatic weapon. If decision makers believed that driving the enemy to the sea was the aim of the war, they faced a serious conflict between reality and intent.

At the beginning of 1951, the USSR gave a signal of great significance to the US: the Soviets would not fight in Korea. The chief Soviet liaison officer in Tokyo told one of the US representatives there that no Soviet military personnel were then fighting in Korea and that there would be none; however, if US troops crossed the Soviet frontier, the whole might of the Soviet army would be thrown into battle.[99] One implication of this message was that, despite the terms of the Sino-Soviet treaty, the USSR would not fight for China if China were attacked by the US—just as they would not fight for Korea. The British Joint Intelligence Committee believed at the time that the USSR would not openly intervene if China were involved in war with the US or UN, but the British Chiefs of Staff believed that Soviet intervention was possible. The Chiefs observed that the long and short of the JIC conclusion was that China, in fact, was not vulnerable to any decisive, or even very effective, extent. A war between the US and China would be like a fight between the whale and the elephant: neither could directly do the other real harm. On the other hand, indirectly China could do the US and the UN far more harm than vice versa. The Chiefs concluded that an open war against China, even without Soviet intervention, would result in a major defeat for the West.[100] The Truman administration believed that it "would be foolhardy to engage in full-scale hostilities against Chinese Communist forces while the heart of Communist world power remains untouched."[101]

Attlee wrote to Truman on 8 January 1951 expressing deep concern over the Korean situation. He said that, from what Acheson had told Bevin earlier the same day, the "US Government may wish to substitute for a policy of localizing the conflict in Korea a policy aimed at developing limited action against China." Attlee said it should be borne in mind that the Soviet Union was the principal enemy, that it was unwise to provoke China to further aggression unnecessarily, and that the US action at the UN would almost certainly provoke China to extend hostilities. Attlee explicitly stated that the British would "oppose condemning China as aggressor in the UN." Truman replied that, though he kept all doors open for peaceful settlement, he would not shrink before aggression.[102]

Meanwhile, Acheson reported to the Cabinet that having the UN cite China as aggressor was a delicate matter. Britain basically went along with the US, but was slow in giving assurances.[103] In order to allay the apprehension of the allies, the US informed Britain and France in mid-January, in strict confidence, that efforts had been made to establish contact with the Chinese delegation. British representative Jebb and French representative Chauvel both stated that if this were made known as soon as possible, it would be an invaluable aid to the British and French governments.[104] The State Department reported to the Cabinet on 15 January that the US had been working on a pact to brand China as the aggressor but was unable to get a majority.[105] In order to persuade them to agree to the US proposal, the US assured other governments that branding the PRC as the aggressor would not constitute authorization to extend hostilities against the Chinese mainland or permission to bomb China. The US, however, reserved the right to bomb the Manchurian airfields which launched planes attacking UN forces.[106]

Acheson was unhappy with the British attitude. He told senior associates in the State Department on 23 January that he wondered if the US were not getting pretty far from the British on the entire Korean matter. All present agreed that he should take this up with British Ambassador Oliver Franks.[107] In fact, Franks himself had expressed to Bevin, in a telegram sent two days before, that the Truman administration was genuinely hard-pressed, by public opinion and by Congress, to declare the PRC the aggressor. The administration agreed with those feelings and could not resist or delay action, for fear of being accused of softness toward the Communists. Franks observed that the American public would be disillusioned with the UN if it failed to brand China the aggressor; this disillusionment would affect British relations with Asia, and especially with India.[108] (Tito, incidentally, told US Assistant Secretary of State Perkins he did not think the Soviets would take any action that might bring the label of aggressor upon themselves.[109])

America's western allies were reluctant to follow the US line, but they ultimately yielded. As Oliver Franks expressed, if Britain did not comply with the wishes of US in this instance, Britain would be thought of by the US as "unwilling to do for the big fellow what we were willing to do for the little fellow and this would have serious consequences for the general relationship" between the two allies.[110]

Around this time, Dean Rusk put before the Far Eastern Subcommittees of the Senate and House four alternatives for the US in Korea: (1) unification of Korea by force, (2) withdrawal of US troops, (3) a military stalemate accompanied by a cease-fire, and (4) a general settlement permitting the withdrawal of all troops. A fifth alternative was also suggested: diversion tactics against the continent, with or without the aid of Chiang's troops. The participants explored these alternatives but no decisions or recommendations were made.[111] Paul Nitze told his State Department colleague Francis Wilcox that the first US objective in the Far East ought to be keeping out of a war on the Chinese mainland. The effects of such a priority were to localize the war in Korea and to require great care to avoid steps that would lead the US into open conflict with China elsewhere.[112]

At this point, the Truman administration did explore the possibility of an attack on the mainland by Chiang's forces. The NSC meeting of 17 January decided to request that the JCS prepare a study of the possible military effectiveness of Chiang's forces against the mainland, including consideration of effects upon the defense of Taiwan. This decision was subsequently communicated to the JCS for implementation.[113]

Also at this time, the NSC was about to undergo a reorganization. Executive Secretary James Lay told Acheson that the NSC staff was having difficulties reconciling differences before matters reached the Council—and such reconciliation was one of the staff's primary purposes. Differences often existed between the State Department and the military establishment. Acheson stressed the importance of joint work by the departments, which would effect a cross-fertilization of ideas.[114] Lovett called Acheson from the Pentagon in early February to discuss the matter further. He stressed getting "someone to head up the Council who has drive and imagination, and would serve as a prodder in order to give guidance and direction to the organization." He said that "a full time man of the stature of Mr. Harriman was essential." Acheson replied that "questions of personality might crop up insofar as establishing the senior man." Obviously, the military wanted to get Harriman, but Acheson did not want him.[115]

Kim Il-Sung and Peng Dehuai met at the united headquarters of the CPVA and KPA on 10 January 1951. It had been decided by the Chinese and North Korean parties that such a headquarters should be set up, and it began to function in early December, commanding "all activities pertaining to operations and the front." Peng was commander and commissar of the united headquarters and Deng Hua was deputy commander. One Korean General was also a deputy commander, and another was a deputy commissar. The existence of the united headquarters was not publicized. During Kim's visit, Peng briefed him on the casualties of the past three campaigns. The troops badly needed a period of rest and readjustment, during which a serious transportation problem could be addressed. Enemy forces still numbered over 200,000, and their front line was wide; it was better for the CPVA and KPA to destroy parts of the line rather than to enter the narrow bottled-neck around Pusan. Unless 70,000 or 80,000 more enemy troops were destroyed or some significant political changes occurred, the UN would not withdraw from the Korean Peninsula.[116]

On the 14th, the Chinese government sent Kim a telegram explaining that the PRC would refuse to call a cease-fire in advance of negotiations that the US and its allies had suggested. Zhou proposed that the PRC, the USSR, the US, the UK, France, India, and Egypt meet in China to negotiate the withdrawal of foreign troops from Korea and ending the Korean War by letting the Koreans settle their own problems. Zhou suggested that the withdrawal of US forces from the Taiwan Straits and other problems related to the Far East could also be discussed, and that the PRC's seat in the UN would be restored on the day the meeting convened. Kim agreed to these terms.[117]

From 15 January until the 29th, the CPVA and the KPA held a meeting of senior officers. On the 27th, the UN troops launched a new offensive, so the meeting was reoriented toward mobilization for the fourth campaign of the Volunteers. The US government had brought reinforcements from Europe, Japan, and the US; the offensive was started with a total of 230,000 men. The CPVA and the KPA forces first resisted the attack, then retreated to the north of the Han River on 14 March. The campaign ended on 21 April; according to Chinese data, 78,000 UN troops were wiped out. Losses on the Chinese and North Korean side were reported at 53,000.[118]

On 1 February 1951, the UN General Assembly passed a resolution naming China as the "aggressor" in Korea. The vote was 44 for and 7 against, with 9 abstentions. Branding China as an aggressor by orchestrating a majority in the UN was an unwarranted action. The UN stood by the South, and China stood by the North, intervening only at the invitation of the North Korean government. Korea belonged to all Koreans, and the UN could not say that one part of Korea was an "aggressor" during a Korean civil war. More than four decades have passed since Chinese troops were sent to fight in Korea, and China's seat in the UN has long been restored. Historical experience shows, however, that relations between countries should be treated with the utmost discretion. From a long-term perspective, going to extremes brings more harm than good.

Though the PRC had been branded as the aggressor, the British government continued to support Chinese representation in the UN. Acheson sent Bevin a personal message on 23 February 1951, asking him to authorize the British delegation to the UN to work out a plan with US delegation, to avoid further public display of disunity between the US and the UK over the issue of Chinese representation. According to Younger of the British Foreign Office, Prime Minister Attlee was firm that the PRC's right to representation should not be compromised.[119] Meanwhile, India's Foreign Minister made known to the US that it might withdraw from UN and be forced closer to the USSR and PRC if the US and UK sponsored a resolution on Kashmir in the Security Council. He implied that the British had yielded to the US. Truman added in longhand, on the brief paper which reported the Indian statement, "India is not doing what it should for peace. Their attitude is not sound."[120]

Mao suggested on 1 March that, in view of possible prolongation of the Korean War, China should be prepared to fight for at least two more years. The UN troops were seeking to fight a war of attrition, and only 60-70 percent of China's supplies could reach the front, with the rest destroyed by bombing. When Mao proposed that Chinese troops should fight in Korea on a rotating basis, a decision was made to divide them into three groups.[121] This arrangement provides hard evidence that Mao believed, at this point, that the war would be a protracted one.

President Truman relieved General MacArthur of all his posts on 11 April 1951. This measure—so at variance with ancient Chinese military teaching, in which changing commanders in the course of a war is taboo—was of course the result of careful deliberations. MacArthur was relieved due mainly to partisan, personal, and constitutional issues. Foreign policy was not a major factor, though the allies did generally approve his removal. In fact, there was not a big difference between MacArthur and Truman on the conduct of the war, and the British Cabinet Meeting concluded after MacArthur's removal that he "had not in fact exceeded the directives given to him on behalf of the United Nations."[122] And MacArthur was not blamed for misjudgment on Chinese intentions during the Wake meeting, since finding out whether the PRC would intervene in the Korean War was essentially a CIA responsibility. What really cost MacArthur his positions was failure in battle. As the Chinese say, "those who win a war become monarchs and lords, those who are defeated become bandits; a general who is defeated should never say how brave he has been."

On 24 April, the State Department reported to the President on the subject of Britain's China policy. The embassy in London concluded that there would be no basic changes in British China policy even if the Conservatives came in; they might cease to support seating the PRC at the UN, but they would not recall the British representative in Beijing. Churchill had favored recognition of the PRC as early as autumn 1949.[123] In October 1951, Acheson would express this same view—that a change in the government of Britain would not have much effect on foreign policy; rather, the Conservatives would simply be more united and responsible.[124]

The CPVA's fifth campaign was launched on 22 April 1951 and ended on 10 June. It destroyed 82,000 UN troops, with the Chinese and the North Koreans suffering 85,000 casualties.[125] In all five campaigns from 25 October 1950 through early June 1951, the UN forces lost 196,700 men, of whom 88,800 were Americans. The situation in Korea had been completely reversed since the Chinese had intervened, and the front line had been stabilized near the 38th parallel.[126] Summing up the five campaigns, Mao remarked on 26 May that it would be best not to be too ambitious. So far, the annihilation of even one entire US regiment had not been possible, because US morale was high. It would be good work if one CPVA army could wipe out one or two US battalions. There were eight Chinese armies at the front, and exterminating eight battalions would be a heavy blow to the US. At that rate, after three or four battles, each US division would have lost three or four battalions, shaking their confidence. By then, the

Volunteers could entice enemy troops farther north, and plans could be made to obliterate entire US divisions.[127]

THE CLANDESTINE WAR

Apart from military operations in Korea, the US conducted another sort of war—a clandestine war in China. As noted earlier, ESD-44 (External Service Detachment 44), the CIA outfit in China, had deployed networks of secret agents before its withdrawal from the mainland, and the CCP authorities had made individual disclosures, such as that concerning the Shenyang spy case and Angus Ward. From the spring of 1951, the Chinese media began reporting a crackdown on US spy networks in cities such as Beijing, Shanghai, and Tianjin. It is still not certain whether these networks were previously known to the PRC security service or exposed only during a housecleaning campaign beginning in late 1950. Each network was generally composed of a principal agent, some informants, and a radio operator equipped with a transmitter-receiver designed for spy activities. The networks included Americans, Japanese, Koreans, Germans, Soviets, Frenchmen, and Russian emigres, as well as Chinese, and they became very active after the outbreak of the Korean War.

The PRC's biggest catch in its crackdown on spies was Hugh Redmond, an intelligence officer for ESD-44 headquarters. Redmond had gone underground prior to the liberation of Shanghai, disguised as a businessman. One can only imagine how much he told the Chinese authorities during his long imprisonment. After he committed suicide in prison in 1970, his ashes were turned over to his mother through the Red Cross and his hometown gave his remains a hero's welcome. His CIA identity was not revealed; rather, in the American media he was reported to be a victim of Communism. Apart from captured spies such as Redmond, the CIA attempted to bring others out by air. For example, CIA operative Thomas Downey and pilot Richard Fecteau were sent to pick up an agent in Manchuria. Their venture failed when Chinese security forces and militia shot down their plane, capturing Downey and Fecteau alive.

NEGOTIATIONS BEGIN

In May 1951, the State Department made overtures to the PRC through go-betweens. US officials warned of the prospect of a tough and bloody war between the US and Russia, which would involve China. After such warnings, American diplomats would wave an olive branch, saying that the US wanted a reasonable and peaceful settlement and was ready to pursue one any time the Chinese leaders came to their senses. The American media cast no aspersions on the Chinese; if the Chinese could come to terms with the US, it would be making an accommodation with a friend, instead of yielding to a foe. The Americans' most telling statement was that the US sought restoration of the Korean situation to what it had been before the aggression. A certian Eric Chow was chosen as a go-between by State Department officials, who believed him to be secretly associated with the PRC and able to reach top CCP officials.[128] According to Chinese sources, Chow was an employee of the pro-China Hong Kong newspaper *Ta Kung Pao*, with no access to CCP leaders.

Kim Il-Sung went to Beijing again on 3 June, to confer with Mao and Zhou on armistice negotiations. Yakov Malik, Soviet Ambassador to the UN, stated on 23 June that the Soviets believed the Korean conflict could be settled, and the Chinese media supported settlement efforts. Armistice negotiations began on 10 July, in Kaesung. The CPVA and the KPA formed a unified delegation. The names of the Chinese and North Korean negotiators were released in newspapers at the time, but has not been widely known who actually directed their work. Although the KPA headed the delegation at the negotiating table, the negotiations were actually supervised by Li Kenong, a Chinese general and Vice Foreign Minister, and also chief of the Chinese intelligence service. Apart from CPVA generals Deng Hua, Xie Fang and Chai Chengwen, Li's close associates included Qiao Guanhua, who became Chinese Foreign Minister in the 1970s.

The negotiations had gone on for only two days when the UN delegation refused to attend, in a dispute over the number of journalists present. The negotiations resumed on 15 July. Then, on 23 August, the North Koreans and Chinese declared an adjournment, because UN ground forces killed a Chinese military policeman in the demilitarized zone and a UN plane bombed and machine-gunned the residence of the CPVA-KPA delegation in Kaesong. Negotiations were not resumed until 25 October, at Panmunjom.

Mao had instructed the CPVA that, if UN forces launched an attack intended to force China and North Korea into signing an agreement, the Volunteers should retaliate with a large-scale counter-offensive. On 14 November, the PRC leadership reviewed the situation in Korea and proposed policies for the future. They observed that, since the resumption of negotiations on 25 October, the US government had faced growing domestic and international pressure for an armistice and that this pressure increased the chances of reaching an agreement. On the other hand, the US still wanted to keep the situation in Korea tense and was trying to delay agreement. The Chinese wanted a conference, to be attended by high-level representatives of the USSR, the PRC, the US, the UK, and both parts of Korea—and perhaps France, India, and Egypt. China would negotiate with flexibility, showing no eagerness to make peace, trying to reach agreement during 1951, and preparing at the same time to fight six months or a year more if need be. China's leaders concluded that "it would be good to have peace, but we should not be afraid of intentional procrastination."[129]

Truman and Churchill met in January 1952. Acheson said at that time that "around January 1950 the US had thought it possible to play on Chinese-Russian differences with a view to fomenting a split between these two Communist powers. Now, however, the US no longer holds this view, this being especially true since the Chinese intervention in the Korean War."[130] Churchill stated that diplomatic relations with the PRC were "essentially a fiction, as the latter had not recognized Great Britain....Had he been in power he would have broken relations with China when the Chinese attacked the UN forces in Korea." But now that the armistice talks had started, such a break would be undesirable. Churchill did not want to see the Chiang government recognized as the legitimate government of mainland China. Eden said he did not agree with the China policy of the Labor Government, especially "with its belief that a Chinese brand of Titoism could be fostered," and thought it "unwise to base a national policy on such a tenuous possibility."[131] As it is common practice for politicians to act quite differently "in the imperial court or in the fields," it is difficult to assess whether Churchill and Eden really meant what they said.[132] It did them no harm to please their hosts in Washington.

US officials continued to devise ways to woo the PRC away from its alliance with the Soviet Union. Chester Bowles, US Ambassador to India, told Truman in December 1951 that:

> against the background of the cold war, China may be more important to Russia than Russia is to China. For several centuries European Russia has had the advantage of a weak and divided China at her back door. This situation is now gradually changing and no man can foresee the implications. A China of growing strength which is even slightly wobbly in its attitude toward the Soviet Union would be a source of grave danger to the [Soviet] Politburo. A strong and unfriendly China would force the Politburo to drastically modify its present policies towards the West....A major long term objective of our foreign policy must be directed towards modifying China's present ties with the USSR and gradually easing her into a more independent position.

Truman expressed appreciation of this viewpoint.[133] But it proved impossible for his administration, and some later ones, to shape a policy on the basis of Bowles's recommendations.

The war dragged on, and the US tried to force China to negotiate. If the GIs and allied soldiers were fighting for democracy and justice, it was a wasted effort: they fought and died for a repressive regime. Acheson reported to the Cabinet in June 1952 that Syngman Rhee was conducting a reign of terror in South Korea to promote his own reelection, and that this was sapping morale among the UN troops as well as the South Koreans.[134] After US aircraft bombed a power installation on the Yalu river, Truman was informed on 25 June 1952 that the bombing caused considerable excitement in the British press and in the Commons. The British opposition saw the bombing as a sufficiently important departure from previous UK policy as to have required prior consultation with the UK, and felt that the bombing would have adverse effects on the armistice negotiations.[135] The Tory Government asked its embassy in Washington whether Lord Alexander had been aware of the bombing.

A high-level Chinese delegation visited the Soviet Union in August 1952; they were met by Molotov and three other Politburo members at the airport. Kennan expected the two governments would reach some new understanding in regard to the Korean War, and recommended careful consideration of America's own diplomatic and military moves in Korea at this time.[136] But the policies of China and the Soviet Union were apparently quite far apart. A member of the Israeli UN mission talked with the Soviet representative, Malik, in mid-October 1952 and came away with the impression that the Soviet and Chinese positions diverged. On 1 December, the State Department briefed Truman on a report from Ambassador Chester Bowles in India. Bowles said that most diplomatic mission chiefs in New Delhi, in addition to Nehru and Indian Foreign Office officials, believed that the USSR and China had not seen eye to eye on the question of the Korean armistice. China was originally noncommittal on the resolution proposed by India, which led the Indian Government to believe that it might be acceptable to them. But Vyshinsky's attitude led observers, including Nehru, to believe that the Soviets were privately imposing pressure on China.[137]

Nehru made a statement in mid-December to the effect that India had first approached China on 2 November regarding the principles on which a Korean War resolution might be based. In Nehru's words, "There was no commitment by the Chinese government, but there was no disapproval indicated at that stage to these principles." According to the US embassy, Nehru believed that the relationship between the USSR and China seemed firmer, but this might well change. Nehru believed that there was considerable conflict within the Chinese government over the Indian resolution, and that China was far too strong to be dominated by the Soviet Union or anyone else. While the Soviet Union wanted chaos and confusion in Asia, China—torn by forty years of war and civil strife—needed peace.[138]

POWs

During the negotiations, the issue of POWs kept coming to the fore. When the negotiations first started on 10 July 1951, this issue did not seem so hard to handle. Mao and the CCP Central Committee, in a directive of 14 November 1951, said that POWs should be exchanged, and that it would not be difficult to reach an agreement. Incidentally, on the same day the Judge Advocate of the US 8th Army announced that the North Koreans and the Chinese Volunteers were killing POWs, and that the person responsible was the Commanding Officer, CPVA 81D, 23R. KPA and the CPVA spokesmen denied this charge, saying that there was, in fact, no CPVA outfit bearing the given designation. The Communists claimed that, from February to May 1951, US planes had bombed POW camps under CPVA/KPA supervision four times, causing sixty-two casualties.[139]

The next argument concerned the POWs' mail. On 31 December 1951, the CPVA/KPA side turned over 9,890 letters from UN POWs; 803 letters had already been turned over before Christmas. The UN side turned over only 43 letters allegedly written by CPVA/KPA POWs. The letters were written on 5x8 cards, and 39 of them said only "Merry Christmas. I am well"—an unusual greeting for Chinese and Korean families! One of the cards was addressed to Pan Jinlian, a notoriously lewd adulteress in the Ming Dynasty novels *Water Margin* and *Jin Ping Mei*.[140]

But the thorniest part of the POW issue concerned how to go about exchanging them. The numbers of POWs captured by the two sides were disproportionate. On 2 May 1952, the CPVA/KPA proposed that the UN side repatriate 132,000 POWs to China and North Korea, getting 12,000 in return. The UN side insisted that the exchange should be on an one-for-one basis.[141] Later, the crux of the dispute surfaced: the Chinese and North Koreans insisted on unconditional repatriation of all POWs, while the UN side insisted that repatriation must be voluntary. Each side argued that its view was in conformity with the Geneva Convention.

The total number of Chinese POWs was a little over 20,000. Of these, 6,673 returned to the PRC, while most of the rest went to Taiwan.[142] How and why some went to the PRC and others to Taiwan is a long story. The UN's version has been circulating in the West for decades; a Chinese version of the story bears consideration.[143]

In April 1952, the UN forces conducted a screening of POWs. Of the 20,000 Chinese, 6,000 insisted they wanted to return to China, despite repeated threats. This group was put in POW Compound 602 on Koje Island, "for direct repatriation." After the Dodd incident (described below), all the POWs in Compound 602 were transferred to the 8th Compound on Cheju Island. Some 2,000 of them were tattooed with anti-Communist messages, which they removed by cutting off patches of tattooed skin. Of the 6,673 Chinese POWs eventually sent back to China, 5,640 designated "for direct repatriation" were repatriated via North Korea between 5 August and 6 September 1953. On the last day, 6 September, "war criminals" were repatriated in a group of 138.

The Dodd incident occurred in May 1952. North Korean POWs in Compound 76 asked to see Brig. General Francis Dodd, commander of all POW compounds on Koje Island. When Dodd came to see them, they took him hostage. Then they convened a meeting of representatives from other camps. Dodd, meanwhile, was being held in a large tent, with his meals sent in by the Americans. The POWs' meeting began the evening of 7 May, with representatives from seventeen POW compounds attending. The Chinese Volunteers had seven representatives. At a rally after the meeting, POWs recounted atrocities committed by camp authorities; Dodd was much affected. A meeting the next day listed conditions for the release of General Dodd—among them, cessation of all barbarities in the camps, protection of the lives and human rights of the POWs, and cancellation of all screening processes. Brig. General Charles Colson, acting commander, sent his reply on the morning of 10 May; it was unsatisfactory. Dodd claimed that the reply did meet with the POWs' conditions, and suggested that it might have been mistranslated. After revision of the reply, Colson and Dodd both signed it, and the POWs were satisfied.

General Mark Clark, who succeeded General Van Fleet as Commander-in-Chief of UN and US troops in Korea, installed a new commander of the POW compounds. The new commander rearranged the management of all POW compounds, and ordered that all the POW representatives, except for women, be detained in Compound 76. He also ordered all Korean civilians to leave Koje Island, and sent for the engineering corps to rebuild the compounds so that each would intern no more than 500 POWs. One month later, on 10 June, several thousand US soldiers in tanks and armored cars washed the 76th in blood, killing or wounding about 150 POWs. All surviving representatives from various POW compounds were accused of war crimes and held in a special prison on Koje.

To celebrate the third anniversary of the People's Republic on 1 October 1952, POWs in the 8th Compound on Cheju decided to fly the five-star Chinese flag. They sent a letter to the superintendent of the camps one week before the anniversary, informing him of their plan. There was no response. At breakfast time on 1 October, ten flags rose as the POWs saluted and sang the Chinese national anthem. Tanks surrounded the 8th Compound. Nearly 1,000 soldiers wearing gas masks jumped from trucks. Mortars, flame throwers and heavy machine guns were set up, and fighters circled in the sky. Captain Brooks, an intelligence officer from 8th Army

Headquarters, demanded that the flags be taken down within five minutes. When soldiers came forward to take them down, a struggle ensued, leaving 56 POWs dead and 109 severely wounded. The US military authorities reported that they had defeated "a plan of escape of 5,784 Chinese Communist troops detained on Cheju Island." Captain Brooks attended the prisoners' funeral on behalf of the camp commander, expressing condolences and admiration for the patriotism of the Chinese POWs.

The US authorities let Nationalist agents from Taiwan operate in the POW compounds, for the purpose of convincing POWs to refuse repatriation; these agents threatened, beat, raped, and killed prisoners to achieve their purpose. A former CPVA soldier by the name of Li Daan collaborated with the Nationalists, committing terrible atrocities against POWs. Li is said to have killed four POWs with a dagger, scooped out their hearts, and eaten them.

From August 1951 to May 1953, the US intelligence service selected 179 Chinese POWs, trained them, and sent them to North Korea on intelligence missions. Li Daan was one of these. He was airdropped into North Korea on the night of 22 April 1953; he and his partner were captured by North Korean security police and turned over to the Chinese. Li was tried by the Beijing Regional Military Court in June 1958 and sentenced to death.

Soon after being welcomed home, returned Chinese POWs were sent to Changtu County in Liaoning Province, where they were detained for a year of observation—in fact, a humiliating and heartbreaking process of interrogation and investigation. In the end, almost all of the Communists and Young Communist Leaguers were deprived of their memberships. All former POWs were expelled from the armed forces and excluded from government jobs. When some appealed this unfair treatment, they were thrown in prison. Lt. Colonel Jin Daying, a Chinese military author who has read nearly 500 such appeals and many of the case files of the former POWs, sadly notes:

> Some say the way that ex-POWs were treated followed the example of a certain country after WWII. I am not familiar with WWII and dare not comment. However, I feel the fate of these POWs had many 'special Chinese features.'...For instance, they were found guilty on moral charges. As a matter of fact, what were these POWs guilty of? And what was the legal basis for treating them like this? The most fearful guilt is this kind of 'guiltless guilt.' Verdicts were announced in the name of morality; violation of morality was the greatest crime in 2,000 years of Old China. But what are we doing in the contemporary

era? Leniency, understanding, and gentlemanly behavior were part of our ancient tradition, but do they exist anymore?

After 1978, when the former POWs appealed for rehabilitation, the post-Mao authorities started to correct the mistakes of their predecessors. Most of the former Communist party members had their memberships restored, and the status of retired officers and veteran soldiers was acknowledged. Their circumstances improved considerably. But the former POWs had spent the prime years of their lives in humiliation and misery.

All wars must end in due course. When all the belligerents feel no one among them can win, war ends. Following the gradual stabilization of the front line near the 38th parallel, the participants in the Korean War came to believe that the time had come to end the conflict. In the US, however, 1952 was an election year. The other side probably considered it advantageous to sign an armistice with the incoming administration. In fact, it was not signed until 27 July 1953, after three years and one month of war.

11

The Echoes of Panmunjom

The signing of the armistice in Panmunjom brought sighs of relief in all the belligerent countries. But what were the real costs and benefits of the Korean War?

Of course, for the Korean people, the war was tremendously costly. Their nation lay in ruins. The damage suffered by the Korean Peninsula compares with the worst killing and devastation anywhere in the world during WWII. And reunification of the two parts of the Korean nation became even more remote.

Equally clearly, there were gains. The young People's Republic could claim that it had fought against the most powerful country in the world, and that the CPVA had driven that country's troops and those of its allies from the Yalu back to the 38th parallel, where the war had started. The United States could claim that it had not deserted one of its weaker allies in time of need. Rather, the US had hastened to help and had stabilized a difficult situation; the resolve of the US to defend its friends would prove very helpful in setting up NATO and other collective security organizations. North Korea could claim that the American and UN invaders had been repelled, and its security assured. South Korea could claim rebirth after near destruction, and its leader, Syngman Rhee, was able to avoid being overthrown.

Judged from a broader perspective and in the context of global events, some of these gains are illusory. Since the Korean War was part of a larger rivalry between the United States and the Soviet Union, the balance sheet for the war must be viewed in terms of this rivalry.

THE UNITED STATES

The United States sent the 7th Fleet to the Taiwan Straits when the Korean conflict started, immediately connecting the Chinese civil war with the Korean War. The US government then openly declared that China was behind North Korea, and ordered the crossing of the 38th parallel and an approach toward the Yalu. This recklessness ultimately led to China's military involvement in Korea. After American troops suffered severe casualties, the US signed an armistice without having touched "the heart of Communism" (i.e., the USSR). Using the flag of the United Nations had given American and allied troops a veneer of righteousness, but the result of their failure was nevertheless a rapid decline in prestige.

Instead of driving a wedge between the USSR and the PRC, the Truman administration pushed them closer together. And, with forces committed in the Far East, the US could not strengthen the defense of Europe against the Soviet threat. This terrified America's Western European allies, who became more attentive to protecting their own territory—and, hence, reluctant to continue participating in the UN venture in Korea.

The biggest strategic mistake the Truman administration made was antagonizing the PRC. In the Cold War, the US should have tried to minimize the number of enemies it faced, so as to focus its attention on the Soviet Union. Once the US and the PRC became opponents in the Korean War, any rapprochement between them became impossible, for a long time to come. To the United States, China was not "lost" in 1949; rather, China was lost in 1950, when the US forced China to enter the Korean War. The Democrats did not lose the White House in 1948, even though the Communist victory in China was imminent; they lost it in 1952, while negotiating the Korean armistice.

CHINA

China suffered heavy casualties in Korea.[1] Taiwan became inaccessible, at least for some time to come. The division of China into two hostile parts has been a tragic experience for people on both sides of the Straits. The war forced China to form a closer relationship with the Soviet Union at the cost of some of her independence. In addition, Korean War debt and interest owed to the Soviet Union would become heavy burdens, when the Soviets demanded payment at a time of severe economic difficulties.

BRITAIN

On balance, Britain broke even in Korea. The British brigade in Korea did suffer casualties, but this appeased the United States. Though the US considered Britain's attitude vacillating, Britain in fact often followed in the steps of the US—after some hesitation. And Britain managed not to alienate China. Apart from agreeing to cross the 38th parallel after the Inchon landing, the Labor government remained very cautious, and continued to seek containment of the war and the designation of a non-military zone in North Korea. Labor insisted that China's seat in the UN should be restored, and that a Chinese representative should attend debates in the Security Council. It opposed the presence of the US 7th Fleet in the Taiwan Straits and continued to station a British representative in Beijing. After the Korean Armistice, therefore, the British position in Hong Kong was not affected, and its China trade continued to develop. Britain made painstaking efforts to defend the *status quo* through very sophisticated diplomatic maneuvers, and displayed Britain's admirable expertise in walking a tightrope.

JAPAN AND TAIWAN

Japan set out on the road to prosperity during the Korean War. By acting as the supply and recreational base for the troops of the US and her allies, Japan profited handsomely. In April 1951, Acheson told Joseph Pholieu, the Belgian Prime Minister, that "at the moment there is no predominant power in the Pacific, but there could be no doubt that Japan could be such a power. We must have the Japanese on the side of the West."[2]

Chiang Kai-shek in Taiwan had similar good fortune. If not for the Korean War, the PRC would have exercised sovereignty over Taiwan in the 1950s. It is wrong, however, to consider Chiang Kai-shek a yes-man to the US. He used foreign nations to achieve his own ends, though he had to pay a price in doing so. For example, Chiang's secret service penetrated the US Consulate-General in Hong Kong as the Nationalists themselves were fleeing to Taiwan, and continued this operation during the Korean War.[3] But Nationalist agents were then implicated in conspiring to sell US visas, in a scandal that came to light in 1951.

The American Joint Chiefs of Staff completely reversed the position on Taiwan that it had held before the Korean War. A March 1952 document confirmed that in the future the US might want Taiwan detached from China, and demanded that Taiwan be strengthened as an anti-Communist base—militarily, economically, politically, and psychologically. Denying Taiwan to Communism was seen to be of major importance to US security interests and to the long-term US position in the Far East. Taiwan should continue as a base for US military operations, and the 7th Fleet should continue its current mission in the region. The JCS believed that its views on Taiwan should govern US policy for the foreseeable future and, specifically, in any negotiations that might follow an armistice in Korea. The US should continue to assist units of the KMT military, to enable them to carry out actions outside Taiwan; KMT forces now interned by the French in Indochina should be released for overt or covert operations and for repatriation to Taiwan. The US could also recruit individuals on Taiwan for covert operations.[4] Clearly, the fate of the Chiang regime changed dramatically over the course of the war.

THE BIGGEST WINNER: THE SOVIET UNION

According to recent Chinese disclosures, in autumn and winter of 1950, thirteen Soviet Air Force divisions entered China to take up defense missions. When these divisions withdrew the next year, China paid for some equipment left behind and turned it over to Chinese Air Force. (The Soviets also supplied free of charge 372 MIG-15 fighters, which at the time were fairly advanced aircraft.) Between 1950 and 1955, these and other transfers of military (some of which had been allocated to North Korean Troops), the Chinese incurred a debt of $1.3 billion. China repaid this, plus interest, by the end of 1965. Hence, the Soviet Union, which did not send troops to fight in Korea, required that China pay for the weapons and ammunition used in defending the socialist camp. One can hardly call this fair.

As the Korean War dragged on, the Soviet Union was doing quite well. In June 1952, for example, US Ambassador Kennan believed that the Soviets were "precisely in their better moments."[5] One might well ask just how these "better moments" came about.

In his correspondence with Bevin in July 1950, Acheson said the US did not see the practical advantage of the Soviet delegate's return to the Security Council, and that it was only in his absence that the Security Council had been able to act on Korea with such speed.[6] It would be naive to suppose that the Soviet absence at the beginning of the Korean conflict resulted from bureaucratic and rigid diplomacy. One should assume the Soviets believed at the time that, if they returned to the Security Council, they would have to challenge the governments and the public of the Western world. They did not want to do this. The usual practice of the USSR in those years was to reap the crops without having sowed the seed.

When Churchill visited Truman on *USS Williamsburg* in January 1952, he said that "the central factor in Soviet policy is fear." Acheson later commented, "So far as the Soviet Union was concerned, it seemed to me the heart of the matter was the concern of the regime to maintain itself in power, first in the Soviet Union, and then to maintain influence in the satellite areas." In April 1952, Stalin himself told India's Ambassador Radhakrishnan, who in turn told the US Charge in Moscow, that the "Soviet Union was concerned only with its own security and the establishment of a belt of buffer countries friendly to the Soviet Union."[7] Nevertheless, the Soviets' true intentions remained an enigma to the United States. Someone in the Truman administration is even reported to have employed a psychic, who predicted war with the USSR in 1952.[8]

The prestige enjoyed by the USSR, and the USSR's attempts to exploit it, are evident in a number of incidents and statements of 1952. For example, contrary to his belligerent speeches made before the Tories returned to office, Churchill was now extremely concerned about a NATO exercise off Bornholm, Denmark. He believed that it was dangerously provocative, in view of the strategic importance of Bornholm to the USSR. From Moscow, Kennan also expressed misgivings about NATO's Baltic movements.[9] In September, *Pravda* attacked US Ambassador Kennan, who was then travelling in Western Europe; in October, Kennan was declared *persona non grata*. A ranking British official believed that the Kennan incident was meant to split the West. In any case, in the past the Soviet Union had never been in a position, or considered it politically advantageous, to denounce an American ambassador.[10]

Near the end of the Truman administration, the Soviet Union was busily driving wedges among the western countries. As early as August 1950, Acheson was already very concerned, saying that "the great difficulty was how to preserve our unity." Truman agreed.[11] In October 1952, the US Ambassador to France reported that serious strains were developing in US-French relations, and that the US might expect difficult days ahead. The French government refused to allow US review of the French defense budget, considering such review an infringement upon the sovereignty of France. The French Foreign Office informed the US that Vyshinsky had said the USSR's "greatest wish" was to reach a general understanding with France as a prelude to a relaxation of East-West tensions. By the end of October, French President Auriol was defending the French attitude—and doing so at the dedication of a dam financed largely by the US. Meanwhile, Kennan derided Vyshinsky's statement as a move aimed at splitting the West; his expulsion might well have something to do with the Soviets' wedge-driving efforts.[12]

In London, US Ambassador Gifford detected fear and suspicion concerning US intentions for the western world. He agreed with Kennan that Stalin continued to place his hope primarily on rifts in the West. And he felt that it was time for a policy of harmony with allies and associates, avoiding an overemphasis on military issues and on everything that smacked of US domination or heavy-handedness, and stressing the economic soundness and political security of all countries in the non-Communist camp. Outside the US, few believed that the US wanted a "preventive war," though many did believe a war might occur as a result of a precipitous or ill-considered action on the part of the US. British fears were intensified by constant publicity about US military developments and by the prospect of Soviet retaliation directed against bases in Britain. Ambassador Gifford noted British perceptions that the US was reluctant to explore possibilities for negotiations and coexistence, and suggested that this perception had entered into the Kremlin's calculations; recent pronouncements showed that the Soviets were counting on it as a powerful tool in dividing the West.[13]

In sum, during the Korean War the Soviet Union did not fight for its ally as UN troops swept in; rather, Stalin took a "hands off" stance, simply watching the situation develop—and forcing China to intervene. The Soviet Union then took advantage of the Americans' difficulties in the Far East, scaring off the Western Europeans with the threat of possible invasion. But the biggest coup for the Soviet Union was that the war destroyed any possibility of rapprochement between the US and the PRC for a long time, keeping the balance of power in the Far East tipped in the Soviets' favor.

All coins have two sides. While China's intervention in the Korean War convinced Stalin that the Chinese were loyal Communists and contributed to his decision to assist China in building up its industry, Soviet behavior during the war taught the Chinese that the Sino-Soviet treaty of 1950, which called for joint defense, was no more than some black ink on white paper. The Korean War was the watershed in Sino-Soviet relations. After Stalin's death in March 1953 and then the armistice at Panmunjom, a process that would eventually split the two Communist giants began.

Conclusion
The Dynamics of the Truman Policy

The previous chapters examined major events in the relations among the United States, the Soviet Union, China and the United Kingdom during the Truman presidency. This concluding chapter attempts to extract the key factors affecting foreign policy decisions in Truman's administration, so as to suggest the dynamics of Truman diplomacy.

TRADITION

Some historians characterize traditional American diplomacy in terms of four principles: isolationism, the Monroe Doctrine, the Open Door, and the American mission.[1] Others name only the first three, viewing the American mission as ideology rather than as a principle of diplomacy.[2] These traditional factors survived into the twentieth century, but often took on new meanings. Isolationism, for example, when it could no longer effectively protect the United States, became a camouflage, worn before the entry of the US into the world wars. Isolationism lost its significance during the Truman period, as the American mission—far from its original sense of manifest destiny within US borders—turned into global "commitments". As Truman said, "the North Atlantic Pact is the last nail in the coffin of isolationism."[3] The Open Door became a policy tool for taking over the interests of the old colonial powers and interfering in the affairs of nations within the Soviet sphere of influence.

Against this backdrop, the preeminent tenet of diplomacy was the Monroe Doctrine. Under the banner of a new American Mission, the Doctrine drew a demarcation line from Norway to southern Manchuria, taking all the major powers of Western Europe—and their spheres of influence—under the wing of the American Eagle. This expanded Doctrine would become the basis for containment theory. In the words of Allen Dulles, the American policy in Europe was a "logical extension of both"—of the Open Door and the Monroe Doctrine. In the words of Ernest Bevin, the superpowers were "two Monroes."

THE ROOSEVELT LEGACY

Truman's diplomacy was heavily influenced by that of his predecessor. In his summit with Soviet and British leaders at Potsdam, Truman completed the postwar design initiated by Roosevelt in wartime exchanges with Stalin and Churchill—notably at the summits in Tehran and Yalta and at the Cairo conference of 1943, which Stalin endorsed. The essence of this design was division of the world into American and Soviet spheres of influence, with peace ensured by unanimity of the major powers in a new United Nations Organization. But the design was made only by a gentlemen's agreement; nobody knew what would be done if either America or the Soviet Union wanted to go its separate way.

Roosevelt and the other two wartime leaders had discarded the principles agreed upon in the Atlantic Charter of 1940. By doing so, they paved the way for interference in the boundaries, rights of self-determination, and internal affairs of smaller nations. Nor was Truman a proponent of the charter, believing it to be another Fourteen Points.

Not until the announcement of the Truman Doctrine in early 1947 did Truman begin to have a foreign policy with his own imprint.

IDEOLOGY

Ideology often acts as a shield for national interest. This was particularly true in the case of the Truman administration. The American government, Truman included, has always trumpeted democracy, freedom, and justice. But Truman appeased the fascist Franco in Spain, supported Rhee's repressive and unpopular regime in South Korea, and aided the corrupt and autocratic Chiang Kai-shek group in China and then on Taiwan. Unfettered elections in Eastern Europe were a matter of serious concern to the Truman administration. But in Italy the CIA mustered its strength and its dollars to see that the Communist Party was defeated in elections.

There has not been a single major war between the Soviet Union and the US since the Bolsheviks seized power in 1917; on the contrary, the Soviets fought alongside the US and its allies in WWII. This reflects the fact that, where immediate national interests were involved, anti-fascism dominated anti-Communist ideology. Thus, the Soviet Union was called a "democracy," rather than a totalitarian state. In 1948, when Yugoslavia was forced to detach itself from the Soviet group, the Truman administration rendered it economic and military aid despite its being viewed as Communist. (Who could have believed in 1946 that Yugoslavia and Greece would plan a joint naval exercise in 1952?[4]) History shows that, in diplomacy, national interest—or, more precisely what decision-makers perceive to be the national interest—is of paramount importance. Ideology often serves simply as handmaiden to the tangibles.

ECONOMICS

Economic development in the US required new sources of raw materials, new export markets, and new supplies of cheap labor. It was only natural that, after industrialization in the nineteenth century, the US should seek expansion overseas. During the Truman period, although not every diplomatic move was directly intertwined with economic considerations, more often than not economics did affect foreign policy. For instance, Truman personally set full employment at home as one of his two objectives; this priority inevitably influenced foreign policy decisions. In the early postwar period, the US aimed for exports of $14 billion per year—the equivalent of total wartime exports, including Lend-Lease, and about six times the average for 1936-1939.[5] One implication of the Truman Doctrine was "management and procurement in the US market." "Greece alone is not large, but add in British, French, Belgian, Czech, and occupation purchases and you will reach a figure not far less than the lend-lease operation. This program will give us a long continued high level of employment whatever else happens."[6] In 1949, the Truman administration was eager to make known to the American people that, under the Marshall Plan for aid to Europe, "ultimately dollars can only be spent in the United States [and] due to current large unfilled requirements for United States goods in Western Europe, the dollars come home rapidly....The money is spent at home for items produced on US farms by our farmers or in US factories using our labor."[7] The US objected to the dismantling of German and Japanese industries as reparations partly because maintaining these industries would lessen the economic burden on US occupation governments.

The state of the economy also determined the possible extent of military build-up, which in turn influenced foreign policy. Truman said in January 1952 that "if we strive for a quick military build-up we will wreck our economy and thereby Russia would win the cold war."

OPPONENTS OF THE US

By now it is clear that the foreign policies and diplomatic actions of the Truman administration were shaped by the presence of the Soviet Union—or were reactions to Soviet policies and actions. Indeed, it is fair to say that all the other factors impinging upon Truman's diplomacy orbited around the USSR. The sheer presence of such a weighty opponent was a new phenomenon for the United States.

As for China, the decisions of the CCP were beyond the control of the US as well as the USSR. Indeed, the establishment of the PRC and the role of the CPVA in Korea embarrassed and puzzled American decision makers and forced revisions in US policy. In Independence, Truman had prayed: "Help me to understand their motives and their shortcomings, even as thou understandst mine."[8] This prayer must have been constantly in his mind as he dealt with the Chinese and the Soviets as President. At the core of the art of politics is winning as many friends and making as few enemies as possible. Truman failed to win the friendship of the Chinese Communists and, as a result, China was one of greatest failings of Truman diplomacy.

ALLIES OF THE US

The US government always wanted its allies—especially its major ally, Britain—to follow the US lead. But in fact, the British were able to significantly influence US foreign policy during the Truman years. And the attitude of the British served as a barometer gauging the efficacy of Truman diplomacy. When the US was not sufficiently firm toward the Soviet Union, the British would support the US in firmer measures; when the US became overzealous, the British would try to cool things down. Bevin once remarked that "fear is sometimes expressed that the US might be tempted to indulge in adventurous policies....If the US were nonetheless to embark on [them, there were opportunities] for the UK to apply a brake to American policy if necessary."[9] Sometimes Britain caused the US considerable worry. In April 1951, John Foster Dulles reported that the British were adopting an independent stance—which was disturbing now that Bevin had died. The new Foreign Secretary Herbert Morrison thought British ought to develop its own foreign policy and ought not rely too much on the US.[10]

SCIENCE AND TECHNOLOGY

In the last year of the Truman administration, Secretary of Defense Lovett said, "Weapons now in sight will result in a war that no one can win...if we get into a shooting war. There would be no similarity with warfare in WWII due to scientific progress."[11] Science, particularly the atomic and hydrogen bombs, influenced postwar international relations and American diplomacy to an extent that cannot be overstated. The atomic bomb was initially a tool for intimidating opponents and imposing the will of the US upon its allies. Truman himself believed that the bomb was a psychological weapon or, at most, a tactical weapon. In Truman's words, "If I had been in that frame of mind [willing to kill noncombatants], I could have knocked out Peiping, Shanghai and Canton and killed 17 or 18 million people. But that would have just been murder. That's why MacArthur and I fell out. That's what he wanted to do."[12] Once one's opponent had the bomb too, fear of retaliation was always stronger than the urge to kill.

CONGRESS

Truman once complained that "this Congress has been described as the axe-and-shovel Congress. Axe to cut it [legislation] up. Shovel to bury it."[13] But as we have witnessed, in critical matters the Congress often went along with his administration's decisions. Whether Democrats or Republicans were in the majority, Truman could do pretty much as he decided—dropping atomic bombs, announcing the Truman Doctrine and the Marshall Plan, entering the Korean War. On the other hand, Truman granted concessions on some items—token military aid to Chiang Kai-shek in 1948, for example. On the whole, the America Congress served as a check upon the Executive's diplomacy, mostly in relatively minor issues.

McCARTHYISM

The first institutionalized anti-Communist measure in the US was the Loyalty System, a measure so ridiculous that even Truman himself had to sign a statement saying that he was not a Communist.[14] The Loyalty System became a hotbed of rampant McCarthyism, "a sort of Frankenstein created by Truman himself."[15]

McCarthyism jeopardized Congressional diplomatic resolutions and nearly immobilized the State Department. Many Senators voted for a resolution urging that Communist China be kept out of the UN because a negative vote might bring upon them accusations of being "soft on Communism."[16] Almost all of State's China experts were removed, and even Marshall and Acheson could not avoid being attacked. Philip Jessup was perhaps the juiciest target, due to his past affiliation with the Institute of Pacific Relations. Harold Stassen charged that Jessup had expressed pro-Communist views during a meeting with the President in the White House. But Jessup had been visiting Dwight D. Eisenhower in New York at the time of the meeting—a fact to which Warren Austin, Chief of the US delegation to the UN at the time, was required to testify.[17] In Truman's words, "the greatest asset that the Kremlin has is Senator McCarthy."[18]

THE UNITED NATIONS

During the initial stage of the United Nations, the US was able to muster a majority in the General Assembly. By the end of the Truman administration, however, Third World countries started to have their own say, and the western allies became less inclined to follow the lead of the US for fear of antagonizing their former colonies or provoking the Soviet Union. The decline of US influence at the UN was hastened by the fighting in Korea and the adverse reaction of the smaller nations to the use of the UN for this purpose. Gradually the US lost interest in the UN.

THE REPUBLICANS

The Republican Party usually supported Truman's foreign policy in Europe and, early on, cooperated in the bipartisan approach to that arena. But for the Far East, it was not until 1950 that a sort of bipartisanship started to take shape. The situation there was one of abandoning familiar rules, and the US was suffering a defeat. It would have been strange indeed had the Republicans rushed forth to plunge into this quagmire. The situation stabilized after the establishment of the People's Republic and the emergence of Japan as a prospective ally of the US. The Republicans then lost no time in coming onto the scene, with Foster Dulles as their agent. In the end Dulles captured the limelight for himself, in successfully concluding the Japanese treaty. This provided the Republicans with a handsome campaign asset and contributed to the fall of the Democratic administration.

TRUMAN'S PERSONALITY

At the first state dinner he hosted, Truman was terrified. Afterwards, he said that "in spite of himself, he had a good dinner."[19] He told Stalin and Churchill in Potsdam what a great pleasure it was for him, a country boy from Missouri, to be associated with two such great figures as the Prime Minister and the Marshal.[20] At the same time, he was sensitive to real and imagined slights, and wary of being dwarfed by the greatness of his predecessor. He once ordered the State Department to have Soviet Ambassador Novikov recalled, because the ambassador failed to show up at a party hosted by the Trumans.

Truman had few political debts and owed favors to no one. This fact, and his simple life-style, gave him a large measure of immunity from outside pressure and a freedom to act without excessive apprehension.

But Truman did not escape the racism of his native Missouri. He would not allow blacks on his White House staff, and he called Hazel Scott a "damned nigger" when the singer refused to sing in Constitution Hall.[21] His racism may have influenced his stand toward the Chinese, and later, the Koreans.

TRUMAN'S ASSOCIATES

As a new president with no experience in diplomacy, Truman badly needed expert advice. Truman had great respect for Marshall, although the latter considered himself a military man, not cut out for diplomacy; Marshall himself once admitted, "frankly, I don't understand half of this business going on."[22] Truman nevertheless asked him to take up the most significant posts in foreign affairs. Harriman was a Truman confidant throughout the latter's presidency. He was ubiquitous: Ambassador to the

Soviet Union, Secretary of Commerce, head of the ERP Committee, special assistant to the President on the eve of the Korean War, head of the Mutual Security Agency. When Acheson was severely attacked by the McCarthyists, it was Harriman who carried the torch for the Democrats in foreign policy. Acheson himself, the most brilliant of Truman's associates, had a business-like relationship with the president. In China, many believed that, owing to his background, Acheson was more attentive to Europe than to Asia. This was not the case: Acheson advocated a China policy in the strategic interest of the US—that is, driving a wedge between the Soviets and the Chinese. It was Truman who approved this policy, only too late.

A FINAL COMMENT

Truman's diplomacy was a legacy left to later presidents. His experience, especially in the Korean War, confirmed that a major war was not feasible. But it also demonstrated the need for a program of military build-up, originally formulated in NSC-68. The fundamental logic of Truman's diplomacy—the theory and practice of containment—was acknowledged and followed by his successors. The Eisenhower administration advocated "liberation" and "roll back" for domestic political consumption, but did not act when East Berliners rioted or when the Soviet Army invaded Hungary.

As Acheson once observed that, "in the Dulles era they were following Truman too slavishly," one of Acheson's aides commented that they overreacted to dangers that the Truman era flushed out. Kennedy and Johnson were influenced tremendously by the notion that Truman lost China and sold the Far East to the Communists. Under their administrations, the Truman legacy exploded in Vietnam.[23]

The most regrettable heritage of Truman diplomacy has been the practice of international power politics. Although originated by Roosevelt, this was further developed during the Truman years. The superpowers have not only pursued their own interests via direct rivalry, but also attempted to impose their wills on other nations and to interfere in their internal affairs. Indeed, this has been the principal cause of the world's postwar troubles. One superpower has acted in the name of democracy and freedom, the other in the name of revolution and internationalism. Though the latter has now receded, we see as yet no end to regional conflicts fomented by their actions.

Notes

CHAPTER 1: FDR'S CHINA LEGACY

1. Steinhardt to Hull, 17 October 1940, *Foreign Relations of the United States, 1940* (Washington, D.C.: United States Government Printing Office), vol. 4, p. 671.

2. Steinhardt to Hull, 17 October 1940, *Foreign Relations of US, 1940*, vol. 4, p. 671.

3. Hull to Johnson, 24 October 1940, *Foreign Relations of US, 1940*, vol. 4, p. 679-682.

4. Johnson to Hull, 20 October 1940, *Foreign Relations of US, 1940*, vol. 4, p. 674-676.

5. Hamilton to Secretary of State, 3 June 1940, *Foreign Relations of US, 1940*, vol. 4, p. 658.

6. Johnson to Hull, 9 November 1940, *Foreign Relations of US, 1940*, vol. 4, p. 688-690.

7. Morganthau to Hull, 10 January 1941, *Foreign Relations of US, 1941*, vol. 5, p. 599.

8. "The President and US Aid to China—1944," China Folder (1), Box 1, George M. Elsey Papers, Truman Library.

9. Memo, 5 September 1945, China Folder (8), Box 2, Elsey Papers.

10. State Department Briefs, 9 June 1945, Naval Aide Files, Truman Library.

11. "The President and US Aid to China—1944."

12. Excerpts from Map Room File, China Folder (6), Box 2, Elsey Papers.

13. The "Precious Jade" story is from the famous 17th century Chinese novel *The Dream of the Red Chamber*. Jia Baoyu, the hero in the novel, had a piece of "Precious Jade." Once the jade was lost, his life would go with it.

14. Excerpts from Map Room File, China Folder (7), Box 2, Elsey Papers.

15. "The President and US Aid to China—1944."

16. David D. Barrett, *Dixie Mission* (Berkeley: Center for Chinese Studies, University of California, 1970), p. 23.

17. Hurley to Truman, 10 May 1945, Hurley to Truman 1945 File, Box 8, Naval Aide Files.

18. Hurley to Truman, 12 September 1945, Hurley to Truman 1945 File, Box 8, Naval Aide Files.

19. Chiang Kai-shek, *Soviet Russia In China* (New York: Farrar, Strauss & Cudahy, Inc., 1958), p. 175.

20. Roosevelt to Marshall, 8 March 1943, China Folder (3), Box 1, Elsey Papers.

21. Marshall to Roosevelt, 16 March 1943, China Folder (3), Box 1, Elsey Papers.

22. "History of the American War Production in China," p. 208, State Department Correspondence, Confidential File, Box 33, White House Central Files, Truman Library.

23. John Paton Davies, *Dragon By The Tail* (New York: Norton, 1972), p. 344.

24. Roosevelt to Hurley, 15 December 1944, *Foreign Relations of US, 1944*, vol. 6, p. 703.

25. Memo, 5 September 1945, China Folder (8), Box 2, Elsey Papers.

26. Hurley to the Secretary of State, 24 December 1944, *Foreign Relations of US*, vol. 6, pp. 746-747.

27. See *Foreign Relations of US, 1945*, The Conference at Malta and Yalta, vol. 6, p. 984.

28. Wilcox Diaries, 4 June 1951, Francis Wilcox Papers, Truman Library.

29. "The President and US Aid to China," *Selected Works of Mao Zedong* (Beijing: Foreign Language Press, 1967), vol. 3, p. 270.

30. Barrett, *Dixie Mission*, Illustrations.

31. General Ismay reporting to the War Cabinet, 9 April 1945, PREM 3 159/12, Public Record Office.

CHAPTER 2: EASTERN EUROPE AND YALTA

1. Press Conference, 17 April 1945, *Public Papers of the Presidents— HS Truman, 1945* (Washington, D.C.: Government Printing Office).

2. *Foreign Relations of U.S., 1945*, vol. 5, pp. 201-204.

3. Memoirs File Box 3, Post Presidential Papers, Truman Library.

4. *Foreign Relations of U.S., 1945*, vol. 5, pp. 213-217.

5. Harry S. Truman, *Memoirs* (New York, 1955), vol. 1, p. 50.

6. *Foreign Relations of U.S., 1945*, vol. 5, pp. 231-234.

7. *Foreign Relations of U.S., 1945*, vol. 5, pp. 252-255.

8. Russia-Molotov File, Box 188, President's Secretary's Files, Truman Library.

9. *Foreign Relations of U.S., 1945*, vol. 5, pp. 256-258; Truman, *Memoirs*, pp. 79-82.

10. See Charles Bohlen, *Witness to History: 1929-1969* (New York: Norton, 1973). On 17 May 1951, Truman's assistant Eben A. Ayers wrote a memo to the President asking him to recall the happenings during Molotov's visit in 1945. Truman's reply was:

> Eben: I had a very pleasant and rather social visit with Molotov on Sunday April 22 '45. We talked through an interpreter. I expected him to call next day. He did at 5:30 at the office in the White House.
>
> He was rather truculent. I had been talking to him about Poland and the UN Conference in San Francisco. Finally I told him in no uncertain terms that agreements must be kept, that our relations with Russia would not consist of being told what we could and could not do; the cooperation was not a one way street and that we would expect agreements to be lived up to.
>
> Molly told Bohlen that he'd never been talked to like that before by any foreign power. But he understood me.

Truman's reply in the file was not the original copy. Ayers noted that "The foregoing written in pencil by the President in reply to my memorandum of May 17, 1945 (?), EAA." Molotov Conference 1945 Folder, General File, Box 8, Eben Ayers Papers, Truman Library.

11. Ayers Diaries, 24 April 1945, Eben Ayers Papers, Truman Library.

12. *Foreign Relations of U.S., 1945*, vol. 5, pp. 263-264.

13. *Foreign Relations of U.S., 1945*, vol. 1, p. 384.

14. Memoirs File Box 3, Post Presidential Papers.

15. Memoirs File Box 3, Post Presidential Papers.

16. Ayers Diaries, 12 May 1945, Ayers Papers.

17. Ayers Diaries, 24 September 1945, Ayers Papers.

18. Daily Appointment Sheets of the President, 15 May 1945, Truman Library; *Foreign Relations of U.S., 1945*, Potsdam Conference, vol. 1, p. 13.

19. Daily Sheets, 18 May 1945.

20. Daily Sheets, 19 May 1945.

21. Press Conference, 13 June 1945, Russian Folder, Box 7, Ayers Papers.

22. Ayers Diaries, 6 June 1945.

23. *Foreign Relations of U.S., 1945*, Potsdam Conference, vol. 1, pp. 7-9.

24. Ross Diary, 5 September 1946, Charles G. Ross Papers, Truman Library.

25. Daily Sheets, 19 May 1945.

26. Ayers Diaries, 25 May 1945.

27. O.S.S. R & A No. 1109, 1 September 1945, Frank Roberts Correspondence File—1945-46, Box 9, Naval Aide Files.

28. Box 134, President's Secretary's Files.

29. Information Memo 374, 5 February 1945, Joint Chiefs-of-Staff

30. Minutes of Policy Committee 81st Meeting, 25 October 1944, Box 138, Notter Records, RG 59, National Archives.

31. Warren F. Kimball, ed., *Churchill and Roosevelt: The Complete Correspondence* (Princeton: Princeton University Press, 1984), vol. 3, p. 371.

32. Edward Stettinius, Jr., *Roosevelt and the Russians in Yalta Conference* (New York: Doubleday & Co., 1949), p. 302.

33. *Washington Star*, 18 March 1955.

34. Stettinius, *Roosevelt and Russians*, p. 301.

35. Department of State, *Bulletin*, 4 March 1945, p. 325.

36. Truman, *Memoirs*, vol. 1, p. 72.

37. Minutes of Policy Committee 81st Meeting, 25 October 1944, Box 138, Notter Records, RG 59.

38. *Foreign Relations of U.S., 1945*, vol. 5, pp. 231-234.

39. Intelligence Reports—Jay Franklin, Box 14, Rose Conway File, Truman Library.

40. Kennan Memorandum, *Foreign Relations of U.S., 1945*, vol. 5, pp. 856-860.

41. George F. Kennan, *Memoirs 1925-50* (Little, Brown & Co., 1967), pp. 211-212.

42. JCS 1313, 16 April 1945.

43. Wilson to Chiefs-of-Staff, 21 April 1945, CAB/105-188-65, Public Record Office.

44. Milovan Djilas, *Conversations with Stalin* (New York: Harcourt, Brace and World, 1962), p. 114.

45. Stettinius, *Roosevelt and Russians*, p. 317.

46. Stettinius, *Roosevelt and Russians*, p. 302.

47. Truman at American Senior Newspaper Editors dinner, 9 June 1945, Russian Folder, Box 7, Ayers Papers.

CHAPTER 3: THE ROAD TO CIVIL WAR IN CHINA

1. Daily Sheets, 14 May 1945.

2. Hurley to Truman, 10 May 1945, Box 8, Naval Aide Files.

3. Folder 1, Box 1, Elsey Papers.

4. Jiang Yongjin, "Chronicles of Sino-Soviet Treaty Negotiated by T.V. Soong and Stalin," *Zhuanjiwenxue* (Biographical Literature), Taipei, vol. 53, no. 4, pp. 76-82.

5. Daily Sheets, April-May 1945 Folder.

6. *Selected Works of Mao Zedong* (Beijing: Foreign Languages Press, 1967), vol. 1, pp. 205-270.

7. *Selected Works of Mao Zedong,* vol. 3, pp. 281-284.

8. *Selected Works of Mao Zedong,* vol. 3, pp. 285-286.

9. *Foreign Relations of U.S., 1945,* vol. 7, pp. 317-322.

10. *Selected Works of Mao Zedong,* vol. 4, pp. 33-39.

11. *Selected Works of Mao Zedong,* vol. 4, pp. 27-32.

12. Folder 1, Box 1, Elsey Papers; Daily Sheets, 15 May 1945.

13. *Selected Works of Mao Zedong,* vol. 4, pp. 47-52.

14. *Selected Works of Mao Zedong,* vol. 4, pp. 53-63.

15. *Selected Works of Mao Zedong,* vol. 4, pp. 53-63.

16. Memo 5 September 1945, China (8), Box 2, Elsey Papers.

17. Memo, 5 September 1945, China (8).

18. Memo, 4 September 1945, China (8).

19. *Selected Works of Mao Zedong,* vol. 4, pp. 53-63.

20. C.F. Romanus and R. Sonderland, *Time Runs Out in CBI* (Department of the Army, 1959), p. 394.

21. *Time Runs Out in CBI,* p. 381.

22. *Time Runs Out in CBI,* p. 381.

23. *Time Runs Out in CBI,* p. 391.

24. *Time Runs Out in CBI,* p. 394.

25. *Foreign Relations of U.S., 1945,* vol. 7, pp. 558-559.

26. Joint Chiefs-of-Staff 1330/3, 27 September 1945; Chester Joseph Pach, Jr., "Arming the Free World: The Origins of the U.S. Military Assistance Program, 1945-1949" (PhD dissertation, Northwestern University, 1981), pp. 122, 150; Romanus and Sonderland, *Time Runs Out in CBI.*

27. Roland Parker Report, 7 September 1945 (sent to Vaughan from China, 15 October 1945), Official File, White House Central Files, Truman Library.

28. Spencer Kennard, Jr. to Joseph Ballantine, 7 September 1945, Official File, White House Central Files.

29. Williams to Connally, 6 November 1945, Tom Connally Papers, Library of Congress, Washington, D.C.

30. Chien Tuan-sheng to Charles Ross, 30 July 1945, forwarded to Ross by Arthur Ringwalt, Far East Division, State Department, Official File, White House Central Files.

31. Ayers Dairies, May 1945.

32. China Folder (1), Box 1, Elsey Papers.

33. Joseph Grew to Stimson, 26 June 1945, Stimson Papers, Yale University Library, cited from Kolko Collection, York University, Toronto.

34. Daily Sheets, 15 November 1945.

35. Patterson to Samuel Rosenman, 11 November 1945, Robert P. Patterson Papers, Library of Congress.

36. "Report on the Accepting of Surrender, Chinese Army General Headquarters, China Theatre," Archival no. (25)675, Military History Society, Ministry of Military Order, Chinese National Government.

37. Memo, Locke to Truman, 19 October 1945, President's Secretary's Files.

38. Patterson to Rosenman, 11 November 1945, Patterson Papers.

39. Hurley to Byrnes, 12 September 1945, Box 8, Naval Aide Files.

40. Daily Sheets, 19 October 1945.

41. Ayers Diaries, 10 November 1945.

42. Henry Wallace to Truman, 19 September 1951, Foreign Relations—China Folder, Box 59, Elsey Papers.

43. Daily Sheets, 15 November 1945.

44. Hurley to Truman, 10 and 29 May 1945.

45. Hurley to Byrnes, 12 September 1945.

46. Hurley to Truman, 21 May 1945.

CHAPTER 4: DEBUT OF ATOMIC DIPLOMACY

1. Truman to Congress, 10 March 1945, General File (A-Bomb), Box 112, President's Secretary's Files.

2. File 345, Box 13, Miscellaneous Historical Documents Collection, Truman Library.

3. Stimson Memo, 6 June 1945, Stimson Papers, cited from Kolko Collection.

4. Subject File (NSC Atomic), Box 199, President's Secretary's Files.

5. Subject File (A-bomb), Box 199, President's Secretary's Files.

6. *Look*, 7 June 1960; John McCloy to Clark Clifford, 17 September 1984, Centennial File 1, Truman Library.

7. Michael Armine, *Report*, 5 January 1954.

8. William Lawrence Interview, Box 1, Lansing Lamont Papers, Truman Library.

9. Daily Sheets, 17 May 1945; William Leahy, *I Was There* (New York: Whittlesey House, 1950), p. 245.

10. Subject File (A-bomb), Box 199, President's Secretary's Files.

11. Subject File (A-bomb).

12. Subject File (A-bomb).

13. Subject File (A-bomb).

14. Subject File (A-bomb).

15. Interview at Kansas City, 26 August 1953, Memoirs File Box 4, Post Presidential Papers, Truman Library.

16. Ayers Diaries, 6 July 1945.

17. Joseph Daniels, *The Man of Independence* (Philadelphia: Lippencott, 1950), p. 280.

18. *U.S. News & World Report*, 9 August 1960.
19. Leahy, *I Was There*, p. 29.
20. Box 422, Stimson Papers, cited from Gabriel Kolko Collection of Research Documents, York University, Ontario.
21. 31 March 1954, Memoirs File Box 3, Post Presidential Papers.
22. Truman Diary, 25 July 1945, Truman Library.
23. Truman Diary, Berlin, 18 July 1945.
24. Charles G. Ross Diary, 5 September 1946, Ross Papers.
25. Box 71, Elsey Papers.
26. Ayers Diaries, 7 August 1945.
27. *Selected Papers of Will Clayton* (Baltimore: Johns Hopkins Press, 1971), p. 138.
28. Truman Diary, 26 July 1945.
29. Ayers Diaries, 7 August 1945.
30. General File—Potsdam, Box 10, Ayers Papers.
31. *Selected Papers of Will Clayton*, p. 139.
32. *Public Papers of President Truman, 1945*, p. 213.
33. Associated Press news item, 29 August 1945, Elsey Papers.
34. Truman to Snyder, 25 August 1945, Army 1945-49 Atomic Bomb Folder, Confidential File, Box 4, White House Central Files.
35. Cabinet Meeting, 31 August 1945, Box 2, Matthew Connelly Papers, Truman Library.
36. General File (A-bomb), Box 112, President's Secretary's Files.
37. Ayers Diaries, 5 October 1945.
38. Daily Sheets, 21 September 1945.
39. General File (A-bomb), Box 112, President's Secretary's Files; Cabinet Meeting, 21 September 1945, Connelly Papers.
40. General File (A-bomb), Box 112, President's Secretary's Files.
41. Ayers Diaries, 24 September 1945.
42. J.W. Pikersgill and D.F. Forster, *The MacKenzie King Record, 1945-1946* (Toronto: University of Toronto Press, 1970), vol. 3, pp. 7-8.
43. *The MacKenzie King Record, 1945-1946*, vol. 3, p. 39.
44. *The MacKenzie King Record, 1945-1946*, vol. 3, pp. 40-41.
45. Ayers Diaries, 1 October 1945.
46. *The MacKenzie King Record, 1945-1946*, vol. 3, p. 42.
47. Memoirs File, Post Presidential Papers.
48. Harriman to Truman, 9 August 1945, Harriman-Truman 1945 Folder, Box 7, Naval Aide Files.
49. Intelligence Reports, 9 August 1945, on Henry Field trip to the Soviet Union, etc., Box 14, Rose Conway Papers, Truman Library.
50. Attlee to Truman, Communications Attlee-Truman 1945-46 Folder, Box 6, Naval Aide Files.
51. Daily Sheets, 18 September 1945.

52. Attlee to Truman, 25 September 1945, Attlee Miscellaneous Folder, Box 170, President's Secretary's Files.

53. Truman to Congress, 3 October 1945, General File (A-bomb), Box 112, President's Secretary's Files.

54. Truman to Attlee, 5 October 1945, Attlee Miscellaneous Folder, Box 170, President's Secretary's Files.

55. Ayers Diaries, 12 September 1945.

56. Stimson Diary, 23 July 1945; *Foreign Relations of U.S., 1945*, Potsdam Conference.

57. Council of Foreign Ministers, London, September 1945, *Foreign Relations of U.S., 1945*, vol. 2; Council of Foreign Ministers—London, September 1945—File, Box 9, Naval Aide Files.

58. Council of Foreign Ministers—London, September 1945—File, Box 9, Naval Aide Files.

59. Council of Foreign Ministers, London, September 1945, *Foreign Relations of U.S., 1945*, vol. 2.

60. Interview in Kansas City, 26 August 1953, Memoirs File Box 4, Post Presidential Papers.

61. *Foreign Relations of U.S., 1945*, vol. 2, p. 558.

62. Council of Foreign Ministers—London, September 1945—File, Box 9, Naval Aide Files.

63. *Foreign Relations of U.S., 1945*, vol. 2, p. 559.

64. Acheson to Truman, 25 September 1945, *Foreign Relations of U.S., 1945*, vol. 2.

65. Attlee to Truman, Communications Attlee-Truman 1945-46 Folder, Box 6, Naval Aide Files.

66. Ayers Diaries, 24 September 1945.

67. Press Conference, 8 October 1945, *Public Papers of President Truman, 1945*, p. 213.

68. Daily Sheets, 14 May 1945.

69. Daily Sheets, 18, 26 and 29 September 1945.

70. Ayers Diaries, 29 October 1945.

71. Ayers Diaries, 29 October 1945.

72. Ayers Diaries, 29 October 1945.

73. Truman to Stalin, 1945, Box 9, Naval Aide Files.

74. Telegram, 7 November 1945, Russia-Stalin Folder, Box 188, President's Secretary's Files.

75. Ayers Diaries, 19 November 1945.

76. Ayers Diaries, 1 November 1945.

77. Ayers Diaries, 19 November 1945.

78. *Foreign Relations of U.S., 1945*, vol. 5, p. 921.

79. Harriman to Byrnes, 27 November 1945, *Foreign Relations of U.S., 1945*, vol. 5.

80. *Foreign Relations of U.S., 1945*, vol. 2, pp. 55-57, 59-62.

81. *Foreign Relations of U.S., 1945*, vol. 2, p. 69.

82. *Foreign Relations of U.S., 1945*, vol. 5, pp. 55-57, 59-62.

83. Foreign Affairs—Russia-Molotov File, Box 187, President's Secretary's Files.

84. Foreign Affairs—Russia-Molotov File, Box 187, President's Secretary's Files.

85. *Time*, 31 September 1945, p. 22.

86. Ayers Diaries, 17 December 1945.

87. *Foreign Relations of U.S., 1945*, vol. 2, pp. 776.

88. U.S. version of the 7th Formal Session, Council of Foreign Ministers, Moscow, December 1945, *Foreign Relations of U.S., 1945*, vol. 2.

89. For reference to the agreements and non-agreements of the Council of Foreign Ministers Moscow Meeting, December 1945, see *Foreign Relations of U.S., 1945*, vol. 2.

90. Diaries, 26 and 28 December 1945, William Leahy Papers, Library of Congress; see Herbert Feis, *From Trust to Terror: The Onset of the Cold War, 1945-1950* (New York: Norton, 1970), p. 55.

91. Memoirs File Box 3, Post Presidential Papers.

CHAPTER 5: 1946—PRELUDE TO THE COLD WAR

1. Daily Sheets, 8 March 1946.

2. Daily Sheets, 16 March 1946.

3. Army 1945-49 Atomic Bomb Folder, Confidential File, Box 4, White House Central Files.

4. Attlee to Truman, 16 April 1946, Attlee-Truman Correspondence 1945-46, Box 6, Naval Aide Files.

5. Harriman to Truman, 12 June 1946, Subject File (Attlee), Box 170, President's Secretary's Files.

6. Army 1945-49 Atomic Bomb Folder, Confidential File, Box 4, White House Central Files.

7. Locke, Jr., to Truman, 21 June 1946, Subject File (NSC Atomic), Box 199, President's Secretary's Files.

8. State Department Briefs to the President (Summary of Telegrams), 3 June 1946, Naval Aide Files.

9. State Department Briefs, 8 July 1946.

10. Baruch to King, 24 May 1946, and King to Baruch, 5 June 1946, Box 17, Ernest J. King Papers, Library of Congress.

11. Eisenhower to Baruch, 14 June 1946, Bernard Baruch Papers, cited from Kolko's Collection.

12. Truman to Baruch, 10 July 1946, Baruch Papers, from Kolko's Collection.

13. U.N. Committee U.S. Staff Meeting, 10 September 1946, Baruch Papers, from Kolko's Collection.

14. Franklin A. Lindsay to Baruch, 21 October 1946, Baruch Papers, Seeley Mudd Library, Princeton.

15. Army 1945-49 Atomic Bomb Folder, Confidential File, Box 4, White House Central Files.

16. Bernard Baruch, *The Public Years* (New York: Holt, Rinehart & Winston, 1960), p. 379.

17. (46)14th Meeting Conclusions, 11 February 1946, CAB/128/7, Public Record Office, Kew.

18. State Department Briefs, 20 February 1946.

19. State Department Briefs, 7 February 1946.

20. State Department, "U.S.-Soviet Policy," 15 May 1946, Box 14, Clark Clifford Papers, Truman Library.

21. C.P.(45)174, 17 September 1945, CAB 129/2.

22. C.M.(46)1, 1 January 1946, CAB 128/5.

23. Allen to Woodward, 23 January 1946, and Connelly to Woodward, 26 January 1946, File 134 (1945-49), Official File, Truman Library.

24. State Department Briefs, 29 January 1946.

25. State Department Briefs, 31 January 1946.

26. State Department Briefs, 25 February 1946.

27. State Department Briefs, 5 March 1946.

28. State Department Briefs, 6 March 1946.

29. State Department Briefs, 12 March 1946.

30. State Department Briefs, 14 March 1946.

31. State Department Briefs, 15 March 1946.

32. State Department Briefs, 16 March 1946.

33. State Department Briefs, 18 March 1946.

34. State Department Briefs, 22 March 1946.

35. State Department Briefs, 9 April 1946.

36. State Department Briefs, 26 March 1946.

37. State Department Briefs, 12 and 15 April 1946.

38. State Department Briefs, 14 May 1946.

39. Stettinius to Byrnes, 20 May 1946, Miscellaneous to Truman 1946 Folder, Box 8, Naval Aide Files.

40. State Department Briefs, 3 June 1946.

41. State Department Briefs, 10 June 1946.

42. State Department Briefs, 11 June 1946.

43. State Department Briefs, 18 June 1946.

44. State Department Briefs, 21 June 1946.

45. State Department Briefs, 25 June 1946.

46. State Department Briefs, 25 November 1946.

47. State Department Briefs, 3 December 1946.

48. State Department Briefs, 10 December 1946.

49. C.P.(47)11, 3 January 1947, CAB/129/16.

50. JCS 1714/1, 12 October 1946.

51. Minutes of 23 July 1945 Meeting, Berlin Conference File, Box 2, Naval Aide Files.

52. State Department Briefs, 19 March 1946.

53. State Department Briefs, 11 April 1946.

54. State Department Briefs, 11 June 1946.

55. State Department Briefs, 27 June 1946.

56. State Department Briefs, 9 August 1946.

57. State Department Briefs, 13 August 1946.

58. State Department Briefs, 13 August 1946.

59. Kennan's Comment on the Clifford-Elsey Paper (draft), Russian Folder (5), Box 15, Clifford Papers.

60. State Department Briefs, 19 and 20 August, 1946.

61. Meeting with Turkish Foreign Minister, 12 April 1949, Box 64, Acheson Papers.

62. State Department Briefs, 26 September 1946.

63. State Department Briefs, 2 December 1946.

64. State Department Briefs, 18 December 1946.

65. State Department Briefs, 20 December 1946.

66. *St. Louis Post-Dispatch*, 29 February 1948.

67. NSC 47-50 File, Box 1, Sidney W. Souers Papers, Truman Library.

68. Samuel F. Wells, Jr., "The Origins of Massive Retaliation," *Political Science Quarterly*, Spring 1981.

69. Intelligence Service Folder, Box 7, Ayers Papers.

70. Ayers Diaries, 27 August 1945.

71. Intelligence Service Folder, Box 7, Ayers Papers.

72. Intelligence Service Folder, Box 7, Ayers Papers.

73. Intelligence Reports Folder, Box 14, Rose Conway Papers.

74. Intelligence Service Folder, Box 7, Ayers Papers.

75. Intelligence Service Folder, Box 7, Ayers Papers.

76. Intelligence Service Folder, Box 7, Ayers Papers.

77. See Bradley F. Smith, "A Note on the OSS, Ultra, and World War II's Intelligence Legacy for America," *Defense Analysis* (Britain), 1987, vol. 3, no. 2, p. 188.

78. David Bruce to Allen Dulles, 10 October 1945, Allen W. Dulles Papers, Mudd Library.

79. Russia 1945-48 File, Box 187, President's Secretary's Files.

80. State Department Briefs, 31 January 1946.

81. State Department Briefs, 25 January 1946.

82. State Department Briefs, 30 January 1946; *Time*, 11 February 1946.

83. *New York Times*, 9 February 1946.

84. Folder 2, Box 63, Elsey Papers.

85. State Department Briefs, 18 February 1946.

86. State Department Briefs, 10 February 1946.

87. Lamkin to Vaughan, 17 September 1945, and Vaughan to Lamkin, 27 September 1945, 1429 File, p-504, President's Personal Files, Truman Library.

88. Churchill Folder, General File, Box 116, President's Secretary Files.

89. 1429 File, p-504, President's Personal Files.

90. Churchill Folder, General File, Box 116, President's Secretary Files.

91. Churchill Trip—Florida 1945 Folder, Box 7, Naval Aide Files.

92. *Time*, 21 January 1946.

93. Churchill Folder, General File, Box 116, President's Secretary Files.

94. Churchill Folder, General File, Box 116, President's Secretary Files.

95. Ayers Diaries, 11 February 1946.

96. Ross Diary, 4 March 1946, Ross Papers.

97. Churchill Folder, General File, Box 116, President's Secretary Files.

98. The Words and the Man (Fulton: Westminster College, 1960).

99. Ross Diary, 4 and 5 March 1946.

100. Ross Diary, 18 March 1946.

101. *New York Times*, 15 March 1946.

102. Vaughan to K.C. Marshall, 19 April 1946, 327 File, p-479, President's Personal Files.

103. Churchill Folder, General File, Box 116, President's Secretary Files.

104. *New York Times*, 9 March 1946.

105. *New York Times*, 9 March 1946.

106. Ayers Diaries, 5 March 1946.

107. Press Conference, 8 March 1946, Truman-Churchill-Stalin Folder, Subject Files, Box 5, Ayers Papers.

108. Pp. 81-82, Clark Clifford Oral History, Truman Library.

109. Truman Diary, Berlin 16 July 1945, Truman Library.

110. *Time*, 18 March 1946.

111. (46)23rd Meeting Conclusions, 11 March 1946, CAB 128/5; (46)25th Meeting Conclusions, 18 March 1946, CAB 128/5.

112. (46)54, 3 June 1946, CAB 128/5.

113. Daily Sheets, 23 March 1946.

114. State Department Briefs, 1 April 1946.

115. Smith to Byrnes, 3 April 1946, Miscellaneous to Truman 1946 Folder, Box 8, Naval Aide Files.

116. Stalin to Truman, 6 April 1946, Stalin-Truman Correspondence 1946 Folder, Box 9, Naval Aide Files.

117. State Department Policy Information and Statement, 15 May 1946, Russian Folder (1), Box 14, Clifford Papers.

118. Ross Diary, 25 March 1946.

119. Ayers Diaries, 17 July 1946.

120. Truman to John Garner, 21 September 1946, Box 187, President's Secretary's Files.

121. State Department Briefs, 26 July 1946.
122. State Department Briefs, 26 July 1946.
123. State Department Briefs, 30 July 1946.
124. Ayers Diaries, 20 September 1946.
125. Ayers Diaries, 21 September 1946.
126. Ross Diary, 23 September 1946.
127. Truman to Garner, 21 September 1946, Box 187, President's Secretary's Files.
128. Ross Diary, 25 September 1946.
129. Carol Briley, "George Elsey's White House Career, 1942-1953," (MA thesis, University of Missouri-Kansas City, 1976).
130. Clifford Papers. Arthur Krock took this document as an appendix of his *Memoirs*.
131. Memo, Acheson to Clifford, 6 August 1946, Box 15, Clifford Papers.
132. State Department Briefs, 24 December 1946.
133. State Department Briefs, 23 and 28 September 1946.
134. State Department Briefs, 31 October 1946.
135. *Time*, 11 November 1946.
136. Russia-Molotov Folder, Box 187, President's Secretary Files.
137. *Time*, 18 November 1946.
138. Patterson to Julius O. Adler, 2 November 1946, Robert Patterson Papers, Library of Congress.

CHAPTER 6: ALL QUIET ON THE WESTERN FRONT

1. State Department Briefs, 31 December 1946.
2. State Department Briefs, 9 January 1947.
3. State Department Briefs, 21 January 1947.
4. State Department Briefs, 13 January 1946.
5. State Department Briefs, 6 February 1947.
6. State Department Briefs, 12 February 1947.
7. State Department Briefs, 18 February 1947.
8. State Department Briefs, 20 February 1947.
9. State Department Briefs, 27 February 1947.
10. State Department Briefs, 27 February 1947.
11. State Department Briefs, 4 March 1947.
12. State Department Briefs, 3 and 4 March 1947.
13. State Department Briefs, 7 March 1947.
14. Subject File (Greece), Box 180, President's Secretary's Files.
15. State Department Briefs, 28 January 1947.
16. State Department Briefs, 13 January 1947.
17. State Department Briefs, 3 February 1947.

18. State Department Briefs, 10 February 1947.

19. Greece and Turkey 1947 Folder, Box 1278, Official File, Truman Papers.

20. Greece and Turkey 1947 Folder.

21. Bennett to Vandenberg, 3 March 1947, Vandenberg Papers, cited from Kolko's Collection.

22. O'Mahoney to Truman, 10 March 1947, Box 386, Official File, Truman Papers.

23. C.M.(47)15, 3 February 1947, CAB 128/9.

24. State Department Briefs, 19 February 1947.

25. Lord Sherfield, formerly Sir Roger Makins who was the last Ambassador to U.S. during the Truman period, in an interview with the author in London, October 1987.

26. Daily Sheets, 10 May 1947.

27. Daily Sheets, 4 June 1947.

28. Truman off-record address at American Senior Newspaper Editors dinner, 17 April 1947, Russian Relations Folder, Box 7, Ayers Papers.

29. State Department Briefs, 5 June 1947.

30. C.M.(47)54, 17 June 1947, CAB 128/10; C.M.(47)55, 19 June 1947, CAB 128/10; C.P.(47)188, 23 June 1947, CAB 129/19.

31. State Department Briefs, 27 June 1947.

32. C.P.(47)197, 5 June 1947, CAB 129/19.

33. State Department Briefs, 1 July 1947.

34. Memo, 26 February 1947, CIA Memo 1945-48 Folder, Box 249, President's Secretary's Files.

35. State Department Briefs, 7 February 1947.

36. State Department Briefs, 21 July 1947.

37. State Department Briefs, 25 July 1947.

38. State Department Briefs, 28 July 1947.

39. State Department Briefs, 4 August 1947; C.M.(47)71, 17 August 1947, CAB 128/10; C.M.(47)72, 19 August 1947, CAB 128/10; C.M.(47)73, 20 August 1947, CAB 128/10.

40. State Department Briefs, 5 September 1947.

41. Daily Sheets, 5 August 1947.

42. Memo, Wilcox to Will Clayton, 6 August 1947, Francis Wilcox Papers, Truman Library.

43. C.M.(47)77, 25 August 1947, CAB 128/10.

44. Memo, Elsey to Clifford, 16 October 1947, Clifford Papers.

45. State Department Briefs, 13 August 1947.

46. NSC 32nd Meeting, 24 January 1949, Box 205, President's Secretary's Files.

47. C.P.(47)340, 22 December 1947, CAB 129/22.

48. Patterson to commanding generals of armies, 4 January 1947, Patterson Papers, Library of Congress.

49. State Department Briefs, 23, 25 and 29 September 1947.

50. Russian Folder (6), Box 15, Clifford Papers.

51. State Department Briefs, 1 October 1947.

52. 12 April 1945, Box 21, Kennan Papers, Seeley Mudd Library, Princeton.

53. State Department Briefs, 29 January 1946.

54. State Department Briefs, 5 June 1946.

55. CIA Memo, 3 August 1950, 1950-52 Folder, Box 250, President's Secretary's Files.

56. State Department Briefs, 1 October 1947.

57. State Department Briefs, 2 October 1947.

58. State Department Briefs, 25 November 1947.

59. Vedeler to Steinhardt, 12 August 1947, Box 55, Steinhaardt Papers, from Kolko's Collection.

60. German Assignment July 1947, bulletin, Joseph M. Dodge, written in Vienna 1 July 1947, Dodge Papers, from Kolko's Collection.

61. Steinhardt to Diamond, 1 August 1947, Steinhardt Papers, from Kolko's Collection.

62. Williamson to Steinhardt, 7 July 1947, Steinhardt Papers, from Kolko's Collection.

63. State Department Briefs, 6 August 1947.

64. CIA Memo, 3 August 1950, 1950-52 Folder, Box 250, President's Secretary's Files.

65. C.P.(48)6, 4 January 1948, CAB 129/23.

66. C.P.(48)35, 5 February 1948, CAB 129/24.

67. C.P.(48)6, 4 January 1948, CAB 129/23.

68. C.P.(48)71, 3 March 1948, CAB 129/25.

69. *Town Meeting* (New York: Town Hall Inc.), vol. 13, no. 50, 6 April 1948.

70. C.P.(48)71, 3 March 1948, CAB 129/25; *Foreign Relations of U.S., 1948,* vol. 4, pp. 745-747.

71. State Department Briefs, 31 March 1948.

72. State Department Briefs, 3 May 1948.

73. Daily Sheets, 13 May 1948.

74. State Department Briefs, 14 June 1948.

75. State Department Briefs, 14 June 1948.

76. State Department Briefs, 21 June 1948.

77. Cabinet Meetings File, Box 1, Connelly Papers.

78. State Department Briefs, 29 June 1948.

79. C.M.(48)42, 24 June 1948, CAB 128/13; C.M.(48)43, 25 June 1948; C.M.(48)44, 28 June 1948.

80. C.M.(48)53, 22 July 1948, CAB 128/13.

81. *Foreign Relations of U.S., 1948,* vol. 2, pp. 950-994; C.M.(48)53, 22 July 1948, CAB 128/13; C.M.(48)54, 26 July 1948.

82. C.M.(48) 19th Conclusions (points not included in the open Minutes), 5 March 1948, CAB 128/14.
83. C.P.(48)162, 24 June 1948, CAB 129/28.
84. C.M.(48)42, 24 June 1948, CAB 128/13; C.M.(48)43, 25 June 1948.
85. Cabinet Meetings File, Box 1, Connelly Papers.
86. *Foreign Relations of U.S., 1948,* vol. 2, pp. 995-1007.
87. Cabinet Meetings File, Box 1, Connelly Papers.
88. Cabinet Meetings File.
89. Cabinet Meetings File.
90. Conversations with Arthur Vandenberg, 11 and 23 October 1948, Box 36, Allen Dulles Papers.

CHAPTER 7: WAR DRUMS IN THE FAR EAST

1. Ayers Diaries, 22 May 1945.
2. Box 428, Stimson Papers, from Kolko's Collection.
3. C.M.(46)1, 1 January 1946, CAB 128/5.
4. For new research results regarding the CCP International-Soviet Communist Party relationship cited here, refer to Yang Kuisong, "Several Problems of the Relationship Between the Chinese Communist Party and the Communist International and the Soviet Communist Party during the War of Resistance against Japanese Invasion," *Dangshi yanjiu* (Party History Studies), 1987, no. 6, pp. 141-148.
5. Ayers Diaries, 17 July 1946.
6. Truman to Locke, Jr., 3 October 1945, Box 1, Edwin A. Locke, Jr. Papers, Truman Library.
7. Locke to Truman, 5 November 1945, Miscellaneous to Truman 1945 Folder, Box 8, Naval Aide Files.
8. Locke to Truman, 5 November 1945.
9. China Folder (1), Box 1, Elsey Papers.
10. *Foreign Relations of U.S., 1945*, vol. 7, p. 770.
11. Yeaton to Wedemeyer, 20 December 1945, *Foreign Relations of U.S., 1945*, vol. 7, pp. 793-794.
12. Shepley to Marshall, 9 December 1945, *Foreign Relations of U.S., 1945*, vol. 7, p. 775.
13. Yeaton to Wedemeyer, 20 December 1945, *Foreign Relations of U.S., 1945*, vol. 7, p. 793-794.
14. *Time*, 31 December 1945.
15. *Zhang Zizhong huiyilu* (Memoirs of Zhang Zizhong) (Beijing, 1985), pp. 739-740. Zhang was a general who became a member of the Committee of Three representing the Nationalists. He led the Nationalist peace delegation to Beijing to negotiate with the CCP in early 1949. He did not return to the

Nationalist side after the negotiation failed. He later became a prominent figure in the coalition between the CCP and smaller parties in the PRC.

16. Marshall's Memorandum to Truman, 1954, Post Presidential Papers.

17. Tai (Dai) Li, Director of the Bureau of Investigation and Statistics, Military Commission (a Gestapo-type organization) since the late 1920s. This facility was strengthened by U.S. support during World War II, via the U.S. Navy Group in China headed by Milton Miles.

18. Wedemeyer to Marshall, 7 July 1946, *Foreign Relations of U.S., 1946*, vol. 9, p. 39.

19. Chiang, *Soviet Russia*, pp. 154-155.

20. State Department Briefs, 29 January 1946.

21. Wedemeyer to Marshall, 7 January 1946, *Foreign Relations of U.S., 1946*, vol. 9, p. 39.

22. Truman to Delacy, 12 January 1946, China—1945 File, Box 173, President's Secretary's Files.

23. C.M.(46)1, 1 January 1946, CAB 128/5.

24. Chiang, *Soviet Russia*, pp. 154-159.

25. Zhang Wenjin, former PRC Vice-Foreign Minister and Ambassador to the U.S., was Zhou Enlai's interpreter during the time of Marshall's mediation.

26. Zhang Wenjin, "Zhou Enlai and Marshall in 1946," *Zhonghua yinglie* (Journal of Chinese Heroes and Martyrs), 1988, no. 2.

27. Zhang, "Zhou Enlai and Marshall in 1946."

28. *Time*, 11 March 1946.

29. State Department Briefs, 6 March 1946.

30. Reminiscing about his days as the Soviet Commander in Mukden, General Kovtun-Stankevich mentioned neither the stripping of Manchurian industries nor his role in it. Quite the contrary, he said that the Soviet troops used their transport facilities to help restore coal mines. He also mentioned negotiations with bankers to lend money to factories so they could restart production, and said that the Soviets acted "with greater determination to stabilize and strengthen the Manchurian economy." See *Soviet Volunteers in China 1925-1945: Articles and Reminiscences* (Moscow, 1980), pp. 285-304.

31. *Time*, 11 March 1946.

32. State Department Briefs, 25 April 1946.

33. Marshall's Memorandum to Truman, 1954.

34. Marshall's Memorandum to Truman, 1954.

35. State Department Briefs, 15 April 1946.

36. Zhang, "Zhou Enlai and Marshall in 1946."

37. Zhang, "Zhou Enlai and Marshall in 1946."

38. State Department Briefs, 20 August 1946.

39. C.M.(46)86, 14 October 1946, CAB 128/8.

40. State Department Briefs, 11 April 1946.

41. Stimson's Rough Notes after Talk with Henry R. Luce, Wednesday, 20 November 1946, Box 434, Stimson Papers, from Kolko's Collection.

42. Marshall to War Department, 28 November 1946, Box 183, President's Secretary's Files.

43. Marshall's Memorandum to Truman, 1954.

44. State Department Briefs, 9 January 1947.

45. There were altogether five charges. Charge 1, rape, was the most serious.

46. The relevant documents of this case were then in the possession of the Department of the Navy. They are now in the National Archives in Suitland.

47. *Zhou Enlai xuanji* (The Selected Works of Zhou Enlai) (Beijing, 1980), vol. 1, p. 269.

48. John Melby, a diplomatic officer in the U.S. embassy, Nanjing, mentioned the case in his published diary, *The Mandate of Heaven* (Toronto: University of Toronto Press, 1968): "Rape being unarguable, the facts will probably remain obscure."

49. *Selected Works of Mao Zedong*, vol. 4, p. 120.

50. State Department Briefs, 2 January 1947.

51. State Department Briefs, 5 February 1947.

52. *Selected Works of Mao Zedong*, vol. 4, pp. 113-114.

53. *Selected Works of Mao Zedong*, vol. 4, pp. 120.

54. State Department Briefs, 3 April 1947.

55. State Department Briefs, 18 April 1947.

56. Eximport Bank.

57. Daily Sheets, 16 to 30 June 1947 Folder.

58. State Department Briefs, 27 June 1947.

59. State Department Briefs, 2 July 1947.

60. State Department Briefs, 12 September 1947.

61. Daily Sheets, 30 September 1947.

62. State Department Briefs, 22 September 1947.

63. State Department Briefs, 7 October 1947.

64. State Department Briefs, 14 October 1947.

65. State Department Briefs, 15 and 23 December 1947.

66. State Department Briefs, 6 November 1947.

67. C.M.(47)92, 2 December 1947, CAB 128/10.

68. State Department Briefs, 24 December 1947.

69. Daily Sheets, 20 December 1947.

CHAPTER 8: THE "LOSS" OF CHINA

1. *Selected Works of Mao Zedong* (Beijing: Foreign Languages Press, 1967), vol. 1, p. 19.

2. In *Soviet Volunteers in China 1925-1945: Articles and Reminiscences*, a book published in Moscow in 1980, in both Russian and English, the period from 1928 to 1936 is very marginally referred to, and the Soviet presence in the CCP and Chinese Red Army is not mentioned. This may not be accidental.

3. Mao Zedong to Georg Dmitrov and Manuisky, 4 November 1940.

4. For new research results regarding the CCP-International-Soviet Communist Party relationship cited here, please refer to Yang Kuisong, "Several Problems of the Relationship Between the Chinese Communist Party and the Communist International and the Soviet Communist Party During the War of Resistance Against Japanese Invasion," *Dangshi yanjiu* (Party History Studies), 1987, no. 6, pp. 141-148.

5. Liu Shaoqi's cable to Mao Zedong, 17 September 1945; The CCP Central Committee Directive to the CCP Northeastern Bureau on sending 100,000 troops to Manchuria, 6 October 1945.

6. Wu Xiuquan, *Wodelicheng* (My Experiences 1908-1949) (Beijing, 1984).

7. CIA Report, March 1948, Intelligence File, Box 259, President's Secretary's Files.

8. 13 September 1948, CAB 129/29-223.

9. Wu, *Wodelicheng*, p. 172.

10. Wu Xinquan, *Wozai waijiaobu baniandejingli* (Eight Years in the Ministry of Foreign Affairs) (Beijing, 1983), pp. 11-12.

11. CIA Report, March 1948.

12. Wu, *Waijiaobubanian*, p. 12.

13. E.M. Zhukov, *History of Far Eastern International Relations 1840-1949* (Moscow, 1956).

14. Wu, *Waijiaobubanian*, p.12.

15. *The People's Liberation Army Chronicle of Major Events, 1927-1982* (Beijing, 1982).

16. Speech, Zhou Enlai, *Jiefangribao* (Liberation Daily), Chongqing, 12 October 1944.

17. Joint Intelligence Committee 230/1, 1 November 1944.

18. *Selected Works of Mao Zedong,* vol. 4, p. 59.

19. *Selected Works of Mao Zedong,* vol. 4, pp. 87-88.

20. Carlos Romulo, "Western Powers and the Far East," *New Statesman and Nation*, 10 September 1949.

21. *New York Times*, 26 June 1950, cited from Paterson, Clifford and Hagen, *American Foreign Policy* (Lexington and Toronto: D.C. Heath & Co., 1988), vol. 2, p. 472.

22. C.P.(48)6, 4 January 1948, CAB 129/23; C.P.(48)7, 5 January 1948; C.P.(48)8, 4 January 1948.

23. *Foreign Relations of U.S., 1945,* vol. 7, pp. 342-344.

24. *Foreign Relations of U.S., 1945,* vol. 7, pp. 323-325.

25. *Foreign Relations of U.S., 1945,* vol. 7, pp. 334-338.

26. State Department Briefs, 9 February 1948.

27. State Department Briefs, 20 February 1948.

28. State Department Briefs, 19 March 1948.

29. 11 March 1948, China Folder, General File, Box 5, Ayers Papers.

30. State Department Briefs, 1 April 1948.

31. State Department Briefs, 11 June 1948.

32. Vandenberg to William Knowland, 21 October 1948, Vandenberg Papers, from Kolko's Collection.

33. Truman dictation, 3 November 1953, Memoirs Box 4, Post Presidential Papers.

34. Marshall Memorandum to Truman, 1954.

35. Vandenberg to Zeimat, 18 January 1949, Vandenberg Papers, from Kolko's Collection.

36. Badger to Halsey, 5 August 1948, Halsey Papers, Library of Congress.

37. CIA Memo, 15 December 1948, 1945-48 Folder, Box 249, President's Secretary's Files.

38. NSC Meetings File, Box 220, President's Secretary's Files.

39. Daily Meeting with the Secretary of the State, 31 August 1949, E 393, RG 59, National Archives. Sun was a West Pointer. He was later put under house arrest by Chiang Kai-shek for scheming with the US.

40. Cabinet Meeting, 3 September 1948, Box 1, Connelly Papers.

41. Cabinet Meeting, 26 November 1948.

42. China—1949 File, Box 173, President's Secretary File.

43. Wedemeyer to Steelman, 20 October 1948, Folder 13, Box 34, Confidential File, White House Central Files.

44. Folder 13, Box 34, Confidential File, White House Central Files.

45. NSC Meeting, 10 December 1948, Box 205, President's Secretary's Files.

46. Memo, 17 December 1948, Box 220, President's Secretary Files.

47. NSC Meeting, 6 January 1949.

48. For summary of above reports from Stuart and the US embassy, see State Department Briefs, January to April 1948 Folder.

49. Liu Xiao, "Ambassadorship to the Soviet Union," *World Affairs* (Beijing), 1987, no. 3, p. 15.

50. *Dangshi ziliao tongxun* (Party Documentary Materials Bulletin), 1987, no. 22, p. 13.

51. There are competing sources that challenge the above version. Former Vice-Foreign Minister Yu Zhan said in an article that he had exhausted research in the archives of the Foreign Ministry, but could not find the record that Mikoyan had persuaded Mao not to cross the Yangtze. (See Yu Zhan and Zhang Guangyou, "Probes on Whether Stalin Had Persuaded Us Not to Cross the Yangtze," *Dangshi wenxian* (Party Documentaries), 1989, no. 1, pp. 56-58. Si Ze, Mao's interpreter, holds a similar view.

52. NSC 34/1, NSC Meeting, 3 February 1949, Box 205, President's Secretary's Files.

53. Cabinet Meeting, 19 January 1949.

54. C.M.(49)18, 8 March 1949, CAB 128/15.

55. State Department Briefs, 10 January 1949.

56. C.M.(49)2, 12 January 1949, CAB 128/15.

57. Yang, "Several Problems."

58. State Department Briefs, 24 and 26 January, and 24 March 1949.

59. State Department Briefs, 29 March 1949.

60. Daily Sheets, 18 February 1949.

61. Daily Sheets, 10 May 1949.

62. State Department Briefs, 31 January 1949.

63. NSC-41, 28 February 1949, Box 205, President's Secretary's Files.

64. Meeting with the Secretary of the State, 8 March 1949, E 393, RG 59.

65. Meeting with the Secretary of the State, 16 March 1949.

66. NSC-37/2, 3 February 1949, Box 205, President's Secretary Files.

67. State Department Briefs, 18 April 1949.

68. Memo, 7 February 1949, January-February Folder, Box 64, Dean Acheson Papers, Truman Library; *The Private Papers of Senator Vandenberg* (Boston: Hughton & Mifflin, 1952), p. 530.

69. State Department Briefs, 19 April 1949.

70. Liu, "Ambassadorship," p. 15.

71. C.M.(49)28, 26 April 1949, CAB 128/15.

72. *Foreign Relations of U.S., 1945,* vol. 7, p. 346.

73. Truman to Vandenberg, 6 July 1950, Vandenberg Papers, from Kolko's Collection.

74. State Department Briefs, 25 April 1949.

75. *Selected Works of Mao Zedong,* vol. 4, p. 438.

76. State Department Briefs, 27 April 1949.

77. *Foreign Relations of U.S., 1949,* vol. 8, pp. 741-742, 745-748, 752-754, 766-769.

78. *Foreign Relations of U.S., 1949,* vol. 8, pp. 756-757, 764, 770-776, 782-783.

79. Luo was a professor and a leading member of the China Democratic League. He played an important role in the coalition of the CCP and the minor parties. He was repudiated during the "Anti-Rightist Campaign" in 1957, and that ended his political activities. He was rehabilitated by the Chinese authorities in the 1980s.

80. Zhang Dongsun was a philosophy professor at Yenching University, a senior member of the China Democratic League, and a member of the Central Government Council after 1 October 1949. It was alleged that he had been secretly involved with the US during the Korean War and was politically ostracized. His case has never been tried or officially publicized.

81. Zhang Zhongbing was a professor of entomology at Beijing University. It is known to his colleagues and students that he once worked for US intelligence in China.

82. *Foreign Relations of U.S., 1949,* vol. 8, pp. 350, 376-377, 443-445, 612-613, 618, 790, 1004.

83. *Foreign Relations of U.S., 1949,* vol. 8, pp. 357-360.

84. *Foreign Relations of U.S., 1949,* vol. 8, pp. 372-373.

85. Conversation with the President, 16 June 1949, Box 1, E 394, RG 59; *Foreign Relations of U.S., 1949,* vol. 8, p. 388.

86. Smith and Bender were US military personnel in Qingdao missing in flight on 19 October 1948. They actually had landed in the Communist-controlled area and were later released and returned to the US in 1950.

87. *Foreign Relations of U.S., 1949,* vol. 8, p. 384.

88. *Foreign Relations of U.S., 1949,* vol. 8, pp. 397-399.

89. *Foreign Relations of U.S., 1949,* vol. 8, p. 385.

90. F 12075/G, 13 August 1949, OF 371/75766/134841, Public Record Office.

91. Guy Burgess was in China Political in the Foreign Office in 1949. He fled with Donald McLean, another F.O. official, to the Soviet Union in 1951. Burgess was considered a Soviet spy but his true identity is yet to be confirmed. However, judging by his comments on China in various F.O. documents, he was doubtless one of the few in the F.O. who really knew something about Marxism and the Chinese Revolution.

92. China—1949 Folder, Box 173, President's Secretary's Files.

93. Wu, *Waijiaobubanian*, pp. 14-15.

94. F 9742, 14 July 1949, OF 371/75761, Public Record Office.

95. F 7222, 13 May 1949, OF 371/75755.

96. Memo, 1 July 1949, July 1949 Folder, Box 64, Acheson Papers.

97. China—1949 Folder, Box 173, President's Secretary's Files.

98. Conversation with the President, 23 May and 13 June 1949, E 394, RG 59.

99. Memo, 25 July 1949, Box 64, Acheson Papers.

100. C.P.(49)214, 24 October 1949, CAB 129/37.

101. Daily Meeting with the Secretary of State, 8 March 1949, E 393, RG 59.

CHAPTER 9: ADAPTING TO THE COMMUNIST ACCESSION IN CHINA

1. Wu, *Waijiaobubanian*, pp. 4-5.

2. Wu, *Waijiaobubanian*, pp. 14-15.

3. Wu, *Waijiaobubanian*, pp. 14-15; Daily Meeting with the Secretary of State, 3 October 1949, E 393, RG 59.

4. Conversation with the President, 3 October 1949, E 394, RG 59.

5. Liu, "Ambassadorship."

6. Svetozar Vukmanovic, *How and Why the People's Liberation Stuggle of Greece Met with Defeat* (London, 1985), pp. 3-4.

7. Conversation with the President, 10 November 1949.

8. Conversation with the President, 10 November 1949.

9 Conversation with the President, 10 November 1949.

10. Conversation with the President, 10 November 1949.

11. See *Renmin ribao* (People's Daily), November and December 1949.

12. "Amtorg" was the abbreviation of the Soviet Trade Mission. Gubitchev was a Soviet official employed by the UN Secretariat. Both were charged by the US government with conducting espionage activities. See Meeting with the Secretary of State, 15 November 1949, E 393, RG 59.

13. Maverick to Jessup, 19 November 1949, Maury Maverick File, A 60, Philip Jessup Papers, Library of Congress.

14. Folder 20, Box 37, Confidential File, White House Central Files.

15. Meeting with the President, 31 October 1949, E 394, RG 59.

16. Memo of Conversation, 17 October and 7 November 1950, Box 64, Acheson Papers.

17. China—1949 File, Box 175, President's Secretary's Files.

18. State Department Briefs, 23 February 1950.

19. NSC-48, 10 June 1949, Box 207, President's Secretary's Files.

20. NSC-48/2, 30 December 1949, Box 207.

21. *Public Papers of President Truman.*

22. 5 January 1950, January 1950 Folder, Box 65, Acheson Papers.

23. Elsey Memo, 6 January 1950, Foreign Relations Folder—China (Policy on Formosa), Box 59, Elsey Papers.

24. Elsey Memo, 6 January 1950.

25. State Department Briefs, 11 January 1950.

26. State Department Briefs, 6 January 1950.

27. Acheson Meeting with Lie, 21 January 1950, Box 65, Acheson Papers.

28. State Department Briefs, 3 January 1950.

29. State Department Briefs, 9 January 1950.

30. February 1950 Folder, Box 65, Acheson Papers.

31. CIA Memo, 18 November 1949, Box 249, President's Secretary's Files.

32. CIA Memo, 21 November 1949.

33. CIA Memo, 21 November 1949.

34. Re Mikoyan's visit to China and Liu Shaoqi's visit to the Soviet Union, see Si Ze, "Accompanying Chairman Mao to Visit the Soviet Union," *Renwu* (Personalities), 1988, no. 5. Si Ze (1905-), a member of the CCP since 1926, and longtime associate of Zhou Enlai and Ren Bishi, also served many times as Mao Zedong's Russian interpreter.

35. State Department Briefs, 4 January 1950.

36. Liu, "Ambassadorship"; Wu, *Waijiaobubanian.* Also see Si, "Accompanying Chairman Mao."

37. Political Consulative Conference, a new version of a conference with the same name in which the KMT, CCP and minor parties participated for the purpose of national reconciliation in Chongqing, 1945. The new Conference convened in September 1949 to decide upon the establishment of the People's Republic on 1 October 1949. It served as the national assembly of the PRC before a National People's Assembly was elected in 1954. The apparatus of the Conference expands from national to county level, functioning like a second house, seated by representative figures from all strata and purported to provide political consultation to the CCP and the government. Luo Luongji was a senior member of the People's Consulative Conference on the national level representing the Democratic League. (See note 79 of Chapter Eight.)

38. *Foreign Relations of U.S., 1949,* vol. 8, p. 539.

39. Gao Gang was then a member of the CCP Political Bureau and Chief of the CCP Northeastern Bureau. It was alleged that he had visited the Soviet Union several times without the consent of the CCP Central Committee. Stalin wanted to win him over. After Stalin's death in 1953, Gao was charged in a CCP National Conference in 1954 as a careerist aiming to secure the highest position in the Party, and was expelled from the CCP. The communique of the National Conference said that he had attempted suicide but there were no follow-up references.

40. Mao had already suffered from Stalin's humiliation for a long time. When He Zizhen, Mao's second wife, went to the Soviet Union during World War II, she had been put into a mental asylum for several years. It is said that she did suffer from a mental disorder, but the Soviet authorities refused to let her return to China when asked by the CCP. She returned to China eventually after the CCP representative to the Soviet Party formally requested her release.

41. Si, "Accompanying Chairman Mao." Among Chinese sources relating to Mao's visit to Moscow, Si reported differently from others on the concluding of a treaty between the PRC and USSR. Si implied that Mao did not directly put his intent of a treaty before Stalin and Stalin was patiently waiting for his proposal, while Wu Xiuquan, a member of Mao's delegation, and Liu Xiao, as briefed by Zhou Enlai, remarked that Stalin was reluctant to have a treaty which would antagonize the US.

42. Si, "Accompanying Chairman Mao."

43. State Department Bulletin, 23 January 1950, p. 111.

44. Statement by Hu Qiaomu, 12 January 1950, *Zhonghua renming gongheguo duiwai guanxi* (Foreign Relations of PRC, 1949-1950) (Beijing, 1957), vol. 1, pp. 92-94.

45. State Department Briefs, 20 January 1950.

46. *Zhonghua renming gongheguo duiwai guanxi*, vol. 1, pp. 97.

47. Daily Meeting with the Secretary of the State, 23 December 1949, E 393, RG 59.

48. Memo, 9 March 1950, Russian Folder (1949-1950), Box 9, Elsey Papers.

49. Department of State Memorandum of Conversation, 24 March 1950, March 1950 Folder, Box 65, Acheson Papers.

50. 26 March 1950, Bi-Partisan Policy Folder, Box 7, Ayers Papers.

51. Truman to Vandenberg, 27 March 1950, Vandenberg Papers, from Kolko's Collection.

52. Randolph Burgess Oral History, 24 August 1966, J.F. Dulles Oral History Series, Seeley Mudd Library.

53. Conversation with the President, 4 April 1950, April 1950 Folder, Box 65, Acheson Papers.

54. When Acheson called Lehman on 5 April, Lehman told him that Vandenberg expressed that he would urge Dulles to accept, and not to haggle about titles, duties, etc., and to pitch in and help to the best of his ability. See April 1950 Folder, Box 65, Acheson Papers.

55. Memo of telephone conversation, 5 April 1950, April 1950 Folder, Box 65, Acheson Papers.

56. Memo of telephone conversation, 6 April 1950.

57. Memo of telephone conversation, 28 April 1950.

58. Memo of telephone conversation, 10 April 1950.

59. Conversation with the President and Lie, 29 May 1950, May 1950 Folder, Box 65, Acheson Papers.

60. C.M.(49)32, 5 May 1949, CAB 128/15.

61. C.M.(49)38, 26 May 1949, CAB 128/15.

62. C.M.(49)42, 23 June 1949, CAB 128/15.

63. C.M.(49)54, 29 August 1949, CAB 128/15.

64. Conversation with the President, 10 and 13 October 1949, E 394, RG 59.

65. Conversation with the President, 17 October 1949.

66. C.P.(49)214, 24 October 1949, CAB 129/37.

67. C.M.(49)62, 27 October 1949, CAB 128/16.

68. C.P.(49)208, 18 October 1949, CAB 129/37.

69. C.P.(49)248, 12 December 1949, CAB 129/37.

70. C.M.(49)72, 15 December 1949, CAB 129/16.

71. State Department Briefs, 9 January 1950.

72. State Department Briefs, 30 January 1950.

73. C.M.(50)24, 24 April 1950, CAB 128/17.

74. C.M.(50)29, 8 May 1950, CAB 128/7.

75. State Department Briefs, 10 May 1950.

76. State Department Briefs, 8 March 1950.

77. State Department Briefs, 3 March 1950.

78. Daily Meeting of the Secretary of State, 1 July 1949, E 393, RG 59.

79. Memo, 28 March 1950, W.H.C. 50-53 Folder, Box 1, Sidney Souers Papers, Truman Library.

80. C.P.(50)73, 20 April 1950, CAB 129/39.

CHAPTER 10: THE BLOOD-TAINTED PENINSULA

1. Cabinet Meeting, 8 July 1950, Box 2, Connelly Papers.
2. Cabinet Meeting, 21 July 1950.
3. Cabinet Meeting, 25 July 1950.
4. Truman-Acheson conversation, July 1950 Folder, Box 65, Acheson Papers.
5. Daily Meeting with the Secretary of the State, 27 July 1050, E 393, RG 59.
6. *Foreign Relations of US, 1950*, vol. 1, p. 329.
7. Cabinet Meeting, 14 July 1950.
8. State Department Briefs, 3 July 1950.
9. State Department Briefs, 14 July 1950.
10. State Department Briefs, 28 July 1950.
11. State Department Briefs, 14 August 1950.
12. State Department Briefs, 13 July 1950; C.M.(50)46, 17 July 1950, CAB 128/18.
13. Commonwealth Relations Office to British High Commissioners, 19 July 1950, 123162, PREM 8/1405, Public Record Office.
14. Daily Meeting with the Secretary of the State, 4 August 1950, E 393, RG 59.
15. State Department Briefs, 17 August 1950.
16. Pearson to Acheson, 15 August 1950 and Pearson to Bevin, 2 September 1950, 123163, PREM 8/1408.
17. Gasconigne to Dening, 8 October 1949, F 15700, FO 371/75773/304, Public Record Office.
18. C.P.(50)156, 3 July 1950, CAB 129/41.
19. C.M.(50)42, 4 July 1950, CAB 128/18.
20. Dorothy Thompson, "On the Record" column, *Washington Star*, 25 August 1950.
21. NSC Meeting, 27 July 1950, July 1950 Folder, Box 65, Acheson Papers.
22. State Department Briefs, 17 August 1950.
23. State Department Briefs, 28 August 1950.
24. State Department Briefs, 30 August 1950.
25. State Department Briefs, 5 September 1950.
26. State Department Briefs, 14 August 1950.
27. State Department Briefs, 7 September 1950.
28. State Department Briefs, 8 September 1950.
29. Wu, *Waijiaobubanian*, p. 39.
30. State Department Briefs, 15 September 1950.

31. State Department Briefs, 18 September 1950.

32. 8 September 1950, September 1950 Folder, Box 220, President's Secretary Files.

33. State Department Briefs, 21 September 1950.

34. State Department Briefs, 26 September 1950.

35. Prime Minister's Personal Telegram Serial no. T156/50, 26 September 1950, PREM 8/1405/123162.

36. August 1950 Folder, Box 65, Acheson Papers.

37. State Department Briefs, 29 September 1950.

38. State Department Briefs, 3 October 1950.

39. State Department Briefs, 4 October 1950.

40. Roger Makins to Prime Minister, "Operations in Korea," 3 October 1950, P.M./50/R.M./61, PREM 8/1405/123162.

41. Lovett to Truman, 7 October 1950, Box 8, Ayers Papers.

42. State Department Briefs, 5 October 1950.

43. State Department Briefs, 5 October 1950.

44. Military History Research Department, Academy of Military Science, Chinese People's Liberation Army, *Zhongguo renmin zhiyuanjun kangmei yuanchao zhanshi* (A Military History of the Korean War) (Beijing: Military Science Press, 1988), pp. 7-8.

45. Xu Yan, *Diyici jiaoliang* (The First Match of Cross Swords) (Beijing: Broadcasting and Television Press, 1990), pp. 18-19.

46. Xu, *Diyici jiaoliang*, pp. 19-20.

47. Hong Xuezhi, *Kangmei yuanchao zhanzheng huiyi* (Reminiscences of the Korean War) (Beijing, 1990), pp. 8-9.

48. Hong, *Huiyi*, pp. 14-15; Chai Chenwen and Zhao Yongtian, *Kangmei yuanchao jishi* (A Factual Record of the Korean War) (Beijing, 1987), p. 55.

49. *Mao Zedong junshi lunwenxuan* (The Selected Military Works of Mao Zedong) (Beijing: 1981), p. 345; *Pengdehuai zishu* (The Self Accounts of Peng Dehuai) (Beijing, 1981), pp. 257-258.

50. Peng, *Zishu*; Yao Xu, *Cong yalujiang dao banmendian* (From the Yalu to Panmunjom) (Beijing, 1985).

51. In 1950, one Chinese "li" was a little shorter than one half of a kilometer.

52. *Zhou Enlai xuanji*, p. 51.

53. Hong, *Huiyi*, p. 15.

54. Yao, *Cong yalujiang*, pp. 25-26.

55. Conversation of Marshal Chen Yi, 16 April 1964, see Yao, *Cong yalujiang*, p. 22; Xu, *Diyici jiaoliang,* p. 22.

56. *Mao Zedong junshi lunwenxuan*, p. 347.

57. Yao, *Cong yalujiang*, p. 22.

58. State Department Briefs, 20 October 1950.

59. Yao, *Cong yalujiang*, p. 25.

60. Chai and Zhao, *Kangmei yuanchao jishi*, p. 62.

61. Yao, *Cong yalujiang*, p. 22.

62. *Mao Zedong junshi lunwenxuan*, pp. 649-650; Military History Research Department, *Kangmei yuanchao zhanshi*, pp. 21-22.

63. Yao, *Cong yalujiang*, p. 31.

64. *Cong yalujiang*, p. 31.

65. Murphy Memo, 9 October 1950, Hawaii-Wake Folder, Box 72, Elsey Papers.

66. Conversation with the President, 19 October 1950, E 394, RG 59.

67. State Department Briefs, 23 October 1950.

68. State Department Briefs, 23 October 1950.

69. *Kangmei yuanchao zhanshi*, p. 34.

70. *Kangmei yuanchao zhanshi*, pp. 43-44; *Mao Zedong junshi lunwenxuan*, pp. 688, 671.

71. *Kangmei yuanchao jishi*, p. 21; *Cong yalujiang*, p. 31.

72. *Kangmei yuanchao jishi*, p. 39.

73. State Department Briefs, 6 November 1950.

74. Memo, 6 November 1950, November 1950 Folder, Box 65, Acheson Papers.

75. State Department Briefs, 14 November 1950.

76. *Kangmei yuanchao jishi*, p. 65.

77. State Department Briefs, 7 November 1950.

78. State Department Briefs, 22 November 1950.

79. State Department Briefs, 24 November 1950.

80. State Department Briefs, 27 November 1950.

81. *Kangmei yuanchao zhanshi*, pp. 50-51.

82. C.M.(50)78, 29 November 1950, CAB 128/78.

83. Statement, 30 November 1950, Box 72, Elsey Papers.

84. From Lord Sherfield's interview by the author.

85. Webb Memo to Truman, December 1950, Army Atomic Bomb Folder, Box 4, Confidential File, White House Central Files.

86. Elsey handnotes of Cabinet Meeting, 10 AM, 1 December 1950, Box 73, Elsey Papers.

87. Marshall to Truman, 16 December 1950, Confidential File, Box 4, White House Central Files.

88. Wilcox to Vandenberg, 30 January 1951, Wilcox Papers.

89. Truman 30 November 1950 Statement File, Box 72, Elsey Papers.

90. Cabinet Meeting, 12 December 1950, Connelly Papers.

91. Cabinet Meeting, 15 December 1950.

92. Boykin to Souers, 12 December 1950, Souers Papers.

93. Cabinet Meeting, 22 December 1950.

94. *Kangmei yuanchao zhanshi*, pp. 76-77.

95. *Kangmei yuanchao jishi*, p. 69.

96. *Kangmei yuanchao zhanshi*, p. 77.

97. *Cong yalujiang*, pp. 47-48, 54.

98. *Diyici jiaoliang*, p. 67; *Huiyi*, p. 110.

99. State Department Briefs, 2 January 1951.

100. P.M.M.(51)13, 6 January 1951, PREM 8/1408/123163.

101. State Department Briefs, 4 January 1951.

102. Attlee to Truman, 8 January 1951; Truman to Attlee, 12 January 1951, PREM 8/1438.

103. Cabinet Meeting, 5 January 1951.

104. State Department Briefs, 15 January 1951.

105. Cabinet Meeting, 15 January 1951.

106. State Department Briefs, 22 January 1951.

107. Daily Meeting with the Secretary of State, 23 January 1951, E 393, RG 59.

108. Franks to Bevin, Telegram 208, 21 January 1951, 123162, PREM 8/1405.

109. State Department Briefs, 15 February 1951.

110. Franks to Bevin, Telegram 208, 21 January 1951.

111. Wilcox Diary, 5 February 1951, Wilcox Papers.

112. Wilcox Diary, 9 February 1951.

113. NSC 80th Meeting, 17 January 1951.

114. Lucius Battle Memo for Secretary of State, 26 January 1951, Box 66, Acheson Papers.

115. Lucius Battle Memo of telephone conversation, 5 February 1951, Box 66, Acheson Papers.

116. *Kangmei yuanchao jishi*, pp. 74-75.

117. *Kangmei yuanchao jishi*, p. 76.

118. *Kangmei yuanchao zhanshi*, pp. 99-119.

119. State Department Briefs, 23 and 26 February 1951.

120. State Department Briefs, 1 March 1951.

121. *Kangmei yuanchao jishi*, pp. 79-80.

122. C.M.(50)71, 4 December 1950, CAB 128/18.

123. State Department Briefs, 24 April 1951.

124. Cabinet Meeting, 19 October 1951.

125. *Kangmei yuanchao zhanshi*, p. 152.

126. *Kangmei yuanchao jishi*, p. 82.

127. *Kangmei yuanchao jishi*, p. 82.

128. For above approaches see *Foreign Relations of US, 1951,* vol. 7, pp. 1653-1664, 1667-1671.

129. *Kangmei yuanchao jishi*, pp. 109-110.

130. *Foreign Relations of US, 1952-54,* vol. 6, p. 782.

131. *Foreign Relations of US, 1952-54,* vol. 6, p. 784.

132. A Chinese saying which means in power or out of power.

133. Bowles to Truman, 11 December 1951, India File, Box 180, President's Secretary's Files.

134. Cabinet Meeting, 13 June 1952.
135. State Department Briefs, 25 June 1952.
136. State Department Briefs, 19 August 1952.
137. State Department Briefs, 1 December 1952.
138. State Department Briefs, 16 and 23 December 1952.
139. *Kangmei yuanchao jishi*, p. 110.
140. *Kangmei yuanchao jishi*, pp. 114-115.
141. *Kangmei yuanchao jishi*, p. 127.
142. Jin Dayin, *Zhiyuanjun zhanfu jishi* (Chronicles of the CPVA POWs) (Beijing, 1985), p. 3.
143. For the following stories see Jin, *Zhiyuanjun zhanfu jishi* and Zhang Zeshi, *Wo cong mei junzhanfuying guilai* (I Came back from the US POW Camp) (Beijing, 1988).

CHAPTER 11: THE ECHOS OF PANMUNJOM

1. According to Chinese sources, the losses of the Chinese People's Volunteers Army totaled 366,000. The break-down is as follows: deaths in combat, 114,000; hospital deaths from injuries, 21,600; deaths from illness, 13,000; hospitalized, 383,000 (hospitalizations, not persons); missing, 25,600. Among the missing, 21,000 became POWs; the remaining must have died in combat or after being captured by enemy troops. The US military alleges that China lost 920,000 troops in the Korean War.
2. Conversation, 9 April 1951, April 1951 File, Box 66, Acheson Papers.
3. John Melby to Raymond P. Ludden, 27 March 1951, John Melby Papers, Truman Library.
4. Joint-Chiefs-of-Staff Memorandum to Secretary of Defense and sent to National Security Council Steering Committee, NSC 114th Meeting, 28 March 1952, Box 216, President's Secretary's Files.
5. State Department Briefs, 20 June 1952.
6. Commonweath Relations Office to British High Commissioners, 19 July 1950, 123162, PREM 8/1405.
7. State Department Briefs, 8 April 1952.
8. April 1952 File, Box 67, Acheson Papers.
9. State Department Briefs, 25 August 1952.
10. State Department Briefs, 29 September, 3 October and 7 October 1952.
11. Meeting with the President, 3 August 1950, E 394, RG 59.
12. State Department Briefs, 13 October 1952, Truman Library.
13. State Department Briefs, 10 October 1952.

CONCLUSION: THE DYNAMICS OF THE TRUMAN DIPLOMACY

1. Robert L. Beisner, *From Old Diplomacy to the New: 1965-1900* (New York, 1975).

2. Yang Shengmao, "Several Problems on Writing U.S. Diplomatic History," *Nankaidaxue Xuebao* (Nankai University Bulletin), vols. 2 and 3, 1988.

3. NSC 31st Meeting, 7 January 1949, 1949 Folder, Box 220, President's Secretary's Files.

4. State Department Briefs, 8 January 1952.

5. Arthur Paul to Bernard L. Gladieux, 11 January 1946, File 93126/64, RG 40.

6. Edwin W. Pauley to Truman, 24 March 1947, Greece Subject File, Box 180, President's Secretary's Files.

7. William C. Foster to Matthew Connelly, 30 August 1949 Miscellaneous Folder, Box 4, Clark Clifford Papers.

8. Anecdotes, Memoirs File, Post Presidential Papers.

9. C.P.(49)208, 18 October 1949, CAB 129/37.

10. Wilcox Diary, 25 April 1951, Wilcox Papers.

11. Cabinet Meeting, 11 April 1952, Connelly Papers.

12. Interview, 22 January 1954, Memoirs Box 3, Post Presidential Papers.

13. Cabinet Meetings, 13 June 1952, Connelly Papers.

14. George Elsey Memo on Truman Signing and form attached, 2 October 1947, 1946-47 Folder, General File, Box 65, Elsey Papers.

15. Lucius D. Battle Oral History, Truman Library.

16. Wilcox Diary, 25 January 1951.

17. Jessup Papers, Library of Congress.

18. Truman Press and Radio Conference, 30 March 1950, *Public Papers of President Truman;* McCarthy Folder, Box 5, D.D. Lloyd Files, Truman Library.

19. Ayers Diary, 29 May 1945.

20. *Foreign Relations of US, 1945,* vol. 2, p. 320-321.

21. Ayers Diary, 13 October 1945.

22. Robert Lovett Oral History, 1971, Truman Library.

23. Lucius D. Battle Oral History.

CORNELL EAST ASIA SERIES

For ordering information, please contact:
Cornell East Asia Series
East Asia Program
Cornell University
140 Uris Hall
Ithaca, NY 14853-7601
USA
(607) 255-6222.

5-93/1M/BB